WOULD
A MAHARAJAH
SLEEP HERE?

DIARY OF A FIVE-STAR TRAVELER
STEPHEN TROY AND LEANNE TROY

iUniverse LLC
Bloomington

WOULD A MAHARAJAH SLEEP HERE?
DIARY OF A FIVE-STAR TRAVELER

iUniverse books may be ordered through booksellers or by contacting:

iUniverse
1663 Liberty Drive
Bloomington, IN 47403
www.iuniverse.com
1-800-Authors (1-800-288-4677)

Because of the dynamic nature of the Internet, any web addresses or links contained in this book may have changed since publication and may no longer be valid. The views expressed in this work are solely those of the author and do not necessarily reflect the views of the publisher, and the publisher hereby disclaims any responsibility for them.

Any people depicted in stock imagery provided by Thinkstock are models, and such images are being used for illustrative purposes only.

Certain stock imagery © Thinkstock.

ISBN: 978-1-4759-8815-4 (sc)
ISBN: 978-1-4759-8817-8 (hc)
ISBN: 978-1-4759-8816-1 (e)

Library of Congress Control Number: 2013909556

Printed in the United States of America.

iUniverse rev. date: 8/12/2013

This book is dedicated to our children, Lauren, Cortney, and Chelsea, our grandchildren, Aideyn and Colin, and our future generations. I hope our journeys ignite your passion to travel and explore. Never stop learning and questioning what you have seen and heard. Shaking hands and smiling at your neighbor is the shortest road to peace and understanding.

TABLE OF CONTENTS

ROAD TO MOROCCO

THE OTHER AMERICA: SOUTH AMERICA

MIDDLE EAST: THE NEW AND ANCIENT

BEHIND THE IRON CURTAIN: RUSSIA, POLAND, THE CZECH REPUBLIC, AND GERMANY

PARIS; THE ONE AND ONLY

CALIFORNIA YANKEE IN CUBA

PREFACE

Would A Maharaja Sleep Here? is the second book I have published as of this date. This and my first, *Business Biographies Shaken Not Stirred with a Twist*, were both born from my two greatest passions. The first is the study of business history, and the second, my love for adventure and travel.

I never planned on writing a book about travel. It just seemed to happen. Originally I started writing about our travels to keep our family back home involved in what we were doing. With the discovery of e-mail, we were able to tell our kids back home about what Mom and Dad were doing. These e-mails tended to be short since broadband was not yet invented and we had to sit in the hotel lobby on a communal computer at the cost of one dollar a minute, while other guests were breathing down our necks waiting to use the only computer in the hotel. You would think a price that exorbitant and ridiculous would keep people away, but it didn't. We always seemed to have a group of people hovering around, waiting for their chance to bang out a lengthy e-mail on a 28.8-kilobyte dial-up modem.

As technology expanded and more people got e-mail accounts, we started to expand our list to a few friends. One friend was my travel agent, whom I obviously have gotten very close to as she has planned our various trips. To my surprise she enjoyed my candid banter and the personal stories I sent back and asked if she could send them to the other agents in the office. That led to a request to send them to clients and eventually to my tour operator. Quickly they all went viral. I would get requests from random people I didn't know asking me, "What happened to day five? I received one through four and six and seven, but never got five." People seem to enjoy reading them. It was then that I decided to spend a little more time making sure I had the facts straight and the spelling correct. The e-mails detailing our journeys started to grow—first a page, then two, and sometimes three pages a day. With that I lost my kids as an audience and won a worldwide stage. Yes, even tour guides were receiving my daily travelogues. We would arrive at a town, and our tour guide who picked us up at the airport had already been reading my previous posts. One experience we had in Russia was most heartwarming. After finishing one of the daily e-mails on Russia, our guide started to cry. We were very taken aback. I asked what was upsetting about what I wrote, and she replied, "Nothing. It's wonderful." She said that she had been showing tourists around the city for ten years and always wondered if anyone actually listened to her.

INTRODUCTION

Reading through these pages, you will discover that this isn't a tour guide, recommending places and giving elaborate reviews of where you can get the greatest cannoli for fifty cents or score cheap first-class train tickets. This is a personal journey of two people who love adventure, history, and the discovery of ancient sites, civilizations, and cultures around the world.

The difference between *Would A Maharaja Sleep Here?* and other published travel books is the description and style of travel. All of our adventures were done in five-star style, and we were constantly on the move. In India, I have to say, our travels were more like seven-star. Our India travels were spectacular in every way, all the more surprising after hearing the many shocking stories of poverty and filth in the cities. Another striking departure is that the book is written as a narrative and contains personal reflections on our daily thoughts and adventures. Each day was originally written for family and a small collection of good friends, so we didn't hold back with our personal thoughts, including our excitement in celebrating the birth of our first grandson. Together, these elements bring more life to the sights and sounds around the world.

As you read through these pages don't expect to find bargains shops. You will not find us galloping through train stations with backpacks on or looking for the cheapest hotels. Our travels were well planned, and immense attention was paid to finding the finest hotels, cars, guides, and restaurants. This doesn't mean that readers won't enjoy or learn from our experiences. If you like luxury travel, there is a great deal of information on the best way to spend your money. If you are on more of a budget, you can easily see where you would want to splurge and where you could cut back. For the person who can't afford foreign travel, we have been told that our stories do make it feel like you are on the trip with us. So whatever level of traveler you are, I am sure you will learn from our adventures. It just may not be where to buy the best gelato.

Our adventures always start three hundred days before our planned departure. The three hundred days was chosen to correspond to the earliest I could book my first-class air for our trip. Working with my travel agent and what I feel is one of the best tour operators in the world, Abercrombie and Kent, I would get itineraries of places to visit, sights to see, and hotels to stay at. Once we were set on the places we were interested in visiting, our next step was getting the timing down to fit all of the important and amazing sites to see. The sights always seemed to be the easiest part to plan. Using a good tour operator who has been around for a while and who knows where all of the not-to-be-missed spots are is imperative. They are the experts in knowing the best times to arrive and to depart. I am not sure if planning trips for us was easy for our agents or if we made it more difficult. I would imagine that the fact that it was only the two of us traveling made it easier, since we were always on a private tour. At times it became embarrassing, such as the time we visited the Amazon. Up to the dock came a large boat that could hold thirty people to pick up just the two of us, while a line of fifty other tourists looked on in frustration. Traveling as a twosome gave us advantages large groups don't have, such as moving quickly to fit in more sights or changing the itinerary when something interesting came up. In addition, we often got special entrances, in some cases avoiding lines stretching blocks. Being only two also gave us special access, as when we were granted an audience with the Maharaja of Udaipur, India, at his palace—an experience we will never forget. Who would have thought we would one day be lifelong personal friends with an Indian Maharaja? (More on that relationship later.)

As I previously mentioned, picking the best hotel is very difficult. Over time I have been delighted with the hotels I have stayed in, but I have also been very disappointed. For me, there is nothing worse than travelling to far-off lands only to be driven to a hotel that we heard wonderful things about—and, not to mention, paid lots of hard-earned money for—only to say to ourselves, "Boy, we wish we were staying at the place across the street instead." I know many travelers aren't as fussy about their hotels. "I only sleep there," they say. Not me. I think the hotel is what separates the whole experience from being just a tour of a city into a true adventure. I am not apologetic that I like five-star luxury and service. So how did I get the best? It is simple. I asked my agent, my tour guide, and the local city representative, "Would you send Elizabeth Taylor there?" Why her? She has for the last half of the Twentieth Century and the first decade of the Twenty-first been known for style, class, beauty, grace, and opulence. My next trip I will be saying "Would you send a Maharaja there?" to prevent being sued by Liz Taylor's estate. I'm sure they will know what I mean.

Trying to find the best hotels and places around the world has proven to be no easy task. How many times have you read a travel magazine claiming to have a complete list of the best of the best, only to find that a competing magazine has a different list? To make things even harder, the same periodicals might publish a completely different list the following year. It makes it almost impossible.

Additionally, the stories you will read in the following pages are compiled backward. That is to say, the most recent trip we have taken is first, followed by the one before that, and so on. My reasoning for doing this was twofold. First, my writing style has gotten better as we have traveled. Secondly, the trips have seemed to get more opulent and longer as the years went on. This was a result of having more money and free time and dialing into what we liked and didn't like. Practice makes perfect, and that goes for travel as well. The quality, detail, and length of the stories were a direct result of my evolution as a writer.

Now, a short note on how I chose my title: I have been asked many times why my second book is called *Would A Maharaja Sleep Here?* The truth is, my original working title was *Would Elizabeth Taylor Sleep Here?* Unfortunately, my publisher would not allow me to use Elizabeth Taylor's name without a release from her estate. Sadly, Ms.

Taylor died on Mach 23, 2011, and I had to talk to the lawyers for her estate. My experience with attorneys told me that their first response would be no. I was right. Not one to be defeated easily, I made one last effort to get my first title choice. I called and e-mailed back and offered to make a $5,000 donation to Ms. Taylor's AIDS foundation. Regretfully that offer was not accepted. I would like to think Elizabeth Taylor would have approved my request for permission and would have enjoyed reading about our glamorous trek around the world. Unfortunately, in the alternative, I changed the title to a more generic *Would A Maharaja Sleep Here?*

Would A Maharaja Sleep Here? harkens back to the days before the Internet—say pre-1991, or even before that. This was a time when people used to keep diaries of their travels, or even their daily lives. Crumpled diaries from the early 1900s and 1800s are found all the time in some old, dusty attic. These journals give wonderful, historic looks at what the world was like, what people were doing, and what they were thinking at that time. I hope the same will be said about *Would A Maharaja Sleep Here?* Now sit down in a comfortable chair and join us on a very personal whirlwind of luxury and adventure.

INDIA EXOTIC

APRIL 2012

DAYS ONE AND TWO

When I mentioned to friends that we were going to India, I was surprised at the polarized responses I received. People who had been there either loved it or hated it. And, of course, there were the ones who had never been and just made up their minds that they hated it.

In any case, getting to India, which is literally on the other side of the world, can be challenging. Traveling to India is not for the novice traveler. I mention that this log is days one and two because we left San Francisco in the evening of April 2 and didn't arrive in Mumbai until the morning of April 4. No matter how much you try, getting to India from the West Coast will take you over twenty-four hours just in travel time. Our trip was closer to thirty hours, and when you add in the ten-hour layover in London, the two-plus hours it took from the Mumbai airport to the hotel, and the ten-and-a-half-hour time difference between the States and India, altogether one can just about burn up a forty-hour workweek getting here. Hey, I bet that was still faster than when Mark Twain made this trip in April 1896, so I guess I shouldn't complain. If you are planning to travel to India, you definitely have to book either business or first class to make it a bit more pleasurable.

Our route took us over the North Pole to London, where, as I said, we had a ten-hour layover. Not content to sit for hours in the first-class lounge, we decided to venture out to downtown London. For those

1

of you who have not been to Heathrow, it's huge. I don't think I have ever been in a larger or more confusing airport.

Leanne had arranged to visit and have lunch with an old friend from high school. I suggested we take a taxi into downtown, and Leanne thought a train would be better. I almost won that discussion until the airport agent told us that London traffic is so bad that it could take four times longer by cab than by train. So a train it was. Dragging a roller bag and carrying our backpacks, we boarded the express to Paddington Station in downtown London, where we took a cab to the restaurant. After a great lunch and lively conversation with Chris Avery, we boarded the express back to Heathrow to wait another three hours before boarding our last leg to Mumbai.

Looking out the window of our Boeing 777, we were struck by the smoggy haze that floated over the city. Upon landing we could already see the stark contrasts India is known for, airport buildings all but crumbling next to new terminals, as well as construction to support India's growing economy. Nearly 40 percent of the population in Mumbai lives in poverty. Driving through the city streets you see the mix of colonial architecture of the British-constructed buildings, slums that seem to grow by the day, and the 1950s-style low-rise commercial buildings all intertwined together, blurring any semblance of neighborhoods. Some of the architecture had been stunning in its day; unfortunately, there has been little done in the way of restoration since the British left in 1947.

The ride from the airport to our hotel was to take an hour and fifteen minutes. Because of the traffic, we had to enjoy a two-hour drive. Leanne commented to our guide how difficult it must be to drive in such a crowded place. He responded that you needed three things to be able to drive in Mumbai: "Good brakes, a good horn, and good luck." Fortunately, our driver had all three, and we arrived safely at the majestic 1903 Taj Mahal Hotel.

The Taj Mahal Hotel sits in front of Bombay Harbor with views of the Arabian Sea. It was truly a welcome oasis after two long days of travel. The resort was a beautiful palace with all the modern amenities one would expect at a five-star hotel, along with the Old World charm of a bygone era, with butlers and valets servicing our room at the touch of a button.

The Taj hotel was built by Jamsetji Tata, the founder of the Tata Group, India's largest company, which manufactures everything from cars and steel to textiles and chemicals. What is little known is they also own Jaguar. The hotel was built in a mixture of Moorish, Florentine, and Oriental styles to assure it was the grandest of all buildings in India. Walking through the main entrance, you are instantly hit with the sweet fragrance of gardenias permeating the lobby. As we checked in, we were greeted with a traditional Indian ceremony and given beautiful leis, and, of course, a red dot was placed in the middle of our foreheads. Although there is a new tower, we had chosen to stay in the original section, where kings, queens, heads of state, and other major celebrities have been staying since 1903. And yes, Elizabeth Taylor slept here. On a side note, this is the same hotel that four Pakistani terrorists attacked and blew up in 2008. When the siege was over, 70 percent of the palace, including the building we were staying in, was destroyed. It took craftsmen two years to fully restore this gem on the harbor.

Gazing out the window at the bay, we could see the dozens of colorful ferries dotting Bombay Harbor, as well as the Gate of India monument that welcomed King George V and Queen Mary of England in 1911 for their coronation as the emperor and empress of India.

Although we had only been in Mumbai for several hours, we had driven through the city and taken a two-hour heritage tour of this fine hotel. From the guide and driver who picked us up to the young man who gave us the most interesting tour of the hotel, we could already feel the welcome embrace of the people of India. We were already feeling that this would be one of our most interesting adventures yet.

EXOTIC INDIA: DAY THREE

Today was our first real taste of India. We started our adventure here in Mumbai, the financial capital of India. Meeting our guide, we set off for a city tour. We still couldn't get over the contrasting architecture along the streets of the city. Many of the buildings looked uninhabitable, as if they were going to collapse any minute. Most cities would have condemned them long ago and torn them down. We were told that the building owners wished they could. Unfortunately, rent control had prevented the owners from evicting the tenants, so it was impossible to tear the buildings down, and with so little rent being paid, they could not afford to renovate or maintain the building to any kind of livable standard. These two issues caused an unfortunate blight on the city.

Mixed between these crumbling buildings were some of the most interesting buildings in the city: beautiful stone structures that, like our hotel, were a mixture of Moorish, Florentine, Oriental, and Colonial architecture, most of the time all mixed in the same building. Our guide called it fusion. Our hotel, the Taj Mahal, was one of the best examples of this interesting fusion architecture in the city. Crossing the street from our hotel, we were able to look back from the Gateway of India and get a complete view of the hotel, the ultimate in fusion. Each floor had a different architectural style, topped with a Renaissance dome in the center with two Islamic onion domes capping each end. The look was mesmerizing.

Back in our thankfully air-conditioned car, we made our second stop at a fruit and vegetable market. Like in most Asian and Middle Eastern countries, there was always a central market, and Mumbai was no exception, offering the Crawford Market, with its rows and rows of stalls selling every type of fruit, vegetable, and spice imaginable. Have you ever heard of a mud apple? It was just a few blocks from here that Rudyard Kipling, the famous poet and author, was born. At one time the market was strictly wholesale, but due to the growing city and competition, it has had to open to retail trade to stay alive.

Back in the car, we headed north of the city. It was here we passed a strange sight of what appeared to be rows upon rows of white drapes blowing in the breeze. At first I thought it was some type of avant-garde art project. When we stopped, we learned that it was an outdoor laundry. Those rows of white drapes were actually sheets belonging to hotels and hospitals. From our high perch we could look down upon rows of four-by-four stalls stretching blocks, where men and woman applied their trade, washing all styles of garments and linens—washing in the morning, drying in the sun at noon, and ironing when the heat subsided in the evening. It's quite possible that those stonewashed jeans you are wearing right now came from one of these local stalls.

Leaving the laundry, we started to see a few more modern high-rise buildings dotting the northern part of the city. Mumbai was originally made up of seven islands. As the city expanded, the shallow waterways were filled, creating one landmass. Where we were driving in the north was the earliest part of the city, which would have been the mainland. Here, the buildings being older, we found that finally some are being razed, opening opportunities for new apartment towers to be built. You would think this model of development would encourage others to move forward with new building. But with property values rising to between five hundred and twenty-five hundred dollars a square foot, it was all too tempting for the displaced tenants to either rent or sell their flats and move back to the same squalid conditions they came from, a situation that must be very frustrating for the government.

Back in our car, we headed to a Krishna temple. I was surprised how ornate it was for a group that denounces personal belongings and work. We arrived just in time for a Krishna ceremony. It consisted of the same banging and chanting we all heard at the airports in the 1970s before the performers were thrown out. Sometimes I think that if it weren't for religion, there would be nothing for us to see when we travel, except the foundations of some mud huts. But I still don't get it.

Our next stop was the Gandhi museum. The museum was once a private residence where Gandhi lived as a guest of a friend—a friend who happened to be a jeweler. I found it strange that a man who took a vow of poverty would be living in the home of a jeweler, whose sole work was to make beautiful things for conspicuous consumption. I also found it odd that so many throughout the world worshipped him. Yes, he fought for freedom for India, and did it in a peaceful way. He also had a political agenda to promote socialism, a system that has kept India in poverty for many years. It wasn't until India's recent embrace of capitalism that the country has shown tremendous growth. It was capitalism that helped India grow and made it one of the four fastest-growing economies in the world, along with Brazil,

Russia, and China. Ten or twenty years from now, you will see a tremendous transformation here in Mumbai, and, I am sure, the rest of India. Travelers coming in the future might very well complain that Mumbai is too modern and westernized. That would be worse than a seeing a few crumbling walls or shanties.

Driving back to the hotel, passing the occasional worshipped cow on a street corner, we no longer noticed the slums or the deteriorating buildings. Our conversations with our guide about India's culture, religion, and history helped us see past its lack of whitewashed exteriors.

Getting back to our room, I was drawn to the window, where the sun was just setting and the moon was rising. Looking out at the harbor, I could see the throngs of people who had come out to the Gate of India as the evening cooled. I grabbed Leanne and the camera and headed back out with them. As we left the fragrant lobby of the Taj, we could see a dozen ornate solid-silver horse-drawn carriages waiting for passengers across the street. (Okay, so they were silverette.)

Anyway, we boarded to take a last slow ride through the city streets. As we rode from the harbor into the town we couldn't help but feel we were back in time, someplace in the 1930s, arriving in Bombay for the first time. That dream came to a halt when we reached the main boulevard and our horse darted into oncoming traffic like a crazed Parisian taxi. I was amazed how calm our horse and driver were, as the traffic came so close we could almost step on the hoods of their cars. We could see drivers behind their wheels smiling from ear to ear. They didn't seem to get very upset here.

Back at the harbor, we stepped down and crossed the street to have one last relaxing glass of wine on the colonial veranda of the most historic hotel in India.

EXOTIC INDIA: DAY FOUR

Ugh! We had to get up early this morning to catch our flight to Aurangabad. It leaves Mumbai at 6:55 a.m., so we have to leave the hotel at 4:50. That means getting up at three. So of course we woke at two. This is when the twelve-hour time difference is to our advantage.

Before we leave Mumbai, I have to tell you about a few things I missed yesterday.

I forgot to mention the very interesting burial site we visited. The site was hidden behind a tall wall located up a long set of steep steps. The exact burial areas couldn't be viewed from the outside for reasons you will learn. Apparently it didn't allow visitors. The sect that uses this burial ground came from Iran centuries ago, and with them, they brought what we feel is their peculiar, if not macabre, burial practices. As we approached the area, what we noticed first were the dozens of crows and other birds flying overhead. These flying predators were a critical part of the burial process and an integral part of nature's plan. Getting it yet? They didn't exactly bury the bodies. They placed them in small, uncovered wells and let the crows and nature take their course. Got it? At least we didn't have to see it.

Okay, back to today. Since the 2008 terrorist attack from Pakistan, security became very tight here in India. From our hotel, which you pretty much needed a visa to enter, to the airports, where you couldn't even enter the terminal without a ticket and ID, security is strict. To assure safety, trained police with automatic weapons guarded the doors and the streets. It's sad that such a peaceful people had to go to such lengths to protect themselves. I don't think I am going to complain about the TSA again.

Leaving the hotel at five in the morning, we made it to the airport in forty-five minutes. Our trip to the hotel a couple days before at noon, if you remember, was over two and a half hours. That will give you some sense of the traffic in Mumbai. We boarded our flight and took our seats in first class at six thirty for our whopping thirty-five-minute flight to Aurangabad. In the States we would have gotten peanuts for a thirty-five-minute flight; here we got menus and a full three-course breakfast on china. We couldn't complain about the hospitality and service here. Everyone was friendly and wonderful. Aurangabad was a smaller town by Indian standards—a mere two million people. That's larger than the Bay Area and yet a small city here. We were surprised to find that it also was once the capital of the entire empire.

After we arrived in Aurangabad, our guide was proud to say

we were traveling in the new part of the city and spoke of how much cleaner and prosperous it had become over the past ten years. (Everything is relative.) Passing the three-wheeled motor taxis we honked our horn and hit our brakes in what was more like playing a game of chicken than driving. As we dodged cows, bikes, pedestrians, *tuk-tuks,* and oxen pulling carts, everyone seemed to have the third element required for driving here: luck! Avoiding disaster, we did safely arrive at another Taj Mahal Hotel.

When the driver said he would pick us up in the lobby at nine, I assumed he was talking about tomorrow. Then, looking at my watch, I noticed it was still only eight o'clock. Feeling like an idiot, I came to realize he was talking about today. He meant this morning.

After a quick check-in and freshen-up, we were picked up for our visit to some of India's most fascinating sites, the Aurangabad caves. As we traveled through the valley, the surrounding mountain, at times, reminded us of the Arizona desert: low mountains and long, flat plateaus (or mesas). Only these mountains were formed by ancient lava flows. As we traveled the highway we passed through one of fifty-seven ancient gates, which once were part of a walled fort in the middle of the valley. The walls surrounded a fortified fort, high on a pointed peak, which jutted up from the flat valley floor. Over time, as the fort fell in battle, each conquering warlord would increase the perimeter of the fort until eventually there were seven surrounding walls encompassing a large portion of the valley floor.

After an hour's drive we arrived at the caves. Calling them caves doesn't do them justice. These were thirty-four ornate temples carved from the volcanic basalt mountainside. These temples and monasteries date from the second century to the tenth. Here you will find Buddhist temples, Hindu temples, and Jain temples. The Jain religion is similar to Buddhism, but is much more restrictive. Apparently the leader of the Jains was born around the time of enlightenment and was a contemporary of Buddha. Both leaders found enlightenment; only the Jain group put heavy restrictions on what followers could do and eat. To keep from ever having the possibility of killing anything, even the smallest of insects, they are not even allowed to farm. They also cannot eat any root vegetables, such as potatoes, garlic, onions, and carrots, nor can they eat any form of meat from any animal.

Our first stop was the seventh-century Jain temple. Carved into the basalt stone of the mountain, it has an open-air courtyard with connecting chamber rooms, all connected deep into the hillside. The outer walls and rooms are intricately carved with figures and designs that defy the imagination—that someone could carve something so perfect with a hammer and chisel from one stone is astounding. Think of Michelangelo carving David while the marble was in the quarry, and then, upon the statue's completion, leaving with his family, David standing, along with his house and belongings, forever attached to the quarry.

Each room had impressive carved figures of the founder of Jainism, flanked by idols, animals, and reliefs, all carved from one continuous stone. When it was originally in use, it would have also have been plastered and painted. Today most of the plaster has been eroded. Sadly, the interior ceilings, which have survived for over a thousand years, have been blackened by soot from fires built by villagers living in the caves. Bats living in some of the caves also did their share of damage. (We couldn't miss the smell of bat urine.) Nevertheless, we could still make out colors and figures in many areas. It's hard to explain the detail and skill used to build these treasures. I can only describe it as Petra, with its stone-carved hillside facades, meets Egyptian story-telling and sculpture. I must say, it was one of the most impressive sites I had ever seen—that is, until we made our next two stops.

Our next stop was the cave of Buddhism. The Buddhists carved their completely enclosed cave straight into the mountain. The idea was to replicate a cathedral with high, arched ceilings, carved to look like it was built and supported by wood beams perfectly spaced, like a gothic church. Remember, this was carved out of one massive mountain. If you made a mistake, you had to start on a new mountain. No do-overs. At the back of the Buddhist cave we found find a twenty-seven-foot-high Buddha. As you walked around the Buddha you could feel the massive size and weight of the stone towering over you. Ringing the walls opposite the Buddha were reliefs of smaller Buddhas and other symbols, again carved directly into the stone. We were lucky to be viewing this cave when someone started a Buddhist chant. He was chanting slowly, demonstrating the amazing acoustics of the chamber.

Our final stop was the Hindu cave. This was the crown jewel of the caves. The Hindu cave was carved two hundred feet back into the mountain and must have been one hundred feet tall. These wonder workers started carving from the very top of the mountain, working their way to the floor of the valley. Again, this was an open-air cave. In the center of the open-air courtyard were three temples, several elephants, and spires, all carved with scenes from the Hindu religion. These carvings were quite intricate and were stacked one upon the other, telling a story like the words on a page. At the perimeter, workers also carved back into the hillside, creating additional rooms for worship, again all meticulously carved with stone figures telling a story. To understand its scale, workers took over seven generations (150 years) working continuously, carving and removing over three hundred thousand tons of rock to create what is today the largest monument cut from a single block of stone.

As we were leaving, Leanne noticed that a group of some ten attractive young Indian women were jockeying close to her, trying to secretly take her picture. When she saw them, they all were very giggly and somewhat embarrassed. It was very cute. When Leanne invited the one holding the camera to take a picture with her, the rest of the girls decided to line up and have their very own personal photograph taken with my gorgeous Leanne. A picture of Leanne might very well be hanging on the walls of ten Indian homes right at this moment.

As a side note, it also was interesting to see the wild monkeys scampering around. Most of them had suckling babies hanging from them. They seemed unafraid of the tourists, so we were able to get quite a few adorable pictures of them also.

I have to say, today was a *wow*, and exemplified exactly why we travel like we do.

EXOTIC INDIA: DAY FIVE

As spectacular as the caves were yesterday, our guide assured us that today would blow us away. We ended up leaving early for a two-hour trip north through the agricultural region for the Ajanta Caves. For today's adventure, as opposed to yesterday's, we find we are viewing strictly Buddhist caves.

Driving down the highway, we passed through many markets dotting the road every few miles. We were astonished at the conditions the people lived and worked in. Not a single attempt seemed to have been made to care for the structures. Sidewalks were simply unheard of. Instead, between the road and shops was a mixture of rubble, dirt, garbage, and old tires. Whether in town or in the countryside, we saw piles of empty plastic water bottles and other various rubbish lining the roads. The country that says it's the third largest and one of the fastest-emerging economies in the world couldn't even clean the streets. For miles I looked for a garbage can or a dumpster and found not one. In San Jose where we live we can't have a paper bag, fearful it will find its way to a landfill. What's happening here in this city is just criminal.

But we were not in India to pick up garbage. We were here to understand the culture, meet the people, and see the sights. Arriving at the caves, we boarded a bus that would take us to the base of the caves. We were happy to hear these sites were precious enough to the people that cars were restricted from getting too close. As we left the bus, our guide explained we had a choice: to climb to the top of the mountain by foot, or to hire porters who would carry us to each cave and back down again.

Leanne felt it was a bit decadent, but how could I pass that up? So, for twelve dollars each, we sat in a chair connected by two poles and had four men carry us to the top of the mountain. In the beginning it was a bit awkward, but once we relaxed and tried to pretend we were the maharaja and maharini, it was kind of fun. The first portion was a switchback trail, but once we got to the top, the path undulated up and down steep stone steps to get to each of the thirty caves carved in the hillside. Going down the steps, they would bring us backward; going up steps, they would turn on the narrow path high on the cliff and take us facing forward. This was repeated again and again for over two and a half hours. All for twelve bucks each! It was all an experience.

The thirty caves were all carved in the upper side of a horseshoe mountainside. As we got to the top we could see all of the caves in a line, each with its own unique façade. From the entry vantage point, we could see how the hillside must have looked when the first artisans showed up to carve in the Second Century BC. The mountainside was jagged both above and below, with meticulously carved cave entries in between. Although this site had the largest collection of Buddhist cave temples in the world, most of these caves were carved as monasteries. Surprisingly, the monasteries were more ornate than the temples.

These caves had one other difference from the caves from yesterday. Many still had their original painted ceilings and walls. Unlike yesterday's caves, these had been undiscovered for more than one thousand years. They were only discovered in 1918, when British soldiers hunting in the jungle for tigers happened to spot a small opening in one of the buried caves and alerted the authorities.

Twenty-five years of excavation unveiled the oldest of the thirty caves: the first Buddhist temple built in the Second Century BC. This temple was unique in that the first sect of Buddhists used it. The second sect then adorned it six hundred years later. What was the difference? The first sect followed the original idea of enlightenment and didn't have or believe in idols. The original decoration was still on the walls, which showed only designs, flowers, fruit, and a few animals. The second sect of Buddhism added more colorful paintings on the ceiling and columns and outer band, which showed stories and fables, moving Buddhism closer to worship of objects. The second sect added these paintings in the Fifth Century AD, some six or seven hundred years after the temple was built.

The temple was built similarly to the temple we had seen yesterday, with its cathedral arch ceiling and columns lining the sides. Remember, this was carved from one solid mountainside, so the adding of columns is totally decorative and not needed to support the structure. Above the columns a band of carved Buddhas circled the cathedral. Once again, monkeys greeted us as we exited the caves. They were so pretty and seem to have quite the life.

Back in our chairs, we were again brought up and down narrow stairways to reach the next cave. It was still almost one hundred degrees outside. Good thing the humidity was low, or we would've been sweating.

We were carried to the various caves one after the other. Each cave was unique in its own way. The second sect of Buddhism built the remainder of the thirty caves. This was evident because of the paintings on the walls and ceilings, as well as from the name of the ruler at the time, which was carved into or painted on the cave. Unfortunately, not a single name of an artisan was found. The painting was fabulous and for the most part very well preserved. Our guide took time bringing us to each panel, explaining the story they told. Vegetable colors were used for the most part, although you could see areas where the color blue, ground from the precious stone lapis, was used, as well as mother-of-pearl. The whole experience was spectacular and exactly what we look for in a trip. We were very happy we came, and it's a do-not-miss on my list.

It was now time to go. Our porters hoisted us in the air for the ride down. This was where we heard all of their sad stories, trying to get sympathy so we would increase the tip. I swear they started sweating and grunting more. What the hell—I gave them forty bucks, a 70 percent tip. That's five bucks each for hauling us up and down the mountain for two and a half hours. Even Leanne, who once got in an argument with a camel driver in Petra over fifty cents, thought I should have given more.

Dodging the mass of peddlers, we made our way back to the bus for the ride back to the waiting car. Stepping onto the bus we noticed a group of thirteen- and fourteen-year-old girls who appeared very excited that we joined them. As we stepped off the bus, for the second time in India a group of girls ran after Leanne and asked to take her picture. It was very cute. We were still not sure why everyone was asking to take her picture. It couldn't be she is an American, because they weren't asking for mine. Could it be because they thought she was a movie star? I didn't think so. Why wouldn't they be asking for mine? With my cowboy hat down low over my face, I could've been mistaken for Brad Pitt. Okay, so that's a stretch. I guess it must've been her natural beauty, inside and out.

Tomorrow we leave early for our next stop. Before I go, I must say a few words about the hotel. I was assured this is by far the very best in town. That said, its being a Taj, I am disappointed. I would give this at best three stars. I do, however, give the staff and service five stars. Everyone here couldn't be more gracious and attentive. I know sometimes chains have to make compromises to be in certain locations, but the very least they can do is provide five star beds. I have slept in better beds at a Holiday Inn. Mr. Tata, you might want to talk to the Starwood chain. They give every guest, even in their budget hotels, a heaven bed. Goodnight—'til we meet again tomorrow.

EXOTIC INDIA: DAY SIX

As we take off from the runway heading to the next city, I always like to take one last look at where we have been. Heading north to Jodhpur, I noticed the city of Aurangabad below was different from what we had traveled through during our stay. The apartments and houses looked newer, the streets looked wider and cleaner, and there wasn't a slum in sight. There was obviously more to India than rubbish-covered dirt roads. I realized that, being tourists, we looked for ancient ruins to explore when we traveled, not middle-class neighborhoods. Historic sites seemed to be surrounded by rural villages, not suburbia. At least from six thousand feet, India looked a little more modern than I have seen so far.

We were heading for Jodhpur. To get there we must first take that thirty-minute flight back to Bombay and catch a connecting flight to Jodhpur. That means another three-course breakfast on silver-rimmed china. Didn't we just have breakfast at the hotel? There must be several airports in Bombay; every one we have been in looks entirely different. The others were pretty old and rundown, but this one was modern and bright. It couldn't have been remodeled in such a short time.

We had a two-hour layover, so we ducked into the American Express lounge. I say that like I do it all the time. Truth is, in all my travels, I had never before seen an American Express airport lounge. Handing over my platinum Amex, we were ushered into the "Platinum Room," where you don't just have nice seats and dry cheese and crackers, but full table service with a full menu and bar. The service is so attentive here in India we just had to order something. So for the third time in three hours we were having breakfast.

After a quick one-hour-and-fifteen-minute flight, which of course included breakfast, we touched down in Jodhpur, the "Blue City" or the "Sun City." Meeting our guide, we made our way to our hotel. At one point Leanne inquired about the large, beautiful building sitting high on a hill; the reply came back, "Why, that's where you are staying."

Driving up the hillside along the tall red sandstone wall, we reached the massive gates of the Taj Unaid Bhawan Palace. All we both could say was "My God!" It was stunning and massive. Set on twenty-six acres, construction on the palace started in 1929 and continued for fifteen years until it was finished in 1944. This was to be the new 327-room palace of the maharajah and his family. Built out of pink sandstone interlocking blocks using no mortar, when finished, it was the second-largest private residence in the world. It may very well still be. Sadly, the maharajah could only enjoy the palace for three years before he passed away in 1947.

The present maharajah still lives in the palace, although today he and his family occupy one large wing of the building. The rest of the palace was converted to a sixty-four-room hotel and was dedicated in 1970 and remodeled in 2005. Today two-thirds of the structure has become a hotel, a museum of the family history, and home to the king's car collection. The cost of maintaining this property for a single family had to be enormous.

Driving up through the motor court, we truly got the royal treatment. Six doormen in typical Indian costume stood along the sides of the staircase holding four gold poles supporting a red canopy for us to walk under. As we proceeded up the grand stairway, rose petals rained down from above. Walking down the art deco corridor we were greeted by butlers with the typical hand-clasped bow of love, a show of respect. If I had known it was going to be this special, I would have worn better clothes. How can you beat an entrance like that?

The entry corridor led to the center reception rotunda. It was breathtaking. Rising 120 feet, the hall was capped with a dome reminiscent of that of a state capital. The hall was long enough to be a basketball court. The room was made totally of pink sandstone, and its scale was impressive. Looking up, we saw two additional balconies, which ran in a continuous circle, giving access to suites and banquet rooms. There was neither reception desk nor a concierge desk. This grand entry was a sitting area created to impress visiting dignitaries, and indeed they came. Prince Charles, Brad and Angelina, Paul McCartney, Richard Gere, Bill Gates, and many others all enjoyed what we were now experiencing. We weren't sure Liz Taylor had been here, but Liz Hurley was married in the gardens, arriving by helicopter.

Receiving a welcome drink and leis, and of course our bindi (a red dot put on your forehead, said to retain energy, strengthen concentration, protect against demons or bad luck, and representative of the third eye), we were shown directly to our art deco suite for check-in. Our suite is large, with four rooms, the bathroom having a large marble tub in the center. This must have been the most magnificent property we had ever stayed in during our travels. The hotel and service were seven stars. We were treated like the king's personal guests. We decided we were not leaving.

Well, we didn't come here just for the hotel; we did come to see the sights. Jodhpur is a wonderful town and doesn't seem to be as dirty or busy as the last places we visited. Being the Sun City, Jodhpur is hot—not humid, just hot. To avoid the midday heat, it was recommended that we start touring at four thirty. This also gave us some time to explore the hotel's indoor and outdoor pool and the shops, restaurants, and, of course, the trophy bar, with its collection of animal heads and tusks from the maharajah's hunts. This was the first time we had seen tiger heads stuffed and mounted.

Picked up at four thirty, we headed to the city market to explore what our guide insisted was the real India. Downtown Jodhpur wasn't downtown San Francisco. It was what you would expect of a developing nation with strong village ties and traditions. My father would have said it had local color; my mother, on the other hand, would have said … Let's just say my mother liked Paris.

The main street with its shops and pushcarts is adjacent to the Fifteenth and Nineteenth Century markets, which might not have changed in four hundred years. Shops lined the narrow streets, selling all types of spices, fruits, nuts, clothes, knickknacks, and any other item the locals could use. This is a local market, and apparently this city doesn't have to depend on tourism. Surprisingly, prices are fixed. You won't find any haggling, begging, or chasing done here. It would have been a very relaxing stroll if it weren't for the constant roar of motorbikes and tuk-tuks running up and down the narrow alleys. Some were so narrow you had to turn sideways to avoid being hit. And why didn't anyone get hit? Just as the driver had told us in Mumbai, all the drivers had good brakes, good horns, and good luck.

We finished shopping—yes, we bought something and had it shipped—and arrived back at the hotel after dark. As we approached our room we noticed our door was open. Stepping inside, we found two valets who had just freshened our room, folded our clothes, and prepared a bubble bath sprinkled with rose petals for us to relax in. You are really treated in royal style here at the Umaid Bhawan Palace. We finished the evening by riding the 1940s hand-carved elevator to the third floor of the dome. We continued by foot up the narrow, twisting stairway to the top of the dome to dine on the outdoor balcony, which circled the rotunda high above the lights of the city fort. Leanne was so pleased to be able to order simple lamb chops—and they actually came without a ton of spices, a much-needed respite for her stomach.

EXOTIC INDIA: DAY SEVEN

We started our day with breakfast on the lower patio just outside the rotunda overlooking the gardens. As the cool breeze blew, we watched the resident peacocks parade back and forth across the grass.

Occasionally they would wander up the steps, hoping to find a treat, only to be quietly shooed away. The service was impeccable here. As we walked through the halls of the hotel the staff members would stop what they were doing to give us a warm smile and the handclasp with the traditional bow.

This morning we headed to the Thar Desert. The Thar is the one of the largest desert in the world in size—behind the Sahara, and bigger than the Gobi.

Our forty-five-minute drive brought us through many of the typical villages in India. I was starting to understand this place a little better. No matter what politicians want you to believe about the expanding economy of India, 70 percent of the people here live in one of these many villages. By our standards, they would be third world. By theirs, it's a way of life steeped in traditions and culture that they are not ready to abandon.

Our first stop was the home and factory of a pottery maker. We had been to pottery factories many times before, but this was different in several respects. First was the ancient way he crafted the pots. Most potters sit on a chair or stool and spin the wheel with their feet. Here they still use a method that must be centuries old. Squatting low to the ground, the potter took a three-foot stone disk and spun it like a top using a thick, pointed tree branch. To get the speed he needed to work the clay, he would place a large pole in a carved-out hole in the disk and quickly stir to increase the acceleration. Just squatting the way he had to, to work on this disk for long periods of time was impressive. This gentleman, as is tradition, learned from his father this craft, which he learned from his father, etc. He was a Muslim with a big smile filled with red teeth stained from years of chewing betel nuts.

The second unusual part was that when he was done making six different individual things, he didn't try to sell us anything. A matter a fact, he gave Leanne a gift of an Aladdin's lantern she was fascinated with. They were all very welcoming here.

The next stop was a weaver. Indian weaving is supposedly very unique. Every time we travel someone tries to sell us a carpet. Truthfully I wouldn't know one that belongs in a palace from one that you can buy in Home Depot. For that reason I never buy. But this time was different. I had been looking for an Indian horse blanket to go with my new saddle and figured this might be the place to get it. It wasn't Navajo Indian, but it was custom-made by Indians, nonetheless.

Now the next stop was very different. We went to have a traditional opium tea ceremony. That's right, opium! This had to have been the strangest thing I had ever done. There is actually a ceremonial contraption for mixing and straining opium tea. There is also an even stranger way to drink it. Kids, don't try this at home.

Apparently our host was a recovering opium addict, of all things. And yes, opium is illegal here. As we sat on the floor, the opium was ground into a paste and mixed with lukewarm water and then strained several times into two wooden bowls. When the tea was finished, get this! It was poured in to another person's hand, and we sucked up the tea with three sips. There I was, sucking opium tea out of a strange Indian man's hand in the middle of the desert. You can't get any more degrading than that.

Want to know what opium tea tastes like? Try putting a used cigar in tepid warm water and letting it sit for a week. Remove the cigar and then suck it up from someone else's hand. For the life of me I couldn't figure out how anyone could get past the taste long enough to get hooked. There was a small amount of tea left, and our recovering addict lunged for the last sips. Our guide tried to stop him, but he was yelling "But it's my opium!" in Hindi. After a friendly scuffle, our guide let our host have three more small sips out of his hand to finish the few drops that were left of this foul liquid. Man, I wasn't expecting that. I just hoped the drug dogs at the airport wouldn't pick up my scent.

After leaving this man's home we had a black buck gazelle run before us. Our guide smiled with delight because it is a sign of good luck to see a black gazelle. Apparently this was the animal that Vishnu himself rode down to earth from the heavens. How lucky are we?

Next stop: lunch. Traveling another half hour over a bumpy desert dirt road, we found we were heading deeper into the desert. Passing small farms, water buffalo, gazelles, cows, goats, and camels, we were beginning to wonder if we were on an African safari instead of in search of lunch. We couldn't imagine there would be anything out here remotely worth driving to, let alone a place we would want to eat at. Then, shortly after passing a shallow watering hole where water buffalo were cooling off from the midday sun, we came upon a brand-new beautiful boutique hotel designed like a Moroccan castle. We had arrived at the House of Rohet. Why on earth would someone build a five-star hotel in, trust me, the middle of nowhere? As we drove up, three butlers and the manager come to greet us with umbrellas open to shade us from the sun as we walked to the veranda.

The Rohet has only eight rooms, all suites. Before lunch we were taken on a very nice tour of the hotel. I could actually understand why people stay here. It was very relaxing, with a pool, hotel spa, and hidden verandas high off the desert floor. I imagine they would provide a spectacular view of the desert to view the sunrise and sunset. Shortly, the stables would be finished, and guests would be able to ride Marwari horses into town. The suites were very well decorated, and I am sure, with the staff-to-guest ratio, that the service is terrific.

Driving back to town, our last stop was the Mehrangarh Fort. Built between 1459 and 1843, the fort served as the protective palace for the maharajah and his family—along with countless servants and concubines, that is. Sitting high on a hill, it, of course, has fortress walls lined with cannons. Above is a truly ornate maharajah's palace perched on top of the massive walls. This fort is very decorative and very well preserved. The palace has been put in a trust so it can be protected for generations to come. Many of the palace rooms are still intact and very colorful, with their gilded ceilings and decorative walls.

Most forts we visit are pretty blocky stone structures. Within this palace, rooms behind the fortress walls are gilded and dressed for a true maharajah. From the fort we could see the new decorative palace where the current maharajah lives and where we have the good fortune to be staying. There also is a beautiful view of the actual Blue City. The Hindu people believe that blue is the color of the top Brahmins, so they paint their houses blue. In the low light of the afternoon, the blue hue shimmers, creating such a beautiful view. Now it was time to weave our way back through the old city once more to get back for dinner and an evening of packing for the next day's adventures.

EXOTIC INDIA: DAY EIGHT

It was time to leave the palace and travel on down the road, literally. We are taking a six-hour drive to our next city, Udaipur. Before we leave Jodhpur—did you know that polo came from here? For you polo people, this is also where jodhpur pants and boots came from. The pants, as you know, are flared out in the upper thigh and have tight fit below the knee. Evidentially the maharajah wore them to Queen Victoria's Silver Jubilee in England and the English went nuts over them, adopting them for their dress. It's not like the English riders needed another excuse to be pretentious.

Our trip will take us through the desert, up and over the mountains, on three national highways and several state highways, and through many small villages. Driving on the national highways here wasn't much different from driving in the villages, except here you play your elaborate game of chicken on a two-lane undivided highway with large trucks at high speed. At one point a large truck decided to pass a farm tractor at the same time another semitruck decided to pass that truck. There we were, staring down the road at three large vehicles taking up the full two lanes and coming straight for us. None of the drivers slowed down, moved, or fell back. We were all confident we would figure it out when we got there, and indeed we did. Half on the highway, half off, two trucks, one car, and one tractor passed side by side on a two-lane road and then continued on down the road, as they say.

The drivers seemed to think that if they honked their horns to alert you to coming death, they were off the hook as far as any consequences were concerned. Before we started the drive I wasn't feeling well and decided to sit in the front seat and put my seat back for a rest. As I put my seatbelt on, the driver, to make me more comfortable, said, "No, no, no, it's not necessary. Trust me." After that, I could only think, *Are you kidding me?*

Driving for six hours, we passed through the real India: small villages with cows roaming, women in colorful saris carrying goods on their heads, and shopkeepers trying to sell their wares out of cramped stalls in cement buildings all jammed side by side. Outlet malls, McDonald's, or Costco can't be found off the highways here—or, for that matter, just about anywhere in most of rural India. This was real India—"local color," my father liked to call it.

We broke up our six-hour drive with a stop at the splendid Jain temple of Ranakpur. Built in the fifteenth century, the Rishabji temples stand two to three stories high. For those of you who have been to the temples of Angkor Wat in Cambodia or seen pictures, it's very reminiscent of that. The temple is elaborately carved inside and out from a mixture of marble and sandstone. The temple has four large, intricately carved domes and copulas held by 1,444 carved pillars all surrounding the center square altar, where four statues of the Jain founder sit in the lotus position looking out toward the worshipers. I liked the Kama Sutra carvings on the ceiling as you enter the temple. I will tell you more about the placement of these later on the trip.

Leaving Ranakpur, we left the national highway to drive down the state highway. The good news was that there were no trucks. The bad news was the highway was washed out by the monsoons last year and left in poor repair. For miles we were rattled and bounced down the road. Along the way we saw farms spread all over the mountainsides. Each one had miles of rock fences. The landscape is very rocky, so I can only imagine that it took centuries of farming to get all the rocks cleared out so they could farm. This is obviously where all the rocks came from to build the miles and miles of stone fencing. We passed a few trees filled with huge, upside down bats. We also saw women and oxen using the ages-old waterwheel, walking around and around in a small circle to bring water up from the deep wells they have built.

The six hours passed, and we rolled into Udaipur. Udaipur is a larger city, yet smaller than Johdpur. Let's not confuse these with cities we are familiar with. You won't find a Hard Rock Café, a Cheesecake Factory, or any department stores. We did see one semimodern shopping plaza at the beginning of town. I also spotted a few modern buildings dotting the city.

Udaipur is a romantic city, built around the clear blue waters of Lake Pichola. Our hotel for this stay is the Oberoi Udavilas. Built as a modern hotel to emulate a maharajah's palace, the hotel sits on thirty-six acres at the edge of the lake. Driving up to the entrance, we were greeted by the hotel butlers, the hotel manager, and a representative from A&K, our tour operator. We were beginning to feel like visiting dignitaries. As we entered the lobby, we were again showered with red and white flower petals from above.

Our room was beautiful with a tremendous view of the lake and the maharajah's summer palace (now a Taj hotel), which sat in the middle of the lake, accessible only by boat. Our hotel would have been an excellent choice for Liz. Opening our rear doors, we accessed a small patio with two chairs and a traditional gold-fringed Indian umbrella, which would be lovely for breakfast or for drinks in the evening. Off the patio, several steps led us directly into our own semiprivate pool, which looked across the lake. The infinity pool was lined with light and dark porcelain tile. It would be a wonderful place to cool down in the evening with a glass of wine to view the city palace lights shimmering off the clear blue water of the lake.

EXOTIC INDIA: DAY NINE

They take service and food service very seriously here in India, as they do all services. The maharajahs might have insisted on having everything done for them, but as Americans we still felt we could butter our own bread just fine, thank you. Just try picking up your own napkin and putting it on your lap here and you will have two waiters descending on you, gracefully taking it and laying it on your lap. Heaven forbid we didn't finish a dish or comment it wasn't to our liking. Within moments our table would be surrounded by the restaurant manager and the chef, backed up by a bevy of waiters waiting for orders on how to satisfy us. Honestly, we were just full!

Udaipur was founded in 1559 by Maharana Udai Singh II as the final capital of the Mewar kingdom. The site was chosen for its proximity to the surrounding mountains, which would protect the kingdom from Moghuls, who were invading major parts of India. As a result, not a single army ever conquered the area. As usual on our trips with the company, A&K set up a very special treat for us here in India. In Russia, we visited the gold and diamond vaults; in Africa, we hunted with Bushmen; and here in India, we will have cocktails with the present maharana of Udaipur, Arvind Singh Mewar, the direct descendent of the founder. We looked forward to the evening.

Udaipur is a clean, middle-class town with a major industry: quarrying marble. There must be hundreds of companies dealing in marble slabs and blocks there. Major factories have not opened in town but are located thirty kilometers away. This has helped prevent the development of the ever-present slums. The slums have invaded other large cities as people from the small villages travel to them, looking for work in the factories.

The day, however, was for visiting the Hindu temples outside of Udaipur. Driving out of the city we skipped the highway and drove into the mountains through tribal villages to arrive at the Nagara temples, dating back to the Eleventh Century. The main part of the temple remains intact, while most, if not all, of its surrounding statues, columns, and smaller monuments have been taken by antique hunters, who ship them around the world to sell. Perhaps you may have a lotus Buddha you wish to return?

Like in the other temples we have seen, the carvings were wonderful. They tell a story of the gods through fables and demonstrations of the life of the times. I paid special attention to the Kama Sutra carvings, as these are obviously timeless. Having these erotic carvings may seem strange to us today, but centuries ago they served two purposes: first, they were a way of expressing the lifestyle of the kings, or more likely their fantasies, and second, they served as a pictorial form of sex education. Men carved these depictions, so I think they allowed their minds to go pretty wild. From what I have read and seen, these carvings are not unique among carvings on Hindu temples. So expect more reports. A guy is writing these, remember.

Our second stop was to the Eklingji temple dedicated to Shiva, the Hindu god of destruction. (To be clear, Shiva destroys evil.) To enter we passed through a row of old women sitting on the floor selling the most fragrant leis and flower garlands. Stopping, our guide purchased three at a cost of ten rupees (twenty cents) each, handing one to each of us, advising us not to wear or smell them. Smelling them will pollute them, making them unfit for Shiva. This is an active temple that the maharana of Udaipur still attends. Entering the temple, having removed our shoes, socks, and camera, we had the great fortune to be in time for the Hindu ceremony. As we waited for the curtain to be removed from the idol, two men rang four large bells in the small room. They rang and rang and rang. Personally, I was surprised people came back. If you didn't have a headache coming in, you sure could have one going out.

Leaving the temple, we couldn't help but notice a parade of women in colorful saris balancing large platters filled with dirt and rock on their heads, walking up and down a steep flight of stone stairs. One after another, each walked down with a full load and dumped it into a waiting trailer, only to disappear back up the stairs to retrieve another load. At the top of the stairs, they were building a new house, and it would have been way too expensive to use men with wheelbarrows to do the job, as women could be hired for half the price.

It was now off to lunch. Driving higher into the mountains we were headed to an eighteenth-century fort, which has been converted into a five-star hotel after being abandoned in the 1960s. Stepping from the car, again we were met as if we were royalty; again rose petals floated from the skies. When would this admiration end?

We headed back to the hotel for a quick cool down before going off for cocktails with the maharana. (All kings are called maharajas except this one, because he was the most successful warrior-king; thus, his title is maharana.) Driving through the city at night was a whole new experience—same game, only this time with lights and in the dark. So many headlights darted in and out down the street that one would swear one was in the belly of a pinball machine. They don't even honk the horn; whom would they warn?

The maharana lives in the old city palace. The palace now has been divided into four parts, two being hotels, one a museum, and the fourth being the actual home of the maharana. Ushered through large private gates, we pulled up to the palace, where the maharana had parked one of his many antique automobiles beside the front door. He was hoping his 1924 Rolls Royce, which the family has owned since it was new, would be accepted in this year's Pebble Beach Concours d'Elegance. If it got in, we would consider attending this year.

{As we later learned, the maharana's 1924 Rolls Royce was accepted into the 2012 Concours at Pebble beach. To our surprise, sometime that June we received a call from the maharana himself informing us that he was accompanying his car to the United States and wanted to get together. For six weeks we communicated and arranged to meet him at the airport when he arrived and to take him to dinner in Monterey, California. During the famous August Pebble Beach Concours, we spent five memorable days with him and his family. Being a guest of a car exhibitor, we gained unprecedented access to one of the premier car shows in the world. Upon the Maharana's return to India we were excited to find ourselves included in the royal newsletter. A copy of my fist book, *Business Biographies*, has also been placed in the royal library.}

Entering his home was like walking into a fine antique furniture store. Every nook and cranny was filled with period furniture and mementos of his family, impressive visitors, and travels. Within a few moments of our arrival, one of the maharana's staff members led us to the lakeside patio, where the maharana and his son warmly greeted us. We were pleasantly surprised that we were the only invitees to meet with His Highness this evening. I have met several presidents, but I do think this was the first time I had the pleasure to meet royalty.

Our conversations crossed quite a few subjects, from horses to politics. When I asked him if he had gone to the United States he replied he had and he didn't like it. Like so many others we have talked to during our years of traveling, foreigners always complain how they are treated in the States, especially at the airports, where they feel they are unfairly singled out. Although I don't think going through security is any easier or more pleasant here in India, I do believe we should figure a way to make visiting the States more pleasant for foreigners.

On the other hand, foreigners have to be more tolerant of the customs, traditions, and procedures of the countries they visit before passing final judgment.

I was especially shocked when his son complained about the poor infrastructure, dirt, and disrepair of New York City. Yes, I know New York has its issues, but had he walked around India lately? Truth is, we all complain about our countries, and I do my fair share; we just don't like hearing it from anyone else. That's how wars start, isn't it?

The evening was charming and special, and we had a delightful time. We only wished the infrastructure was better going back to the hotel.

EXOTIC INDIA: DAY TEN

Wow! When we arrived back to our room, on our bed was another package from the maharana. (Remember the difference between a maharajah and a maharana? They are both kings of their respective kingdoms, the maharana being a great warrior-king.) The package on our bed, with the official seal of Udaipur, contained several pictures commemorating our evening with His Highness and his son, the prince, along with a nice letter on official stationary that I could keep in my collection. I hoped it wasn't a secretarial. I guess he liked us— New York, not so much.

We had just returned from a morning tour of the king's palace and museum when we received the gift. The king's palace was a sprawling complex built on a hillside on the opposite side of the lake where we were staying. We had a magnificent view of the palace, and this morning we got to see it close up.

The building of the palace was first started in 1559 by the maharana of Udaipur. His successors have built onto it for twenty-two generations of maharanas. The last of the structures were added in 1911. The Royal House of Udaipur has had one family ruling since 600 AD to the present, making it the longest-ruling dynasty whose descendants still retain their position. One thing we found interesting was that to make this happen, there were about six maharanas that had been adopted from close relatives' families when the sitting maharana was not able to produce a son himself.

We toured the many buildings of the palace, from the king's chambers and rooftop gardens to the queen's chambers. The past maharanas, being polygamists, had many bedrooms for their concubines in the queen's wing. I found it curious that the bedrooms all seemed to have mirrored ceilings. As a man, I would guess that the king must have visited, rather than the other way around.

About 40 percent of the palace has been transformed into a museum with many collections of antiques and paintings. It also houses a very large nineteenth century crystal collection from a manufacturer in England. The collection has only recently been put on display. One of the nineteenth century maharanas visited a British exhibition of crystal in Calcutta. He was so enamored with the fine-cut glass that he commissioned over six hundred pieces of furniture and accessories to be installed into his palace. Unfortunately, he passed away before the delivery, and the shipment was locked away for a hundred years before our friend, the current maharana, discovered it in a warehouse. It is now on display and is the largest collection of cut crystal in the world, which includes even a totally crystal bed. There were many other things to see from past maharanas. I personally liked a couple of portable steam-powered fans from the late nineteenth or early twentieth centuries.

While here, we also discovered some other interesting facts. Did you know that zero came from India? I had thought it was the Arabs or the Chinese who had created it, but no, it was India. I think everyone has claimed to have discovered "nothing" over the years. No, it's true. I looked it up: the Indians were the first to use zero. The Babylonians only used a placeholder for "nothing." The Indians filled in the empty space. Another myth debunked. Other things the Indians invented were the games of chess and Parcheesi. I believe Parcheesi is the oldest board game still played in the United States.

I have to say, the palace could use some restoration and care. The hotels located at the palace I found a bit bland, and I wouldn't recommend them for a five-star stay. The maharana's private quarters, on the other hand, which we did pass by today, were in perfect restored condition. Leanne and I attempted to take a picture in front of the gates during daylight; unfortunately without a pass we were denied. I felt like Cinderella after the ball.

After the palace we continued on with our city tour, visiting a three-story temple built in 1691. More carvings, more Kama Sutra; let's move on. The rest of the afternoon we spent visiting shops and a few homes showing life from the eighteenth and nineteenth centuries before heading home for a quick rest.

At five o'clock, we were off again for a boat tour of the lake. Walking onto the dock we passed a group of people waiting for a boat and boarded a twenty-four-passenger skiff for our evening cruise. When we shoved off from the dock, we were the only ones on board—a private boat for the Troys. Word of our new friendship with the maharana must have been spreading through the kingdom. Or maybe the people on the dock were going someplace else. Or perhaps we should thank A&K once again.

A pleasant evening breeze passed over the boat as we circled the lake, making a stop at one of the maharana's private islands. The island was originally created as a pleasure island for the maharanas and the nobles. Today they are struggling to find a more profitable use for the island as a hotel and restaurant complex.

Back on our private boat (maybe we are special), we were headed back to shore to continue our adventure. The day wasn't over for us just yet. We had one special dinner before we retired for the evening.

Tonight we were having a special dinner on the hotel barge in the middle of the lake, accessible only by a boat. Arriving at the dock at seven thirty sharp, our speedboat was waiting to take us to our romantic dinner on the water. Pulling up alongside the barge, we were greeted by the Indian staff that helped us aboard. This was going to be very romantic, since we were the only ones onboard besides the staff of five: two waiters, two band members, and the chef. The front of the barge was set up with cushions on the floor and three small, low dining tables. With a drum and flute playing in the background, our first course arrived along with two fireworks explosions from another city palace nearby. Nice touch, Maharana.

Then the food started to come ... and come ... and come. At one point there were three full baskets of naan bread sitting in front of us. The chef was going crazy with his tandoori oven at the back of the boat. Between the never-ending wine and the food cooked for ten, we just couldn't stop laughing. We even had the waiter in stitches as well. At one point Leanne asked if he had chutney. Next thing you know, the skiff was speeding back to the hotel for chutney. Dinner took almost three romantic hours, mostly because I asked for English breakfast tea. Again we heard the boat go speeding away.

Back on shore we were greeted by staff members and led by flashlight to an awaiting cart to drive us back to the front of the hotel (a trip that maybe takes thirty seconds). Heaven forbid they should expect us to walk! We definitely could have used the walk. No wonder they call India the diabetes capital of the world.

EXOTIC INDIA: DAY ELEVEN

This great road show wasn't unlike the others. We had to break down the tents, pack the gear, and move to the next town. The next town this morning was six hours away. We were driving to Jaipur, the capital of the state of Rajasthan.

The highways we were driving today were luckily all four-lane divided roads. That doesn't mean the drivers were any different. They still bounced around, cut between trucks to pass, and for some strange reason, when the traffic wasn't bad, drove down the middle of the road over the dotted white lines. Maybe they were just positioning themselves for the next quick maneuver. There must be traffic rules here, but certainly no one follows them. Driving on our four-lane highway we constantly saw cars, motorbikes, and tractors heading the wrong way up the highway. Instead of using one of the openings in the median to make a proper U-turn they would just drive the wrong way up the shoulder. No one seemed to care about all this bedlam. If people drove like this in the States, guns would be blazing. Here everyone just smiled and moved over. You have to wonder which of us is civilized.

Six hours passed and we finally entered Jaipur. I would like to say that, being the capital, it's a very modern city, but I can't. There are a few modern buildings and a small seven-story shopping mall, but the rest of the city is similar to the rest of the towns and villages we have visited. When it comes to development, India still has a long, long way to go.

Oh my! Passing the golf course and polo grounds we turned to pull through the large ornate iron gates of our hotel, the Rambagh Palace, where we were stopped by security. Rolling down our window, we were greeted by a friendly smile. "Hello, Mr. Troy, we were expecting you. Would you please step out of the car?" We were than led to a vintage V8 Ford convertible driven by an Indian chauffeur for our final approach to the palace. I have to say, the receptions were getting more and more elaborate. Pulling up to the entry, an entourage of staff members were on hand to greet us like visiting dignitaries. There were three butlers, two A&K representatives, the hotel's executive manager, two lovely Indian assistants, and a doorman with an Indian fringed umbrella to protect us from the sun. This is something you would expect for the head of state at the White House. As we walked to the lobby, a beautiful Indian maiden threw the traditional welcome flower rose petals from a silver tray as we navigated the stairs, followed by an entourage. It was pretty cool.

The Taj Rambagh Palace was originally built as a hunting lodge and was transformed into a palace sometime in the twentieth century by a reigning maharajah. It's still owned by the royal family and has been lovingly restored by the Taj Group, which has done an incredible job returning it into its former glory—and so much more. The palace, gardens, and many period restaurants and bars are just magnificent. The service is just splendid and way beyond anything we have every experienced as well, as you can see. I couldn't say enough about this property, and we had only been here a few hours.

Entering the jasmine-scented lobby we were handed cool towels and adorned with a lei and the traditional red bindi on our forehead. After a brief introduction, an adorable Indian hostess escorted us through the lobby to our room for check-in. I have to say, if I were a maharajah looking for concubines, I would be shopping at the Taj Hotels. Every woman working at the palaces we have stayed at has been stunning. I wonder if the maharana of Udipur could make me an honorary maharajah?

You know, I had never been in a hotel where I was so drawn to taking a picture as I walked down the hallway. These hallways were incredible, from the Old World light system outside the door used to alert the staff of your wishes to the elaborately hand-decorated walls. These walls were covered with delicate and colorful floral patterns, all hand-painted. There were portraits of the maharajahs in various poses and beautiful carved wooden period doors. The hallways were a delight to look at as we walked to our room. Approaching our suite, we saw three staff members waiting patiently for our arrival. We found our personal butler for our stay, a stunning tall beauty with a tray of champagne, and a second butler with pitchers of juice and assorted fruit. This was a first.

We stepped through the doorway into the entry hall of our suite gazing into the main salon of the room with its dark wood interior and Indian motif. If you are looking for decadence, India is the place for you. Being guided through the salon, our hostess led us to the main bedroom with a bed that was so inviting with its rich fabrics, I couldn't wait to kick my shoes off and jump in. As everyone exited with customary bows, our butler, Himmat, presented his card and advised us he was at our disposal for the remainder of our stay. What a country!

After taking a quick rest we returned to the lobby for a six o'clock tour and explanation of the history of this fine palace. We learned so much from these excursions, which usually familiarize us with properties very quickly. This tour was no exception. Our tour ended at one of the most beautiful rooms of the palace, the Japanese pavilion. There waiting for us were glasses of fine champagne and hors d'oeuvres—and, of course, our trusty butler to show us back to our room. With the evening song of eighty-two species of birds chiming in from the garden, we sipped champagne and listened to the sounds of the palace.

After freshening up, we were off to dinner. There are three restaurants here, and each has a very distinctive flair and cuisine. Tonight, for us, it's Continental. Being greeted by name, we were led to a comfortable table beneath the portrait of the last queen who resided in the palace. For the next two hours we were pampered with service. Even the chef came from the kitchen to greet us by name and assure us we could alter the menu to our liking if necessary. As we left the restaurant our butler greeted us with a warm smile to ask if dinner was to our liking and to escort us back to our room. Not only did he put us in the elevator, he greeted us when the elevator doors opened when it arrived on our floor. I am telling you, this man was everywhere. Opening the door to our room to retire, we just couldn't believe what we saw. While we were off eating, a pattern of red and yellow rose petals had been placed on the floor for our arrival. Also, a bath sprinkled with roses had been drawn. This is so over the top we couldn't seem to stop laughing. If Brad and Angelina got better service than this, it would be embarrassing.

India so far had left us breathless, and we couldn't wait for tomorrow.

EXOTIC INDIA: DAY TWELVE

Pulling from the driveway with the Taj Rambagh Hotel fading in the distance, we were already missing our butler, Himmat. Thankfully we were in good hands with our A&K guide Gajendra, who assured us we were going to have a fun-filled day in Jaipur. The city of Jaipur was founded in 1727 by Jai Singh and named in his honor, *pur* being the Hindu word for city.

We started our day early to have breakfast with elephants. We were headed to the outside of town to an elephant polo club, where we were to take an elephant trek through the mountains. Heading from the city, we passed through the old city of Jaipur. Here we saw shops and markets already bustling even at this time of the morning. They call Jaipur the Pink City. We could see why, as all of the buildings in the old city were painted a pinkish terra cotta color. The color choice came from the king's orders. The terra cotta color was a favorite of the king, and he signed an order to paint all of the buildings for a visit from the prince of Wales in 1876. To this day the only color that can be used in the old city is Jaipur pink, by legal decree. The streets were so interesting I just had to take some pictures. Jumping from the car with Gajendra, our guide, by our side, we all tried to make our way to the other side of the street for a better perspective. If you think driving is a challenge here, you should try crossing the street. Cars don't slow down, move, or stop for pedestrians. They expect you to figure it out. The safest way to cross here is like an elephant: go in a large group, move together, don't run or fall back—and be brave.

Back on the road, after traveling half an hour we turned off the road onto the rugged landscape, heading to the hills for the polo club. The elephant polo club is an oasis in the middle of the rocky terrain. As we came through the trees we could see the large arch gate with four staff members waiting for us with chilled juice and cool towels, along with an elephant trunk raised up to greet us.

After feeding ten bananas to our noble ride, we mounted our elephant. Our elephant handler rode in front on the neck, guiding us into the hillside. The sound of elephants, various birds, and, of course, peacocks rang through the trees. We heard more sounds here than we had deep in the jungles of the Amazon. Twenty minutes into our ride our handler hopped off and left us alone on this gentle giant. Grabbing our camera, he spoke commands to our pachyderm, putting him into several poses for those Kodak moments. It was amazing. Traveling farther down the trail we were surprised to find a staff member set up with a champagne station. Popping a fresh bottle of bubbly, he poured two crystal glasses and handed them up to us, where we toasted to the good life. We enjoyed the bubbly as we rode back up toward camp.

Back at camp, a staff of six was waiting to prepare breakfast for the two of us. Sitting under a thatched hut next to the polo field that hosted elephant competitions, they served our favorite dishes. They even served my favorite, Lyonnais potatoes. What an experience.

It was now time to tour the forts and palaces of Jaipur. Driving down the city street leading to the fort, we were just in time to see the elephants return from their work, bringing visitors up the steep mountain road. There must have been forty animals returning, making the streets look like an old-time circus coming to town. It was fun watching as motorbikes and cars zipped around them. The Hindu commander in chief of Emperor Akbar built the fort. Akbar was the Mughal ruler at the time. Akbar, a Muslim, teamed up with the commander, a Hindu, in a deal that guaranteed that the commander would get the title of king. He was also promised riches by way of the spoils of war. Akbar got fewer uprisings from the Hindu population and more land to rule. It was a very successful relationship for both. The fort is massive and very well preserved. I particularly liked the harem, with its raised bathing platform positioned in the courtyard strategically beneath the king's window. It was here, interestingly, that another lovely Indian woman requested a picture with Leanne. They seemed to find her fascinating.

The finest craftsmen from India and the surrounding countries were brought to Jaipur to build the commander's new palace and fort, with its inlaid mirrors, stones, and hand-sculpted marble. Looking from the roof of the fort you can see the still-intact walls meander through the mountains, up and down jagged cliffs, all to protect the palace. The view is one of a miniature Great Wall of China. Mind you, this wall is still five miles long. The craftsmen were so talented that when they finished the king's palace in Jaipur, they were sent to their next assignment at the Taj Mahal.

After lunch we were off to the royal observatory, built in 1728, and the Chandr Mahal palace, where the royal family still resides. The open-air observatory was very unique. The kings, being obsessed with time, brought in architects, astrologers, and engineers to create some very interesting sundials. These weren't your everyday in-your-backyard sundials. One literally rose two hundred feet and was accurate to two seconds, looking like a stairway to the stars over a skateboard half-pipe. They could tell time by watching where the shadow from the point of the tower crossed the ramp, which was etched with quadrants broken into hours, minutes, and seconds. In addition to the main tower, there were a variety of smaller dials in several shapes, all with varying degrees of accuracy. At the observatory we also found various designs that could map the skies and locate astrological signs. This is very important to Hindus, since the number-one requirement for two people to get married is how their signs match up. About 85 percent of Hindu marriages are arranged, and 80 percent of those are based on horoscopes. We found all of this very, very interesting.

Heading to the palace, we were informed that A&K had arranged another special treat. In addition to touring the palace grounds open to the general public, we were given access to the private residents' section of the palace. Although we weren't going to sit with the royal family and have tea and cookies, we were given access to the private reception and entertainment rooms, which are still in use. The king resided in the palace up until his passing the year before. His daughter, her husband, and his grandson, the future king when he finishes school, still reside here. The tables were still filled with pictures of celebrities who had been entertained here.

As we left the palace we passed through a large entertainment courtyard, where they were setting up for a wedding. Weddings are big here. Over a thousand people could attend, and they are big Bollywood productions. This one was going to be huge and lavish. We also saw the behind-the-scenes food preparations. Trust me when I say the health department in the United States would have shut down this Bollywood wedding.

Driving back to the hotel, we again passed through the old city. It was busier than it had been in the morning. Cars, motorbikes, bicycle rickshaws, tuk-tuks, pushcarts, cows, camels and horses pulling carts, men in formal dress on white horses going to a wedding, people hurrying each and every way—it was all very exciting. Either this city was cleaner than the past ones we visited, or we just didn't notice anymore. It was really a little of both. Out of the old city, as we got closer to the hotel, the streets got wider and the buildings and houses got nicer. The government seemed to be doing some good here with the money available after corruption.

When we arrived back at the hotel we had a warm welcome from the staff. We were a little disappointed our butler hadn't greeted us.

The executive manger did scoot across the room when he spotted us. When had we gotten so popular? Upon exiting the elevator on our floor, who should be standing there but Himmat? The little dickens had been busy running our rose petal bubble bath and placing a bowl of fruit on the table for us to enjoy before dinner.

This evening we decided on a casual dinner at the outside-themed railway station restaurant. Of course, as we opened our door to leave, there came Himmat around the corner with a flashlight to show us the way. The evening temperature couldn't have been more perfect. Following Himmat onto the platform, everyone seemed to know our name. During dinner, even the sous chef and executive chef came to our table to meet us and chat. We were holding court over pizza and margaritas. This wasn't the first time the chefs came out to greet us. It happened at most every meal. Ready to go back to the room, we walked down the platform beside the 1895 train cars. Whom did we see? Of course, there was Himmat walking toward us to escort us back to the room. My god, we might just pack him up and bring him home with us!

EXOTIC INDIA: DAY THIRTEEN

We were on the move again—destination: Ranthambore for a three-day, two-night Indian tiger safari. Half the staff of the hotel must have followed us out to say good-bye as we packed up the car. It was almost embarrassing how many times I said I love this hotel. I bet Brad and Angie think all the attention when they travel is only for them. Well, it's not—the Troys get it too.

As we pulled out of the gate of the Rambagh Palace, I felt like an eight-year-old kid leaving home and my trusty butler behind for summer camp for the first time—okay, a rich kid leaving home. I am going to miss the palace.

Pulling out of Jaipur we had one last look at the changes in the city. We could see that the city was struggling to modernize. A newly elevated metro was nearing completion, roads were being widened, and new buildings are being erected. Controls had even been put in place to protect the surrounding mountains from totally disappearing from sandstone and marble mining. As we departed, we did see a man hanging off a cliff with a large metal rod, trying to break free large pieces of sandstone. What a dangerous job that looked like. One wrong move, and either he would fall from the cliff, or the cliff would wind up on him.

Ranthambore National Park was a three-and-a-half-hour drive away, so we settled back to enjoy the countryside. Normally I try to avoid these long drives, but passing through the many local villages that dot the road was fascinating. Harvest was just finishing up, so all the villages were teeming with excitement as the trucks, tractors, and animal-driven carts passed through each village. It was thrilling to see.

The drivers of the trucks here in India like to decorate and personalize their vehicles with paint, streamers, rags, and even hubcaps, of all things. They spend so much time in them that they love them more than their wives. In some of the more rural villages, you will even find a unique truck called a Jaugard. A Jaugard is a home-built, unregistered truck crafted using old salvaged car and truck parts. It appears a bicycle or two may be thrown in as well. They look like something homemade in 1912, not 2012. The trucks are used to haul anything from crops to people. They also try to dress up and personalize these simple machines. Seeing one of these homemade vehicles coming down the road straight at you, loaded with people, makes you feel you are in an episode of *The Beverly Hillbillies*. These trucks make the Model T look cutting-edge.

As we traveled through the smallest of the villages, children would run out into the street to wave and greet us as we slowed down. Looking into the fields off the highway, we could see the last of the crops being harvested. Most of the work was being done by women wearing brightly colored saris as the men played cards and talked in the shade of thatched canopies outside the local shops. We spotted many having a shave in one of the many open-air wooden barber chairs. These villages were very primitive. Driving through the main market, I saw a middle-aged woman carrying a large pile of sticks on her head as two men walked beside her empty-handed. Even the men admitted the women do all the work here. It made me shake my head in bemusement.

We pulled into Ranthambore, where an A&K representative joined us for the last few miles of the ride to the Oberoi Vanyavilas Luxury Tent Hotel. The Oberoi was once the grand hunting lodge of the maharajahs. As we exited the car, two large elephants walked from the gate to greet us with their trunks up. Accompanying them were staff members with cold towels, cold drinks, and a handful of bananas and sugar cane to feed our welcoming pachyderms. Being showered of flowers feels like so yesterday.

The lodge was just beautiful. The hotel was on twenty-six acres and had a total of twenty-five permanent tents. These tents were built for luxury. Being permanent, with solid walls and canvas roofs, the tents had the ability to give us all the grandeur and amenities of a fine hotel. A four-poster bed was a focal point of the room, which also featured a private bath area with a large tub, shower, and walk-in closet. Let's not forget the minibar, Wi-Fi, and big-screen TV. Now, this was camping.

We got to our private tent and garden by strolling down one of the winding stone lanes through the dense green trees and colorful bougainvillea while the birds sang us a song. It was all very romantic, especially at night when the small lanterns lit our way.

Finishing a quick lunch, we met our safari guide and hopped in our private open-air jeep to photo-hunt for tigers. The Ranthambore National Park was once the maharajah's backyard hunting grounds for our hotel. Today, of course, it's a protected sanctuary for India's endangered tigers.

The park was different from the African Serengeti in that it was a very rugged forest terrain. This made it much harder to see other vehicles whose passengers might've spotted something interesting. The park also lacked a radio system, unlike the guides in Africa.

We zigzagged through the park, climbing over rocks, and drove through rocky riverbeds. It made for a wild ride. For three hours we felt like we were on Disney's Indiana Jones Temple of Doom ride. During that time we found large troops of black-faced monkeys, herds of white-spotted deer, mongoose, wild peacocks, some very colorful birds, and a type of wild cow/deer thingy, but, alas, no tigers. The guides thought that because of yesterday's unexpected rains, the tigers moved up-country. This may have been so. We did have two more safaris to go, so we thought we might get lucky. I just had to make sure I went to the restroom before climbing back into that jeep.

EXOTIC INDIA: DAY FOURTEEN

Sometimes writing about a safari can be very difficult. After all, how many times can you mention a mongoose if you don't see any big game around? Driving through the forest is interesting for an hour or two, but after a while you'd like to see something more than you can see in your own backyard—especially when you got up at five in the morning to get there.

When the jungle is quiet, the guides always fall back on the birds. "See the pretty yellow bird in the tree there? Aah, you missed it! Well, how about the owl over there? You see it? It looks just like that branch he is sitting on." I'm half kidding. Birds are very interesting wildlife—if you're seventy! (Just kidding, again.) The bird life is very varied and colorful here. One in particular has the same coloring as tigers. It is known as the "tiger's dentist." When tigers are lazing around, it will come over and pick at the tigers' teeth and gums, giving them a good brushing. I am not sure how its camouflage tiger coloring fools the tigers.

When Leanne saw our open-air jeep yesterday, she was very concerned that a tiger might jump in. I thought that after five hours of jarring roads, she would welcome one sitting on her lap. There were only forty-five tigers left in this park, and they could wander over 131 square miles. It was like finding a needle in a haystack. Finding a needle in a haystack can be done; *Myth Busters* proved that. Now that I thought of it, this was going to be harder.

Truly, going through the jungle was interesting. Today we had permits to search zones four and five. Yesterday we were in zone one. Four and five were much different terrain, with their large, serene, crocodile-infested lakes and tree lined shores. Here the waterfowl stood in the shallow water as crocs looked on until dinnertime.

The maharajas built many stone structures here to hide in during hunts or to celebrate the kill in. Over the years, moss has grown on them and the banyan trees have grown around and over the ruins, making them look like fabulous scenes from *Raiders of the Lost Ark*.

Three hours had passed and even the monkeys had moved on, so we headed back to the main gate. Today was going to be another bust as far as viewing tigers was concerned. Checking out, we heard of a male tiger sighting in zone one, the zone we had a permit for yesterday. Luckily, anything can get done in India if you know the right people or price. In this case it was both. Within moments our guide was back in the jeep, and we were speeding through the gates of zone one for a second time. They were right. Shortly after entering, we jumped out of our seats to view a six-year-old male tiger walking on the road, marking his territory. The guide told us this particular male had devoured a villager two weeks ago. That was either true or his way of telling us to stay in the car. He swore it was true—even described the grisly details.

More jeeps descended on the area. The cat was off into the dense woods, and we were in pursuit. Our driver spun the car around and told us to hold on, and we were now on Mr. Toad's Wild Ride to catch the tiger coming out of the brush on the other side of a dry creek. The road actually felt smoother as we flew over the rocks at thirty miles an hour. Taking a sharp U-turn across the creek, we were right in time to catch our tiger emerging from the trees and watch him cross the road. We had found our needle! It was now back to the hunting lodge to celebrate our shoot.

Waiting for our afternoon safari, we relaxed under the colorful umbrellas of the Oberoi pool. Doing a safari in an open-air jeep in the middle of the day would just be brutal. Even the tigers were smart enough to take shade during the noonday sun.

By three fifteen we were ready for the next adventure into the park. Our guide was so confident we would be seeing a tiger he brought along his five-year-old daughter—"99 percent," he told us. A&K even used its pull to get us back into zone one, the only zone over the past several days that had a tiger sighting. If the male had been there this morning, he was bound to be there this afternoon. Having to stop every few hundred yards to mark his territory (i.e., pee), how far could he get?

Driving for two hours up and down, down and up, bumping and jogging back and forth, we wandered with no luck. The guide fell back on the bird-watching. We were down to peering at owls' eyes shining out from the knots in the trees. "Yes, yes, we see it." I swear we both said we saw something when we didn't just to move on. We were here for the tigers! Given that there are only forty-five tigers in a hundred-thousand-acre park and tigers sleep most of the day, this was going to be like winning the lottery.

Exasperated, the decision was made to just wait at one of the two watering holes in zone one. Tigers must get thirsty. So we waited and waited and waited some more. It was clear: lightning wasn't going to strike twice. We did see our share of birds.

Our last night at the Oberoi, the management had a special farewell for us. After having drinks in the bar, a lovely hostess requested that we follow her to our table for the evening. As we followed her outside we could see a special table for two set in the garden beside the pool. Our table was set into a bed of flowers circled with candles on the ground with colorful lanterns hanging above. An Indian flute player sat crossed-legged serenading us just under a nearby tree. This was to be our special private dining experience reserved only for special guests of the lodge.

Ready to retire for the evening and prepare for yet another day of adventure, we approached our tent and there at our front door, spelled out in flowers, we saw a very special thank-you.

EXOTIC INDIA: DAY FIFTEEN

For the second day in a row the alarm sounded at five thirty. Today was a special day on our adventure; the Taj Mahal awaited us. From Ranthambore we traveled by train to Bharatpur and then by car to Agra. It was going to be a long day.

Arriving at the rail station was probably no different today than in Gandhi's time. Pigs and monkeys were seen roaming the station with the poor and beggars sleeping on the platform. When the first train pulled into the station, it looked like something out of a Humphrey Bogart movie. Except for a coat of paint that was applied in 1960, nothing seemed to have changed here since the British pulled out in 1947. *If this was our train,* I thought, *shoot me.* It was not.

At precisely 7:00 a.m. a train pulled into the station, the same as the first. The second-class compartments were stuffed with people, who were even flowing out the doors. With all of the windows open, obviously there was no air-conditioning in these cars. I couldn't tell whether the bars of the windows were to prevent passengers from climbing in or from jumping out. I would have done the latter.

As the train stopped, our A&K representative motioned us to board. I was a bit puzzled; I was expecting the Orient Express. What I got was the midnight express. Oh, god! I got the middle seat! Didn't they know I was an honorary prince from Udaipur? I knew that eventually I would have to fulfill my duties and get up close to the local color and mingle with my people. Luckily we were in the first-class car. What was the difference? Air-conditioning. I have to say, if you close your eyes, the train was as smooth as Amtrak. I think. I have never been on that either.

We pulled into Bharatpur after two and a half hours and walked off with our backpacks just like two poor college kids. The local A&K representative immediately recognized us as the royalty we had come to believe ourselves to be. Outside the station, our driver was waiting with our luggage, which had been sent on ahead to make the trip easier. We were now in the state of Uttar Pradesh. With its 200 million people, it's the largest state population-wise. If Uttar Pradesh were its own country, it would be the fifth largest. The United States has 350 million people, and it's forty times larger in size.

We had several stops to make before making the pilgrimage to the Taj. Our first stop was the deserted city of Fatehpur Sikri. Getting to the fort was almost as exciting as the fort itself. Again, we were among crazy drivers. The fort bus swerved so violently through the traffic it was like being in a Keystone Kops comedy. Like all drivers here he did get us to the entrance safely. Built in 1569 by the Moghul emperor Akbar as the new capital fort and palace, it was abandoned after only twelve short years. Only 10 percent of the city still exists, and it boggles the mind that it could have been bigger. The amount of work that went into such a place only to be abandoned for some inexplicable reason seems insane.

What remains of the fort and palace is just beautiful, built completely out of red sandstone. In its prime it would have been decorated with colorful drapes, carpets, and painted plaster walls. It would have been exactly how one would imagine a Moghul emperor would have lived. Over the short life of the city fort, Akbar experimented with several architectural styles. Craftsmen designed buildings out of red sandstone and painted plaster, eventually building out of white marble and gold. It is said the last addition was the artisan's practice area for the intricate work seen at the Taj Mahal. We could just imagine the emperor sitting in the grand courtyard using the young and beautiful slave girls as pawns to play a game of life-sized Parcheesi on the inlaid floor. Akbar was very wise and impressive for a totally illiterate man with no education. He unified India by welcoming the advice and counsel from learned people from all religions around the country. Being a Muslim, his closest religious adviser was a Jesuit priest. Only when his great-grandson, a hardline Muslim, focused on one religion did the empire fall apart. Hello, anyone listening out there?

Back in the car we were now off on a one-hour drive to Agra. Pulling into Agra I really couldn't figure out where the local village ended and Agra began. The only difference there seemed to be between the village and the city of Agra was that the water buffalo were stopped from crossing the street by the cement median. It seemed like pure chaos. The prince's infrastructure was a bit older in the town. The streets were teeming with water buffalo, old model tuk-tuks painted green, horses, cows, donkeys, and people—lots of people. Over 50 percent of the people here are shoemakers, so we passed men on bicycle-powered carts piled with shoes moving through the city. Just about everything moved through this city by human power. This place was crazy. Every type of business is done right off the street, including women collecting cow patties with their bare hands to dry and sell as fuel. The flowers in India were the most fragrant I had ever smelled; unfortunately, it couldn't mask the sweat of hundreds of cows, horses, camels, and donkeys. This part of the city smelled like a stable. We're cowboys, though, so we felt right at home. It doesn't get more primitive than this; you have to love incredible India.

We pulled into our hotel, the Oberoi Amarvilas, with just enough time to check in and have a quick lunch. Like most of the hotels, it was dripping in opulence. Walking up the steps to the front doors, we entered a massive courtyard comprised of four large pools with sixty-four individual fountains shooting gently into the air. We were escorted to our room, which had a magnificent view of the Taj Mahal. We only had time to change and get back on the road. Wait a minute—I just realized we didn't get showered with flowers. Maybe the hotel had been alerted to our time crunch.

We were told the best time to see the Taj Mahal is at sunset and sunrise, when the soft shimmer of light bathes the white marble, giving it a glow. There was just one more stop before we descended on the Taj: the Agra Fort. Akbar also built the Agra Fort only five short years before he built the fort in Bharatpur. This fort seemed smaller and much more fortified. The fortification consisted of two miles of seventy-foot-high walls, two moats, and, apparently, caged cheetahs that could be set loose in the event of trouble. The fort seemed impenetrable. Expanding their empire, the Moghuls must have built dozens of these forts around India. In the process they amassed a treasury that represented nearly 25 percent of the world's wealth at that time.

It was now time to see one of the most recognizable landmarks in the world. The Taj is the main attraction for people who visit India, and here we were. Going back to the hotel, we traded our chauffeured car for a chauffeured golf cart. Due to security and ecological reasons, cars have been banned from the streets within a quarter mile of the entrance. We were dropped off at a checkpoint and made the short walk to the Taj. Our guide Yogi recommended we not look at the Taj until he set us up at the place the designers had originally envisioned visitors would enter. He was right; our first encounter with the Taj Mahal was magnificent.

Lined up at the great entry gate we had our first view through the gateway arch. In the distance we could see the arched doorway of the building. As we slowly walked closer, more and more of the façade appeared, eventually unveiling the complete structure as we entered through the doorway.

The Taj was breathtaking. Set on a riverbank at the far end of a garden and accentuated by a long reflecting pool in the foreground, it looked like a painting hanging in the sky. The white marble from this distance didn't reveal its beauty all at once. From here we could see the symmetry and scale of one of the most historic buildings in history. As the sun was setting, we could see why Yogi recommended coming at sunset. The marble seemed to change color and texture as we strolled around all four sides of the building. Getting closer we could see the detailed inlays done by craftsman some 350 years ago. The different shades of inlay on the small columns on the sides appeared to shimmer as we walked by. After taking what must have been one hundred pictures, we sat on a bench and watched as the sun changed the lighting on the grand dame of India. We would be back tomorrow at sunrise to view the Taj in a different light and see the intricate detail inside.

EXOTIC INDIA: DAY SIXTEEN

Sunrise at the Taj Mahal is supposed to be a very special time in India. The downside to enjoying it is you need to awaken at four thirty in the morning. So, bright and early, we awoke and got dressed to stroll over to the Taj. Yogi recommended we get there as early as possible to avoid the lines. What other crazy people would do this? We arrived at the Taj at five thirty for a six o'clock opening, and I was a little surprised that there were actually six people already in line. Shockingly, within fifteen minutes of our arrival, there must have been two hundred standing in the queue. Yogi was right. Waiting was not without peril. Between the flies attacking us and the smoke from shopkeeper burning garbage on the street, it was just a typical India morning.

The doors opened, we entered and went straight to the entrance to the Taj. Most of the guests stayed at the back of the garden as we had done yesterday to take their multitude of pictures of one of the New Seven Wonders of the World. We had taken our photos the evening before, so all we had left to do was to photograph the inside of the Taj. As we walked along the fountain path we still couldn't resist taking more shots of this famous building. This time there was nearly no one in back of us blocking our view.

It was now time to enter the main mausoleum. This was a memorial for Queen Mumtaz Mahal by her husband, the Mughal emperor Shah Jahan.

Again Yogi was spot-on in his timing. Not a soul entered the temple when we did, and for a good twenty minutes we were alone with the queen and her husband. Taking pictures inside the mausoleum is strictly forbidden—unless, that is, you are the only ones inside and have fifty rupees to "gift" the custodian. The interior is fabulous. The inlaid stones are of such detail that you would think the leaves are blowing in the wind. Craftsman took great pains to grind the finest of detail into the inlay. There are even microscopic veins made from mother-of-pearl in the leaves. The use of a different color gives the impression that the leaf is partially turned; no detail was ignored. It was obvious that the emperor saved his best artisans to work inside for his queen.

Our time was short in Agra, only one night and two half days. Having done the Taj, we were now on our way to Orchha. Heading out of town we saw the most peculiar sign. There in a vacant lot was a sign that read Clean Agra, Green Agra, with the largest pile of garbage you could imagine right behind and underneath it. Yogi explained it was a campaign slogan for the city to "go green." The mayor's idea of going green was to paint all the tuk-tuks, garbage cans, and benches green. Sure enough, every tuk-tuk in the city was green, but the streets were still not cleaned up. That was India.

Our train for Orchha was leaving the platform at eight ten. Can you believe it? Up at four thirty, taking pictures of the Taj at six, and luggage packed and on the train for our next stop at eight ten. Now that was timing. The train wasn't the Orient Express, but it was better than the one we had arrived on: bigger seats, a tiny bit more modern, and still very smooth.

As usual our A&K representative was on hand as we stepped off the train. It was great having someone meet us to speed things along. It was now a forty-five-minute ride to the village of Orchha. Orchha is a holy city famous for its temples and palaces. What sets these apart from some of the other forts and palaces we have seen are the well-preserved frescoes. We visited two palaces here. The first, Jahangir Palace, was built in the sixteenth century. The palace was built combining both Muslim and Hindu architecture. It took twenty-two years to build, but as we heard, it was only used for one day. Now all red sandstone, this palace was once covered in blue tiles and a yellow and cream-colored paint. A newly painted mosque, in the original colors and fully restored, gave us a good idea what the palace must have looked like five centuries ago. What a pity the emperor only spent one night there after its completion.

The second palace was the Raja Mahal, the palace of the king. Not as ornate as the Jahangir Palace, it did have the distinction of being continuously occupied by kings for over a 250-year period. The long occupancy, I'm sure, helped with preserving the 500-year-old frescoes on the ceilings and walls. The frescoes tell the story of the reincarnation of Shiva. Our guide went through each panel one by one, explaining how the reincarnation of Shiva matched with Darwin's theory of evolution. Shiva started as a fish and transformed to a land turtle, then to a mammal, then to a midget (I had to think about that one), then to a man, and so on ... I was starting to get the hang of this Hinduism thing. There was much more to see in the village, but we didn't have the time. We were now off on a five-hour drive to Khajuraho. This village is a popular tourist destination because of its magnificent carved temples, 10 percent of which are of a Kama Sutra nature.

Since it was a five-hour drive, we decided to put my new iPad 3 to the test and watch a couple of movies. There are no highways going to Khajuraho, only narrow bumpy roads that barely fit two cars passing side by side. We tried to stare at the screen and concentrate on the movie, but it was hard to ignore the big semi-trucks aiming head-on for us, or the cows strategically standing in the middle of the road. At times the asphalt seemed to disappear from under our car. Watching our iPad on an Indian road gave new meaning to motion pictures.

We pulled into Khajuraho around six that evening to check into our hotel. I think we had become very spoiled here in India. Although the Lalit Temple View Hotel is very nice and the best in town, it's not a wonderful palace, which we were getting used to staying at during these past two weeks. I would describe the hotel as a basic Hilton or Marriott you would find in a small U.S. city. It is attractive, but nothing special. Service is adequate, but again nothing special. I suspected I would have to butter my own toast in the morning.

EXOTIC INDIA: DAY SEVENTEEN

Originally, when planning this trip I had picked Khajuraho as one of the destinations I wanted to travel to. I just couldn't resist the tenth-century temples with their intricately detailed, deep hand carvings—especially the ones dedicated to the education of Kama Sutra. Everyone knows the importance of education.

There were originally eighty-five temples here in the village. Only twenty-two still stood, through a little luck and a bit of restoration. Surprisingly, one thing that helped them survive was that the forest grew around them, hiding them for over eight hundred years, which protected them from villagers, treasure seekers, or worse, destruction at the hands of the Moghuls. The Moghuls would have defaced or dismantled them for sure. They were first discovered in 1832, but weren't really acknowledged and saved until the forest surrounding them was cleared in the early 1900s.

We only had the morning to explore these temples, which I was told outshine those found in Angkor Wat. We toured the largest and most well-preserved structures in both the east and west sections of the temple area.

The army, to help keep the men busy when war wasn't being waged, originally conceived the idea of constructing the temples. The army wanted to ensure that the men stayed physically active and in shape—and to make sure that they wouldn't think too much. I guess mutiny happens if your soldiers have time to use their brains.

Sixteen thousand craftsmen were brought to the area to assist in the carvings of these temples, while the army did the physical labor of moving and organizing stones. Each temple took up to twenty-five years to complete, and multiple sites were worked on at one time to speed up construction.

The temples were impressive, rising an average of one hundred feet in the air. With the inside chambers being only twenty-eight feet high, we quickly understood that the remaining height was made from solid sandstone blocks with their outer edges carved with scenes of everyday life. Leanne thought the ancient Hindus must have invented silicone implants since all of the woman statues and paintings had perfectly round Beverly Hills breasts.

If it were not for the fact that the entire area stands on a surface of solid granite, the temples would have long ago collapsed under their own weight. Each temple has over seven thousand different scenes from life, 10 percent of them being erotic Kama Sutra carvings. These scenes depict everything from putting on makeup to sexual positions that would make a porn star blush. The three temples we visited would have had in excess of twenty-one thousand carvings.

After photographing the 10 percent of the carvings of the Kama Sutra nature (that would be 2,100 carvings), it was time to blow this town.

It was time to fly off to Varanasi, the holiest city for the Hindus. Varanasi is for Hindus like Mecca is for Muslims, Jerusalem for Jews, or the Vatican for Catholics. We were traveling from sex to nirvana. Varanasi is the place all Hindus want to go one day in their lives to pray or to die and be cremated.

The flight was a short forty minutes. We were lucky we booked business class, since all the carvings we purchased would certainly have put us over our baggage weight limit. After a thirty-minute drive from a very modern airport, our driver informed us we were passing through the new section of Varanasi. When he later told us we entered the old city, Leanne and I just stared at each other with amazement.

What was the difference? Unlike the villages we passed through on the road, Varanasi is a very, very old city. The religious books put the age of the city at 5000 BC. The oldest authenticated record documents the city at three thousand years old. This would date Varanasi to around 1000 BC. No matter which source you believe, they both refer to a very old city. In fact, it is the oldest continuously inhabited city in the world.

We were staying at the Taj Nadesar Palace. There we were, feeling like we were back home. As before, we were showered with flowers, adorned with leis made from the mud of the Ganges, and welcomed with the sounds of the conch shell. As we approached our room, an Indian musician was at our door playing the flute. The Taj has only ten rooms, each named after a famous guest who stayed here. The king of Bhutan once occupied the room we stayed in. How appropriate, since we will be going there the last few days of this trip. Inside, the king's registration page hung framed on the wall. I would love to have that for my collection!

We barely had an hour in the room before we had to leave for our sunset boat ride down the Ganges. From the boat we could see the traditional ceremony of giving thanks to Mother Ganges. This ceremony has been performed each evening for the past three thousand years.

Cars are not allowed to drive up to the river, so we had to make the final pilgrimage on foot through the old city. Since there wasn't a master plan to build the city, buildings line the riverbank, leaving only one main street ten blocks long, which leads to the water. All other access is through one of the many small narrow streets or alleyways, four to six feet wide, which all end at steps that lead directly into the water.

The streets were the most crowded I had ever experienced. Every one of my senses was on alert—especially my sense of amazement that a city like this still exists in the twenty-first century. Varanasi was crowded chaos. It was amazing traffic could move at all. Even more amazing was the realization that there were no accidents and not one instance of road rage. They had tried installing a few traffic

51

lights several years back, only to turn them off for lack of compliance with the traffic laws. As we approached the river, our guide handed us both jasmine garlands for our necks. Coupled with the mosquito spray we had put on before we left the room, we were ready for the Holy River. You could write a whole book on just the goings-on in this one ten-block stretch of road.

Walking to the river, we dodged beggars, cows, sleeping dogs, peddlers, rickshaws, and the thousands of motorbikes that were all still allowed down this narrow street. Our guide Dharam was so excited about his city it was infectious. I couldn't help but to get in the spirit and try to dance with a cow. The cow, on the other hand, tried to bite my leg—not very holy of her.

Taking the stairs at the end of the road we turned and strolled past colorful lights, umbrellas, candelabras complete with flames created by burning clarified butter, and a huge crowd of people. All was passed before climbing aboard our own private longboat to view the ceremony from the river. With the sun nearly set, our boatman rowed us up the Ganges to view one of the two crematoriums, which have been in use continuously for centuries. Hindus cremate their dead. Coming from near and far to be cremated in the holiest city, on the banks of the holiest river in India, pilgrims were everywhere. Here, it is believed, their spirit can go directly to heaven. As our boatman rowed toward the crematorium, we could see five large fires burning just off the edge of the river. Bodies have been burned this same way for the past several thousand years. Twenty-four hours day, open-air fires cremate the remains of the dead. There are over three hundred cremations a day—over one hundred thousand a year. As you would suspect, these cremations use a lot of firewood, which was thus stacked in gigantic piles everywhere. Most of the wood is brought in by boat, as the streets are too narrow to move the enormous volume required.

Back at the hotel we decided to celebrate our anniversary, which just happened to be today, by getting a spa treatment. After talking to the spa manager, we settled on the ceremonial treatment. This treatment was given to the king and queen the night before coronation.

How could we resist that? The treatment consisted of getting rosewater footbath and then sitting on the edge of the tub while our feet soaked in dense rose petals and warm water. Two people then poured milk, honey, and purified holy water from the Ganges over our bodies. We were then scrubbed with spices and sandalwood paste, rinsed, dried, and massaged for an hour. Aah, nirvana!

EXOTIC INDIA: DAY EIGHTEEN

The phone rang at four with a wakeup call so we could get ready early for another holy trip down the Ganges at sunrise, just as we had done at the Taj Mahal. Sunrise on the Ganges is a sight not to be missed. Our spa date the night before wasn't over until eleven thirty; we just hoped we wouldn't fall asleep and fall overboard.

Leaving the hotel at five, we made our way to the river. The morning traffic was much lighter, and we arrived just in time for the sun to peek over the horizon. After we stepped into our longboat, our oarsman pushed off for our trip down the river to view the holy ceremonies up and down the river's edge. The mornings bring men and women to the river to bathe in the holy waters. It might be holy, but it isn't clean. The Ganges must be one of the most polluted rivers in the world. Chemicals from factories upstream and sewage are released daily, creating a toxic brew. To the holy swimmers it's as pure as the Himalayan water that flows into it. As we watched the oars of our boat dip in and out of the greenish water, the Hindu followers dodged the garbage on the shore for their morning bath.

The sun was now just above the horizon as we rowed down-river to the second crematorium on the river. The colorful buildings and the dozens of brightly painted boats parked on shore made for some fabulous pictures.

Drifting away from the main steps we saw Varanasi's laundry works: ten stone slabs jutting into the river from the banks of the shore with five people slapping the stones with large sheets and towels. The workers alternate between soaking laundry in the waters of the Ganges and smacking it on the stones over and over until it is clean enough to hand to women on shore to sort for drying. I do think our hotel used a more modern service.

Past the laundry the crematorium was already operating this early morning. We arrived just as a body had been placed under the firewood. Stopped on the river, we watched as they coated the wood with clarified butter (used as a fire starter) and then set the pile aflame. We could clearly see the body of a deceased woman wrapped in a traditional red and gold sari. According to Hindu tradition, the soul gets released as the body burns. It was a bit overwhelming to watch.

After rowing back up river we stepped off our boat and climbed the stairway to a small alleyway. Leanne was still a little queasy from watching the cremation. We traveled down the alley past enough stacked wood to power a small city, winding our way back to the main street. Even here, in alleys four or five feet wide, those darn motorbikes came roaring down beeping that bleepin' horn. It was hard enough walking down these streets in early morning, dodging cows and cow patties, without having to pin ourselves to the wall for a motorcycle. Couldn't I just have clotheslined him?

Our next stop was Sarnath. Sarnath is the city where Buddha lived and gave his first sermon. To Buddhists this is a very holy spot. Only the foundation of the city and a large, round stupa, a mound-like rock that contains remains of Buddha, still exist here where Buddha once lived and spoke in the Third Century BC.

Back at the hotel we took an opportunity to take a final carriage ride around the forty acres of gardens of the property. The hotel carriage was 210 years old and was once used by the king, and our driver was a third-generation coachman for the royal family. Champagne in hand, we stopped at every tree and flower, our excited coachman jumping off the carriage every few yards to bring us back mangos, roses, jasmine, and what he called a "good apple fruit." It was very cute.

It was now time to leave Varanasi. Mark Twain's observation about this city was "Varanasi is older than history, older than tradition, older even than legend, and looks twice as old as all of them put together." Mark, it hasn't changed since you were last here.

Leaving the Taj in Varanasi was one of the most heartwarming experiences since our arrival in India. As we prepared to leave the lobby, the manager of the hotel explained it was tradition in Varanasi that a holy man bless us with a spoonful of curd and sugar before our departure, something we just had to take part in. After our brief ceremony, we boarded our car as the whole staff assembled on the hotel steps, hands clasped, wishing us *namaste* for a safe journey. We just loved this place.

Flying into Delhi I had a window seat to view the last city we would visit in India. I have to say, from the air it looked much nicer and more modern than the cities we toured. There were large park areas, trees, wider roads, and modern buildings. I swear I saw a shopping mall.

Landing at a very modern airport we were greeted by our A&K representative and shown to our car. We were excited to see that our regular driver Satish, who had to leave us in Agra, had arranged to meet us in Delhi. I wasn't sure which one of us was more excited to see the other! He has become part of our family.

Driving from the airport we noticed the roads were better, the boulevards were wider, and, shock of all shocks, everyone paid attention to the traffic laws. The cyclists even wore helmets. Delhi is a true world-class city. Driving down diplomat row, we could imagine being in London, Paris, or Rome. We were in awe of the wide, clean, treelined streets. We just love this city.

After we pulled up to our hotel our car door was opened by a uniformed doorman who greeted me, "Welcome home, Mr. Troy." How did he know who I was? This was just a first example of the service provided by the Imperial Hotel in Delhi. A British architect redesigned Delhi in the 1930s, and the Imperial was the only hotel he created for the royalty of England. Stepping into this impeccable hotel brought us back to a bygone era of classic elegance. We were delighted to learn we had been upgraded to a suite.

Our first night in Delhi we enjoyed a fantastic meal at the Spice Route Restaurant, voted one of the best restaurants in the world, and deservedly so. Man, we just loved Delhi. Tomorrow we would get to explore the most modern, international city in India.

EXOTIC INDIA: DAY NINETEEN

This would be our final day in India, before moving on to Bhutan. We were so glad that our trip started in Mumbai and slowly progressed until we reached the more cosmopolitan city of Delhi. The way we did it made it seem as if Delhi was progressing right before our eyes.

Our last day was spent doing a full-day tour of the old and new wonders of this beautiful city. Our first stop was Old Delhi. Now, only a fraction of the main city continues to look like most of the towns and villages we had explored along the way. Old Delhi was the seventh of the cities that were built here. The other cities, dating back over three thousand years, are now gone or lie in ruin. Shah Jahan built Old Delhi, originally called Shahjahanabad, in 1650. He was the emperor who had just completed the Taj Mahal. Shah Jahan was the Steve Jobs of his time; he had a great eye for design.

While building the city, Shah Jahan also built his fort palace, the Red Fort. This fort is a monster of a complex, completely designed by the emperor with high walls, lush, manicured gardens, palace halls, fountains, and waterways, which he could enjoy aboard small boats. To get to the Red Fort we explored Old Delhi by bicycle rickshaw, pedaling through the small streets and alleyways before emerging on a large boulevard that led to the Red Fort. We didn't have the same experience with the motorbikes zooming up and down the streets, and that was a nice change.

The fort originally housed the Peacock Throne until invading Persians looted the palace and brought it back to Persia. The shah of Iran held the title of king of the Peacock Throne, but in truth that honor belonged to Shah Jahan, the Mughal king of India. The palace in its day must have been the most opulent place on earth. Ceilings were decorated with silver and gold. Colorful tapestries hung from the walls, and translucent marble and mirrors reflected in the many waterways, which meandered through the garden. This planned palace was different from the ones we had seen around India in that more attention was paid to the gardens here than at any of the older palaces. The emperor even had an underground piping system that could divert the river water for the fountains and waterways, which passed through the halls of the palace to act as a natural air-conditioning system. Shah Jahan came into his own as a designer here in Shahjahanabad.

Leaving the old fort, we toured New Delhi. The wide boulevards, tree lined streets, parks, new buildings, and government plaza were as impressive as in any other world capital. It gave us the feeling that we could have been in Paris, London, or Rome. If India arrived on the world scene, it was here in New Delhi.

Our next stop was to Humayun's tomb, a monument to Emperor Humayun who reigned in the Sixteenth Century. It is said by historians that this tomb was the inspiration for the Taj Mahal. Approaching the arched gates we could see the tomb veiled and unveiled by the trickery of the arched entrances, only to see what appeared to be a smaller yet simpler Taj as we entered the final gardens. I had no doubt the historians were correct about where Shah Jahan's inspiration came from.

After lunch in a fashionable section of New Delhi, we continued the tour on to our last stop, the first city of Delhi. Built in the twelfth century, the focus of the area is the 238-foot tower that stands in the middle of what remains of the old mosque that once stood there. The tower is very ornately carved and has a distinct tilt, making it appear as a taller version of the Leaning Tower of Pisa.

The remains of the mosque are also ornately carved and very well preserved. This is not from Islamic craftsman, but rather Hindu artisans who carved intricate designs only to see them plastered over and hidden by Muslim invaders, who did their own form of recycling. The plaster cast on the walls now has fallen off or been removed. The plaster that covered the old temple carvings that the Muslims had used to build their mosques was what saved these beautiful columns from destruction over the past eight hundred years.

Our last evening in India we were fortunate to have been invited by the managing director of A&K India and his wife, Mr. and Mrs. Madhok, for dinner at their home. The evening was filled with wonderful conversation, giving us a chance to fill them in personally on our fabulous adventures throughout India. The evening at their lovely home was magical. Typical of homes in India, it was shared by multiple generations of family. I would like to thank them for a wonderful evening. Being a bit more European in their culture, they kept serving us the best food and wine until close to midnight. We knew we had our next plane to catch at four in the morning, but we just could not tear ourselves away from their wonderful company. We must suffer sometimes to enjoy the good life!

I will leave you with a thirteenth-century poem by Amir Khusrau, inscribed on the wall of the palace at the Red Fort.

If there is a paradise on earth,
It is here, it is here, it is here.
If there is bliss on earth,
It is this, it is this, it is this.
Next stop: Bhutan!

MAGICAL BHUTAN

DAY ONE

Bhutan. This is where the people measure GDP by happiness. Tucked into the eastern part of the Himalayas and bordered by Nepal to the east, India to the south, and China to the north, Bhutan is a very small landlocked country.

We boarded Royal Bhutan Air for our two-hour flight, which brought us directly over Nepal and right past Mount Everest. Flight over the Himalayas afforded us a view that was what you would expect it to look like. We saw jagged, snowcapped mountains with narrow valleys shaded by a light fog. In the close distance there appeared two large peaks rising from it all. One of these is the great Mount Everest.

As we reached the eastern end of the Himalaya range, the mountains got much drier, the snow disappearing as our plane turned north into the narrow valley to Bhutan. Our pilot warned us not to be alarmed as we saw the cliffs appear within a stone's throw of the wings. This was a normal approach. In 2010, only eight pilots were certified to make the tricky approach to the Paro airport. First banking left, then right, and back left again, our pilot weaved our Airbus 319 through the narrow pass like a bush pilot. Only during the last, short part of the final approach to the runway did we finally straighten the wings for a landing.

Bhutan is made up of twenty districts seventy-five hundred feet up in the mountains. Each district is situated in one of the many narrow valleys, surrounded by mountain peaks up to fifteen thousand feet.

Bhutan is the size of Switzerland with a population less than eight hundred thousand. There is evidence through carbon dating that Bhutan has been inhabited since 2000 BC.

Until the early seventeenth century, Bhutan existed as a patchwork of minor warring fiefdoms. It was not unified until the Tibetan lama and military leader Shabdrung Ngawang Namgyal, who had fled religious persecution in Tibet, came in around 1653. The present monarchy was established in 1907, which makes Bhutan a very young country.

Up until recently agriculture made up most of the economy of Bhutan, with 80 percent of the population living on farms. Today hydropower created by the twenty rivers running through the valleys is the major driver of the economy, together with the slow increase of tourism.

Met by our guide, we were driven to the capital city on the only two-lane road in the country. Apparently this road wasn't expanded from one lane to two until 2010. There is very little flat land here in this small country hidden in the Himalayas.

As we drove down a winding road carved into the mountainside with the river below, the farmhouses that dot the hillside reminded us of a Tyrolean village. It was very picturesque. Many of these homes were built in the fifteenth century and are still occupied by family descendants. This doesn't mean that life is easy or calm for these people. Up until the 1990s the average life span was less than fifty years, mostly due to poor nutrition and the inhalation of smoke within their own homes. Seems they were late to invent the chimney. Today the average life expectancy is moving up into the sixties as Western technology reaches Bhutan and new construction and retrofitting has added smoke stacks over the stoves.

Entering the capital we were surprised at the amount of construction going on. Tourism has been allowed here since 1974, and foreign investment for only the past several years. Bhutan is becoming modern, I fear a little too quickly. Or at least it appeared this way here in the capital. The monarchy is concerned with the quick pace of change and does have some safeguards in place so as not to spoil the culture and environment.

Checking into the two-year-old Taj hotel, we were greeted with white scarves and brought to the Buddhist temple in the garden for a welcoming ceremony before being shown to our room. We only had a couple of hours to rest before our first tour of the city, and they were spent checking e-mail. We have to say that our bed looked very inviting after only getting three hours of sleep. We are no mere mortals; we were ready to keep going.

Our first stop was the large palace erected by King Jigme Dorji Wangchuck in 1641. These buildings would all look at home in the mountains of Switzerland or Germany. The most distinctive features are the roofs, built of crisscrossing slats of wood all kept in place with large rocks. It makes the rooftops look like a large, far-flung rock garden. Even the new buildings used this medieval construction method. With a closer look at the decoration on the buildings we could see the definite Buddhist paintings and carvings distinguishing the building style from what one would see in Bavaria.

Our next stop was a large stupa with the relics of the king, which was in a different style from the ones we saw in India. In India the stupas were round; here they were square. Visiting in a Buddhist country we did the traditional three clockwise circles around the stupa, but no more than 108, before we were on to our next site. Next stop, we were to buy a pair of Adidas hiking shoes for Leanne —much needed for tomorrow's hike. Good night!

MAGICAL BHUTAN: DAY TWO

Bhutan was very different from our adventure through India. I have to say, it was much different from most anyplace we had traveled. A cloistered country in the middle of the Himalayas, it received very little influence from the outside world over the centuries. Here, ancient history is anything pre-1973. That was when the first paved roads came and the first tourists were allowed into Bhutan. Bhutan would have remained a closed, hidden kingdom for centuries if it were not for the fear of the Chinese. The king of Bhutan, seeing the invasion and takeover of Tibet by China in the 1950s, figured it was only a matter of time before his kingdom was next. Opening the country to tourism and investment, coupled with joining the United Nations, was his plan to keep the country independent. The ploy has worked thus far: Bhutan and China have been trading partners since 2005. We could attest to that—I think Leanne bought Chinese knockoff Adidas.

There was no electricity in the country until the 1980s, and the only education available up to that time was available in a monastery. Today the government mandates that certain children in each family must attend primary and secondary educational schools. Even money is new to Bhutan. Before the 1960s all commerce was done by barter, and taxes were paid in grain to the king.

Our first stop on the tour was the massive golden Buddha that faces east high above the city. He can be seen from every part of the valley. The golden sitting Buddha was constructed just two short years ago, and when its stone base is completed it will sit atop a brand-new modern monastery. From this vantage point you can view the whole valley and see the sprawl of development, which has taken place over the past thirty years. Most of the buildings crowding the capitol have only been standing since 1976. For the most part Bhutan is just now writing its history.

Driving down from the golden Buddha we stopped at an arts and crafts boarding school sponsored by the government. Here students are taught the ancient crafts of Bhutan's rich heritage of painting, sculpting, woodcarving, and embroidery. Going through the school, we could see the step-by-step training students get to master the different disciplines of the arts. Many of the excellent examples produced by these students are either destined for the many monasteries dotting the mountaintops or one of the many government gift shops established by the queen of Bhutan. We were shocked at the prices these shops charged. Evidently the government of Bhutan was trying to raise money quickly. I think we increased Bhutan's GDP by 2 percent with our purchases. My GDP wasn't very happy though. In a country where the average wage is $400 a month, Bhutan is a very, very expensive country. What did we expect from a country that charges tourists $250 a day per person just for the privilege of visiting? Bhutan is going after quality tourism as opposed to quantity, by inflating the prices of everything to keep out the riffraff.

A short walk from the crafts school is a two-hundred-year-old heritage farmhouse that was saved from demolition by the queen of Bhutan. The home, which was once owned by a wealthy Bhutanese family, has been turned into a museum preserving the agricultural way of life of Bhutan pre-1973.

This was a four-story home, the ground floor reserved for the animals, the second for storage of grain and supplies, the third for living quarters, and the roof for drying vegetables—especially chilies, a big crop here in Bhutan. The whole structure was topped with the traditional wood slat roof covered by large rocks. Most of the newer buildings in the country now use corrugated metal, which was introduced to Bhutan in the 1980s. It was explained to us that the traditional roof boards that were used for centuries had to be flipped after three years and completely replaced after six due to the harsh weather of the Himalayas, unless a monsoon did the job sooner. The Bhutanese have realized that cutting one hundred trees for one house and replacing the wood roofs every six years was not exactly environmentally friendly. The adoption of metal was a vast improvement to save the forest. Every home in Bhutan also includes a spiritual room. The one here was located on the third floor. The room would be used by a visiting monk, who would bless the home. For his convenience, a small toilet was installed. It consists of a small box with a hole and a lid. When used, everything drops to the ground for the pigs. For that reason I have stopped eating the bacon.

One of my favorite stories we were told while walking through the home was that of Lama Drukpa Kinley, the divine mad monk who came to this area in the Fifteenth Century. Lama Drukpa came to Bhutan to spread Buddhism sexually by deflowering the virgins in the kingdom. Legend has it that he could fight off enemies with his penis and even turn it into a rope and use it as a bridge. Today in Bhutan you will find penises painted on the walls of houses or hanging from rooftops. We had to duck under a complete wooden phallus that graced the doorways of the museum. Buddhists believe that the lama's penis will protect them from evil. In the United States, as in most of the developed world, Lama Kinley would be in jail as a sexual predator. His private parts would be hung over the doorway, just not voluntarily.

Another surprise we discovered here in Bhutan was that the country was an active participant in slavery as early as 1650s, and it continued here right up to 1961. That's one hundred years after slavery was abolished in the United States. That's shocking. Most of the slaves were untouchables brought from India to work the fields. To continue slavery for that long, there must have been a strict disciplinary system to keep the slaves in line. To me it seems in direct conflict with my understanding of Buddhism. With seventeen sects of Buddhism, I guess you can justify just about anything.

After lunch we visited the king's wildlife preserve where he raises takin. For those of you who don't know what a Takin is, it's a cross between a mountain goat and a cow. The takin is an endangered animal here in the Himalayas. They live in herds high on the mountainsides like goats, living as high as seventeen thousand feet. If you ask me, they look like a combination of a cow, goat, bear, buffalo, and horse—it's one strange, smelly animal. Legend has it that the takin is the reincarnation of the Divine Mad Monk. Supposedly, to prove his magical power, he devoured a goat and a cow whole and reappeared as the takin. They are incredibly superstitious.

There is another interesting tradition: the practice of putting up flags of prayers all over the mountainside. Looking up at the hillside, you can see white strings and poles that display colorful flags. These flags are put there to pray for good health and long life, or to celebrate births or any number of events the Bhutanese would like to commemorate. There must be millions of flags; most are worn by the harsh weather. The only way they will ever come down is with deterioration and age. It doesn't seem to be environmentally friendly to me.

The end of our day was devoted to a trek through the Himalayas. Many of the tourists who come to Bhutan do it for a three-to-thirty-five day trek through the high Himalayas. We settled for a three-mile hike to a monastery located at eighty-six hundred feet. Getting to the monastery was a piece of cake. The climb down was much more challenging, as we had to navigate the narrow trails and steep terrain. This was a good test for our six-mile, two-thousand-foot vertical trek to the Tiger's Nest monastery the day after tomorrow. We can now cross trekking across the Himalayas off our bucket list.

MAGICAL BHUTAN: DAY THREE

We packed up our tent and are moving on. Next stop: Paro, Bhutan. Heading out of the capital, we made a quick stop to see the ancient art of papermaking. For centuries the Bhutanese have used the bark of the willow tree to make paper. They first soak it for days, and then they mash the bark into pulp, boil it, and turn it into parchment. The process is very interesting. The crushed pulp is mixed in a vat of water. Then an operator uses a screen to scoop up the mixture. As the water runs through the screen a small residue of fine pulp is left on top of the screen. The number of times the screen is dipped will determine the thickness of the paper. It's a process similar to candle making.

Driving along the river, we made our first stop on the highway. We were off to see an ancient monastery built in 1420 on the other side of the river. To get to the other side we had to cross a fifteenth-century chain bridge. Made up of six fifteenth-century iron chains tied to two towers, it was made safer recently with the addition of chain-link fencing. In olden times (i.e., pre-1973), one would have to balance on the chains to cross. We, being modern visitors, could cross walking on the chain link. Stepping off onto the chain-link and looking straight through to the river was nerve-racking at first, but we quickly got used to seeing water rushing below our feet.

Now we were off to Paro. As we approached the city we were stopped right before the airport. The road into town runs right beside the airport runway. Due to many crashes in the past, cars can't proceed until the takeoffs and landings are complete. The Bhutanese government is building a bypass road with the help of the Indian government. India provides almost two-thirds of the Bhutanese budget. India is just as worried about China and would hate for Bhutan to fall and for China to thus be a neighbor. China doesn't give anyone the warm fuzzies here. When the traffic was finally allowed to proceed, twenty to thirty cars, coming from both directions, tried to navigate past one another on a poorly maintained one-lane road.

Before checking into our hotel, we made one last stop at the summer palace and fortress of the great unifier. First constructed in 1646, the palace was rebuilt in the early twentieth century after being destroyed by fire. Fire seems to have claimed many of the buildings and monasteries here in Bhutan. When you build your monasteries out of dry seasoned wood, drape them with thin hanging fabrics, light thousands of candles fueled by butter, and finally cook on an open-pit hearth—I can't imagine why they have such bad luck. Suffice it to say, many of the monasteries and homes here have been rebuilt due to one disaster or another. That begs the question—why does a culture whose people pray constantly to thousands of gods for good luck and long life die early and have their homes and monasteries destroyed by floods, monsoons, earthquakes, or fire? Just asking.

The summer palace was transformed into a Buddhist monastery after the restoration, and we had the good fortune of being there during one of its many ceremonies. The chanting, the clanging of cymbals, the banging of drums, and the playing of what looked like a didgeridoo filled the room. We were invited to take part in the service by drinking a liquid that tasted a lot like Vicks VapoRub out of the palms of our hands.

Our hotel for the next two days in Paro was at the Uma Lodge Resort. The hotel is perched high on a hill overlooking a dense forest. It is a lovely rustic lodge rated the best hotel and resort in Bhutan by Travel Advisor. It's a nice hotel, but I wouldn't go as far as that review. The hotel lobby and spa are very rustic and charming, but the rooms are a little too small and basic for my taste. The service and facilities at the Uma didn't hold a candle to the stays we experienced in India.

After I enjoyed a yak burger in the resort's wonderful dining room, we were off again—destination: a seventh-century monastery. This temple also had the great fortune of never having been hit with a natural disaster. Maybe the people chanted better here. Built in the Himalayas by a Tibetan king in 659 AD, the monastery looks very much like the ones we have visited in the past. We were happy to know that the restorations have all been very authentic. The only major difference seemed to be that the paintings on the ceilings and walls of this seventh-century monastery were blackened from centuries of smoke.

Next up was a drive into the mountains up a one-lane road to an ancient fortress built to protect the mouth of the valley. The most stunning part of the drive was the scenery—soaring snow-topped mountains and Bhutanese-style architecture dotting the hillside. Even here we couldn't get past the onslaught of construction that was even happening away from the city. New schools and homes were being built for families who were moving out of their generational farms, and the road was being widened to accommodate the growth. Unfortunately, we could only admire the fort from afar. Fire and earthquakes have made the structure too weak to accept visitors. The road ends at a major trailhead where all of the long Himalayan treks begin. We couldn't resist setting out on our own three-day trek. We can now say we started a three-day trek though the Himalayas. Only you and I know we didn't finish.

MAGICAL BHUTAN: DAY FOUR

The big day had finally arrived. One of the main attractions of Bhutan aside from its fabulous unspoiled landscape is the Taktsang Monastery, also known as the Tiger's Nest. Perched precariously on the edge of a granite cliff 10,200 feet above the valley, it's one of the most sacred Himalayan monasteries.

According to legend, Guru Rinpoche flew to this location from Tibet on the back of a tigress in the Eighth Century, giving the monastery the name Tiger's Nest. The guru meditated in a cave on this site for three months, after which he was the first to spread Buddhism to Bhutan. The first monastery building enclosing the cave was added in the Ninth Century, and the larger, most famous of the buildings was added in 1692. All of these are an incredible feat in dedication to one's religion.

We left our hotel at eight to get an early start on our six-mile, 1,700-vertical-foot hike to this incredible monument. There are three ways to get to Tiger's Nest. You can climb the more gradual but still steep rock switchback trail, you can supplement your climb with much steeper shortcuts through the trees, or you can take a horse. You didn't think we would hike 1,700 vertical feet if a good horse could be had for ten bucks, did you?

Of course we decided on the horse. The horses were small, and the saddles were very primitive. Adjusting the stirrups only required twisting the strap several times to the desired length. Mounting was done strictly from a rock and not the stirrups as I was used to. Climbing on my mounting rock, I stretched my leg across to reach my horse. The rock was placed way too far away, causing the rock to go one way and me to go the other. *Splat!* I went embarrassingly to the ground. On my second try, when the horse was properly lined up closer to the rock, I was much more successful. Once in the saddle, I couldn't resist pulling out my iPhone and showing the Bhutanese wrangler holding my horse a picture of me boxing cows. I just had to prove I wasn't a total spaz.

Solid in the saddle, we made our way up the trail through the dense pine forest. Midway up the trail I was happy we hired the horses. Seeing the red-faced climbers we passed along the way convinced me we could have made the climb if we were willing to miss our flight tomorrow. Who says sweating and suffering like that is fun? Even our Bhutanese guide, who is used to the elevation, was breathing hard. A thousand feet up I think every one of them was rethinking their decision of not hiring the horse. We were happily snapping pictures as we went along; the climbers were watching their footing on the loose dirt.

Arriving at 10,200 feet, we had to dismount and continue the remainder of the trail, about a half mile, by foot. This was the end of the line. Evidently my five hundred ngultrum (or ten dollars) was only for a one-way trip. We were on our own getting down.

We were now eye to eye with Tiger's Nest. The only problem was that we were on the opposite side of a canyon from the monastery. The remainder of our hike was down steep rock steps carved into the side of the cliff around the canyon, across a bridge over a two-hundred-foot waterfall, and then back up rock steps 250 feet to the monastery. When you consider that we had to do this going and coming back, it was equivalent to walking up and down a fifty-story building. I am beginning to think the horses got the better part of the bargain.

We at least had well-maintained stone steps with railings, thanks to a trail renovation completed in 2000. The monks who built this place only had a small rock trail with a seventeen-hundred-foot sheer drop to the valley below. The climb wouldn't have been half as bad if it were not for the ten-thousand-foot-plus altitude.

Like most of the monasteries here in Bhutan, this one has been rebuilt as well. In 1998 a fire broke out and destroyed the two main structures built in 1692. They suspect that a butter-fueled candle ignited a hanging tapestry. Who would have guessed? The Bhutanese government rebuilt the burned-out structures using the same medieval methods, and by 2005 the monastery was welcoming visitors again.

It was now time for our three-plus-mile walk back down. Easier than up, it was still pretty hard on our shins and knees. We had to constantly watch our footing, because we were walking on solid granite with a light dusting of dirt, making the trail quite slippery. Overall the trail was in pretty good shape considering it's a waterfall during the monsoon season.

The scenery and views were spectacular here, and the monastery was a wonder to see. We are very happy that we came to Bhutan—and even happier that we had a ten-dollar horse. Although we only did three and a half miles of a six-mile hike by foot, we feel we earned our spa treatments back at the hotel.

EPILOGUE

Our India and Bhutan adventure was beyond our wildest expectations. We had a fantastic time. For years when we have finished our trips we always ask ourselves whether they were as good as our adventure in

2002 when we visited Turkey, and we have to say this trip was just as good, if not better.

India was a tremendous surprise. We had never stayed at such fabulous hotels—and the service! The service was like nothing we have ever encountered at any of the finest hotels we have previously stayed. India has a rich history and culture, and the people are the nicest you would want to meet. Even driving in the worst of traffic, getting run off the road, and having people cut you off with horns honking, they never get mad, ever. It's amazing.

India is not the place your friends described to you twenty years ago, and it's not the India you will see twenty years from now.

India is still a place with a big gap between rich and poor. We found that 70 percent of the population still lives in the villages, while 30 percent are in more urban settings and have the bulk of the wealth. Twenty years ago it was ninety-ten. Twenty years from now it will be fifty-fifty.

Indians surely have a lot of work to do to bring the country into the twenty-first century, but when they do, you might just miss the best time to visit India.

There are some facts that I never mentioned in the blogs that I would like to lay out here. Hindus have over thirty-three million gods and deities they worship in their religion. I'd like to point out that most refer to Hindu as a lifestyle more than a religion. We tried to really figure out whether they believed in all these stories.

Most of the more educated we met seemed to say they were all fables used to illustrate ways to live or to help people understand situations in life. I can go with that.

There are over 1.2 billion people in India. Over the past sixty years they have added almost a billion people. The good news is that the government is working hard to slow down and control the population growth. This is very important if Indians want to wipe out poverty and upgrade the lifestyles of the villagers—although I can't really say they are truly interested in improving their lives. This might be the number-one reason India's progress will be held back. No one is interested in tearing down the house or business his father's father's father's father built.

Lastly, I would like to meet the person who manipulated the numbers to make India the fourth-largest economy in the world. I think that's ridiculous. Some political economist has created what they call parity GDP, adjusting GDP to the value of local goods by currency valuation. This manipulation brings India from number eleven in the world to four. That sets an actual GDP of India at 1.6 trillion, one-tenth the size of the United States. I had the opportunity to bump into a Stanford economics professor here, and he agreed with me that it's very misleading.

India was truly amazing. Every inch we traveled fascinated and surprised us. I truly think it got much cleaner while we were there. It is of course better to come as a maharaja than a budget traveler or backpacker.

Our last stop in Bhutan was also a surprise, although I don't think either of us knew what to expect.

An example of one of our surprises was how new everything is, such as the homes, palaces and temples. Fires, floods, and monsoons wiped out many structures over the centuries, making life very difficult for the Bhutanese. The other surprise was how quickly things are changing. Most of the growth has been over the last twenty years. The whole country has only had electricity for thirty years.

The kingdom does have a plan to keep the Bhutanese culture. Six percent of the land in the country has been preserved for forest, and 40 percent of the land has been designated as national parks. They have also passed laws requiring all new construction to be in Bhutanese-style architecture. In addition, all citizens must wear the national attire while at work, at school, or in monasteries.

One of the strangest things I heard was that the government no longer enforced the seatbelt laws. We could see that no one wore a seatbelt here. The thinking is that if you drive off one of the country's many cliffs, you can't jump out of the car as it flies down the hill if you are strapped in. I just had to send that one to *Myth Busters*.

The hotels here were not the five-star service we had come to expect on this trip, but they made up for any shortcomings with their spectacular unspoiled landscapes. As you may expect, hikes and treks are a pastime here and the reason most visitors come. I think you can get a much different experience here trekking several days into the remote villages high in the Himalayas. We only had time to visit two of the twenty valleys here in Bhutan. The next nearest one to us was in central Bhutan, and that is 170 miles away, or a fifteen-hour—yes, fifteen-hour—drive from where we are. Planes are limited.

With all their effort, I think growth will be difficult for the Bhutanese. Only 8 percent of the population has a car. As the wealth grows, so will the automobile population. In these narrow valleys, pollution will have to be tackled or restrictions will have to be placed on car ownership. For these reasons I recommend you come to Bhutan soon, if only to hike to the Tiger's Nest. Don't expect to smoke here, as smoking is illegal and punishable by three years in jail. Also, don't pick the wild marijuana growing everywhere; that's illegal here too.

ACKNOWLEDGEMENTS

I would like to warmly thank the many people involved in planning and executing this trip, from the staff in the States to the airport welcoming personnel and the drivers and guides.

I particularly want to thank Jan Morris of Peak Travel for all of her hard work coordinating and booking our India adventure.

This trip also would not have been possible without Vikram Madhok and Cynthia Reed of Abercrombie and Kent and their vast network of wonderful people throughout the world, who, with military precision, pulled off a flawless adventure once again for the Troy's.

Not the least, I would like to thank all of you who have followed us for twenty days, through two countries, ten cities, seventy pages of blogs (28,157 words), and thirty-five hundred miles through India and Bhutan.

CREDITS

Jan Morris	Peak Travel
Vikram Madhok	A&K
Cynthia Reed	A&K
Satish Yadav	Our fantastic driver in India
Yogi Sharma	Guide in India
Shakti Kolyari	Guide in India
Dharam Rajpal	Guide in India
Sangay Khandu	Guide in Bhutan
Taj Hotels	Multiple cities
Oberoi Hotels	Multiple cities
Imperial Hotel	New Delhi, India

Aurangabad Caves

Aurangabad Caves

Hindu Temple carving Khajuraho, India

Maharana Arvind Singh Mewar visiting with his
Rolls Royce at the Pebble Beach Concourse

Oberoi Hotel entrance, Udaipur, India

Taj Hotel Umaid Bhawan Palace, Jodhpur, India

The world famous Taj Mahal just after dawn

Banks of the Ganges, Varanasi, India

Banks of the Ganges, Varanasi, India

Tigers Nest, Bhutan

ROAD TO MOROCCO
APRIL 2011

ROAD TO MOROCCO: DAY ONE

Like Bing Crosby and Bob Hope, we were on the road to Morocco, and I was traveling with Dorothy Lamour. The younger folk should just look this one up. As you may have guessed, we left for Morocco today, which just happened to be our twenty-fifth anniversary. I don't think there was any trip we anticipated more. Morocco just seemed so exotic. When we started telling people we were going to Morocco, we were surprised how many of you have been here. I thought it was a pretty far-out place to go. I guess I was wrong. To all of you who have made the trip here, sorry, but we didn't have time to visit all of your friends. For a while I was thinking you all had more friends in Morocco then you had at home.

To get here we traveled on Air France. I was actually looking forward to this airline. International carriers most of the times are much better and give better service than our domestics. I thought a nice French anniversary meal thirty-five thousand feet over Paris was a nice touch for our twenty-fifth. Unfortunately, I was disappointed on both accounts. The business class on Air France was very basic. In an age of technology, one always expects a good variety of entertainment. Wrong. They played the same two movies over and over for eleven hours. Even I got bored seeing Angelina pout her lips and swing her hips in *The Tourist*. Thank goodness we brought a few of our own movies. The meal was even more underwhelming. I wasn't expecting a Michelin star-rated meal, but let's get real. These were the French. They take their food very seriously. They served the same crap as everyone else. Don't get me started talking about the Air France airport lounge. Comparing it to the one we visited in Dubai flying Emirates is like comparing the Ritz to a dentist waiting room.

The eleven hours tossing and turning toward Paris was all worth it when we entered French air space. I have flown here a few times, and I always forget how beautiful the landscape is below—very green with lots of forests. You don't think of dense green forest when you think Paris. We landed in Paris right on time, and after a short layover, it was on to Casablanca. Getting on Air France again for our three-hour trip to Casablanca, I mistakenly thought this flight would be better. Wrong again. A business-class seat on Air France is simply a regular coach seat without a seat where the middle one would be. Hell, I could get this kind of business seat on Southwest by putting my coat on the middle seat and telling people passing by my wife was in the bathroom. This was a European thing. The food didn't get any better leaving out of Paris. Okay—enough bashing of Air France. When we approached Morocco, I could see large waves crashing on the African coast. It was very reminiscent of flying into Lima last year. Flying closer inland, I was surprised to see so many green, manicured farms. There were multicolored green farms as far as the eye can see. What happened to the desert? I was expecting desert. Well, I guess that's why we travel—to learn and correct our preconceived notions of other lands.

Driving to the city from the airport, we could have been traveling through the central valley in California. I was surprised how good the roads and bridges were. Even as we traveled through the center of the city, we could see that money had been spent on infrastructure. In these difficult times around the world, it looked like they are still improving Casablanca. Going to our hotel, we passed a massive new marina project I was sure would be beautiful when done. We arrived at our hotel some twenty hours after we left San Francisco, very tired and excited. We were taken to Le Doge, a small boutique hotel with only sixteen rooms. Our room was a charming, modern, Moroccan-style with jelly-green carpets and white leather couches. The elevator we came up in was an experience. Have you ever been in a hotel elevator that has a max capacity of three people? It was tiny.

Even though we only had a few hours of sleep on the plane, it didn't hold us back—we hit the town with great enthusiasm. First stop was Rick's American Café, Humphrey Bogart's haunt in the movie *Casablanca*. Humphrey and Ingrid weren't there, and if truth be told, they have never set foot in the place. We did have a chance meeting with the present owner and a piano player named Sam. We just had to make the pilgrimage to one of the most famous movie spots of all time. The food was typical American, not very exotic. Then again, *Casablanca* translates to "white house." We have one of those, and it's not exotic either. As we prepared to leave Rick's, Sam sat down to play "As Time Goes By." Leaving, I just had to say, "Leanne, this is going to be the beginning of a beautiful anniversary."

ROAD TO MOROCCO: DAY TWO

Well, we are off on our first day of touring. I was surprised when I saw our itinerary and we were only staying one day in Casablanca. Casablanca might be the biggest city in Morocco with seven million people, but it's also the newest. The city, when the French colonized it, only had nineteen thousand people in 1912, so not much went on before that. Our first stop today was—what a surprise—a mosque. Casablanca is home to the third-largest mosque in the world and the largest outside of Saudi Arabia. In keeping with Casablanca's history, it's all of eight years old. They started building it in 1987 and were done six years later in 1993. It is a magnificent achievement. It took three thousand workers and ten thousand craftsman working 24-7 for six years to complete it. It's built in the Moroccan style with all the modern comforts. Electric heated floors and 354 loudspeakers hidden cleverly in the columns keep the twenty-five thousand people who can worship at a time warm and informed. The ritual washroom, which is just under the main hall, has dozens of lotus flower fountains for washing 2,800 people at a time. Figuring the average of three minutes per person all twenty-five thousand can be in and out in under a half hour.

After the mosque we traveled up the coast into some of the nicer and newest sections of the city. Like in most third world cities, there is definitely a contrast between the haves and have-nots. I still can't get over how good the infrastructure was everywhere we went. When I asked about it, I was always told it was all built in the last ten years, and it showed.

Morocco, it seems, was one of the winners of the financial meltdown. What I mean by that is this: a lot of that easy, pre-meltdown Lehman Brothers money found its way here. Without that bubble, Morocco wouldn't have the modern roads, trams, and bridges we saw today.

Our next stop of the morning was an open-air market for meats, vegetables, and spices. We had been to many of these markets, and most were swarming with flies and not very clean. This market, on the other hand, was old, but very sanitary. An indoor area housed the meats and fish. Anything you could think to cook was displayed, from prime rib and horsemeat to tuna and fresh live turtle. I still have my turtle soup recipe from China if anyone is interested. It was very interesting. The visit segued to lunch at the marina. Since we were on the ocean, seafood was recommended. We thought it would have been better if we had been able to read the menu or speak French. Since we were just across from Spain, Leanne pulled out her Spanish. I recognized langoustines, and salmon is pretty much the same in every language. In the end, we managed to get by, but we ordered like kindergarteners. After lunch, we made a quick stop to take a picture at the king's palace, and then we were done with Casablanca.

Our next stop was Rabat, about a ninety-minute drive south from Casablanca. Rabat is now the political capital of Morocco. Rabat is around nine hundred years old and is situated on a major river leading to the ocean. Our first stop was the political seat of Morocco. As we pulled up to the main gate, Leanne's good looks and personality got us in without the usual document check. (That was the guide's observation, not mine.) What struck us here were the long rows of large full ficus trees all growing together like a suspended hedge, all leading to the palace. I don't know about your experience with ficus, but mine always lost their leaves.

The palace dates back several hundred years. The early kings used it as a residence; the present king uses it as an office and for government administration.

Of course, if there is a present king, you just have to stop and see the past kings. What was our fascination with seeing the burial places of famous dead people? In Egypt, where royalty goes back three thousand years and was buried with gold and jewels, I get it, but someone buried in a marble building or in the ground—not so much. The previous two kings here in Morocco were buried in a modern mausoleum on the site of an incomplete mosque. Seems that a monarch nine hundred years ago started the foundation of what would have been the world's largest mosque, only to be stopped by a death in the family: his.

The mosque is a beautifully crafted building approachable by a tall flight of marble steps. Once inside, we could see a viewing gallery looking down to the marble caskets of Mohammed V, Hassan II, and his brother. For some reason, everyone was hurried out at noon; for what I don't know. It's not like he was on display like Lenin and had to be spruced up.

Our next stop took us to the Kasbah. The Kasbah was not a romantic playground; it's another name for a fort or a desert castle. This Kasbah was situated on the ocean. Inside the walls were narrow winding streets painted ocean blue on the bottom and white on top. If you didn't know, you would think you were walking the streets of Mykonos in Greece minus the colored doors. We wound around the streets, climbing until we reached a restaurant patio, where we stopped for a traditional Moroccan mint tea.

After our short break, we were off to Fez, another two-hour drive. Fez is the oldest city in Morocco, having been established around 800 AD. We were to camp here for three nights. Our travel here brought us through landscape that could have been anywhere in California with its rolling hills, cows, agriculture, and a modern highway, less the potholes. Over 40 percent of the population is employed in agriculture here. Almost 70 percent depend on it for their livelihood.

Passing through the new city (only six hundred years old), we arrived at our five-star hotel, the Sofitel Palais Jamai. The Sofitel Palais Jamai started as someone's house in 1872 and was expanded and turned into a hotel in 1932. It was very nice—the best in the city—and truly Moroccan. On my Elizabeth Taylor grading scale, I would give it four stars. Liz and I have high expectations. I gave it a slightly higher rating than I might have because of the service and the view from our room, which overlooked the pool courtyard and the medina, *medina* being Arabic for *city*.

We covered a lot of ground today, traveling almost two hundred miles to three different cites in a day and a half. I like to move it (move it). She likes to (move it move it). Tonight, though, we ate at the Moroccan restaurant in the hotel. When we walked through the door and the heard the musicians playing and saw the belly dancer, we both thought for the first time, *We are in Morocco*. The language barrier again seemed to trip us up. The ambiance was what we have come to expect, but the food wasn't. Being a frequent visitor to Moroccan restaurants in the States, I think we do a better job on Moroccan food. Then again, I think we include a lot of Arabic foods in our cuisine. I decided to take our guide to dinner with us as a translator. I was not going to leave here without that powdered sugar lamb dish created in crispy phyllo dough!

The overall observation after two days was that this was a community created from generations of diverse peoples moving here. It started with the very fair-skinned Berbers, and then got mixed with the Arab influence and then spattered with Spanish and a lot of French. There wasn't a true look. The mixing of many customs has created a modern cosmopolitan Arabic society with definite European influence. One thing that struck us while touring the large mosque yesterday was how tolerant the people are of differences here. We happened to team up with a group from Israel at the mosque. Our tour leaders loved each other and tried to translate Hebrew and Arabic back and forth. This was as it should be. Somehow, with all the angst that goes around about Arabs not liking Jews, it stuck out what good friends this whole group was. It seemed that this country has been one of the safest areas for Jewish people. During the war, when the Germans came here, the king stood his ground and forbade them to segregate any Moroccans, no matter what their faith. He stood his ground, saying there were no Jews, Christians, or Muslims living here—only Moroccans.

ROAD TO MOROCCO: DAY THREE

Our Third day in Morocco took us on a day trip out of Fez through the beautiful agricultural countryside. Our drive was very picturesque with rolling hillside fields, and wagons pulled by donkeys and sheep and goat herders shared the highway with us. Our destination was Volubilis, which features the best preserved and restored Roman ruins in Morocco. As I have mentioned many times, the Romans were everywhere except Dubai. The Romans built the city of Volubilis in 40 AD and last occupied it in 262 AD, abandoning the city as the Roman Empire deteriorated.

Leanne and I have seen many ancient ruins, Greek, Roman, and Egyptian. Many of those have been better restored then these. The striking difference here was the location and the preservation of the mosaic floors in many of the destroyed villas inside the city walls. The city is set in the middle of fertile farms that must have existed when the Romans last occupied the area. Most ruins you see today are buried in the middle of cities and discovered by construction projects or unearthed in the middle of deserts. This city stands—or should I say stood—surrounded by a green fertile valley.

After Volubilis, we headed to the city of Meknes. Meknes is one of the imperial cities of Morocco and was built by Sultan Moulay Ismall. Surrounded by miles of great walls with graceful, Moroccan-style entrances, the city features wide streets and large plazas that took us aback as we entered. Our only explanation for these unusually wide roads was that the sultan was trying to build a court to rival the French King Louis XIV. Think wide Parisian boulevards.

There were many sites to visit in Meknes: storage rooms for of all of the grains produced in the region, a stable that was built to house twelve thousand houses (there wasn't a horse left—or a roof, for that matter), several museums, and, of course, the mausoleum of yet another famous dead person, the sultan himself. It was at the mausoleum that we did hear some interesting information about Islam that we didn't know. There are no pictures in any of the mausoleums or in the mosques. Everything inside these religious buildings is done in the abstract. That's how the Arabic style came about. No idol worshipping here. It sounds much like Judaism to me and much different from the Catholic Church, which seemed to instill symbolism into everything. We had never thought about this interesting difference between the religions before. It's unfortunate that a small group of Muslim religious extremists have hijacked Islam, or at least the global dialogue regarding the religion. When you get to know the religion, it sounds very accepting and peaceful. I know someone is going to come up with some comment about everyone wanting to kill the Jews. Interesting enough, here in Meknes, there is a large Jewish quarter with a synagogue and a Jewish school dating back to the founding of the city.

As we left the old city, our guide told us he had a surprise for us that was not on our itinerary. Knowing that we have and love horses, he was arranging for us to visit the royal government stables just outside the new city of Meknes. The stable was not home to twelve thousand royal horses, but it was home to dozens of Arabians, Berbers, and Arabian-Berber mixes. As Leanne's luck would have it, it was also the day of a jumping competition. Although it was raining and cold (we harkened back to the Amazon trip), we decided to stay and watch the competition.

Before they started, we did have an opportunity to meet one of the competitors, a very nice Moroccan man who had spent time jumping and training in Boston. We casually and politely said we loved Boston, and he replied that he liked Morocco better, as he was not free in Boston and felt he was freer in Morocco. This was the second time we had heard this in the last two years from foreigners. Leanne and I told both people we totally understood. When you travel, you realize how we have paralyzed ourselves with so many laws. When foreigners see our shows on TV, they see citizens being held down over cars by the police for doing nothing.

When they see people get tickets in the United States for things they could do freely back in their home country, they get fed up. There are other competitive places to go now, so many vote with their feet. If we want to grow our economy and attract the best and brightest people, we need to change our image and stop restricting our every movement. I guess this is a conversation we need to have back home with a bottle of Cabernet. By the way, the rain stopped just in time for the competition. Our new friend "Mr. Boston" did pretty well.

Driving back to Fez, we made one last stop. High on a hill overlooking the old city, or medina, of Fez, there is a ruin that once was the burial site of the early kings of the city. From this vantage point, we had a great look at the city, our hotel, and the sun setting over the mountains, a pleasant way to end our third day of touring.

But wait—there's more. This evening we took another shot at finding my lamb-pastry-powdered-sugar dish. This time I brought the guide. This dish just may turn out to be like chicken chow mien—an American dish. Our restaurant for the evening was Palais de Fes Dar Tazi, which was on the complete opposite side of the old city from our hotel and is considered to be one of the best Moroccan restaurants in Fez. The restaurant and its banquet rooms are housed in what was once a beautiful private Moorish villa just off the plaza. Dining on the top floor, patrons are able to get a wonderful view over the old city. To reach the top floor, we climbed a narrow, twisting staircase for about four stories. I don't recommend it for people with heart problems or for the elderly. The stairway and most of the restaurant is decorated in white and green (Prophet Mohammad's favorite colors).

Mosaic tiles and ornate wood and plaster carvings decorate the space as we have come to expect in Moorish architecture—all in the abstract, of course.

I'm not sure why Moroccan restaurants have menus. We have been to three, and they all have the same four items. Do you want lamb with prunes and almonds, chicken with lemon and olives, lamb with couscous, or chicken with couscous? We didn't have to think much here.

I did find something close to my pastry, lamb, and sugar dish. It was called pigeon pie, and everyone serves it. It's fried dough stuffed with chicken, fish, or pigeon. Someone someplace might use lamb. No powdered sugar, though. I mentioned the dish to the guide and to the waiters, and no one has heard of my American version. Maybe I needed to chalk this dish up to being an American creation. Alas, we still had over ten days to look. I just didn't think I could eat lamb or chicken for that long. Even though the menu was thin, the food was not. It was very, very good—the best of what we had eaten so far.

Well past ten o'clock, we wound our way back downstairs after dinner, and children of all ages were still playing in the plaza. As we approached our driver to get into the car, I couldn't help but think that maybe Mr. Boston was right. In the States these kids would be rounded up and ticketed for being out after curfew. Just food for thought.

ROAD TO MOROCCO: DAY FOUR

I found it! I found it! I felt like Columbus finding America. I found the pastry stuffed with chicken topped with powder sugar with cinnamon. It was here all the time. There was definitely a communication issue at times. The pigeon pie, or what the Moroccans call it, *pastilla*, I had last night was what I was looking for. I just had one stuffed with seafood, so it didn't have the sugar. At lunch I thought I would give it one more shot, and presto! But all of you who have been there knew that, didn't you? I mention this first because I am sure all of you were shaking your heads and yelling at your computer that I was an idiot. Now you know one of my favorite dishes.

The rest of the day we spent discovering the old city of Fez el Bali. Our first stop was the market, or *souk*. It's changed little over 1,200 years. There were over two thousand shops here in the market where you could get anything and everything. When it was built, it was somewhat of a planned community. Each part of the market specializes in something. There are areas for foods, Moroccan clothes, and Western clothes.

Belts here, electronics there—it became even narrower, with aisles featuring thread down this way and cloth down that way, merchants selling metal in stalls, and workmen making pots and pans around the corner. Each craft was in a distinct area. Another thing we noticed was that except for a candy store here and there, none of the crafts mixed with each other. The belt guy didn't sell next to the clothing shop. Surprisingly, we didn't see every other shop being a souvenir store or T-shirt shop. They just were not there. There were sections for Chinese knockoffs and chukkas. They just didn't mingle. There were a few guided tours of tourists, but most of the shoppers seemed to be Moroccan.

We started our journey through the market walking down the narrow aisles of the food section. Here one can get anything that is edible in Morocco: steaks, vegetables, cow legs (yes, I said cow legs, severed just above the knee), fish, snails (baskets and baskets of them—they looked like the ones in our garden), live chickens (until they were bought, of course), spices, and a very interesting-looking dried spiced beef stored in solidified beef fat and packaged in plastic containers. This was a specialty of Fez and was sold in many of the stalls; it looked pretty gross in solidified form. I am sure it was pretty tasty cooked. The dried meats can last a year in these containers with no refrigeration.

We had walked so long in the food market that I thought we were done. Unbeknownst to me, we were only getting started. Winding through the covered narrow halls past specialty shop after specialty shop, laden donkeys passing us, we arrived at the tannery section. Here on the edge of the market they received goat, sheep, lamb, and cow skins and turned them into finished products. Twisting up a narrow staircase, we reached the third floor, where we had a bird's-eye view of the process of soaking and dying the skins. Before us must have been a hundred clay caldrons where men washed and stomped the skins into the softness and color they desired. The presses started in white water vats that contained lime, which is used to soften the skins and to remove any unwanted material such as pigeon poop before the skins are dried and ready for one of the many colors in the dye vats. The tannery was right on the river, where the water could be diverted to fill the vats, which we were told took place every two weeks. You see what's coming? To fill the vats with new water, you have to dump the old, untreated and directly into the river.

That didn't make us want to take part in the process, so we left without buying anything. As we were leaving, we noticed many horses, donkeys, and mules stacked with hides being delivered to the tannery. On second glance, we saw these beasts of burden hauling all kinds of goods through the market.

The method of transportation in the market for pedestrians was by foot. For shippers of goods, donkeys were the preferred method— unless their shops were near a holy site. Clever five-foot-high wood bars mark no-equine zones. One distinct memory from the souks was the variety of smells. It was so bad and foul in and around the tannery that they gave shoppers a bushel of fresh mint to hold to their faces to keep from throwing up. I can just imagine what these men who soak themselves in the vats with the skins must smell like. We loved the sounds and smells of Morocco—the tannery area, not so much.

Our next stop was a factory area. This was a collection of small stalls, one after the other, where independent owners sat pounding copper with metal and wooden hammers until they had shaped a pot, a pan, or a cauldron that might be used in the home or someone else's shop. The sound of hammers banging was everywhere. Shortly after we arrived, the street started to fill with smoke from someone starting a coal fire to soften metal. When I looked in the direction of the smoke, I noticed a man sitting on the floor reaching his bare hand into the hot coals, bringing handfuls out, and placing them in the cement in front of him to work his pot as the smoke got thicker.

Smoke and all, we stayed in front of the pot stalls as our guide pointed out and explained the university building we were now standing in front of. Here was the oldest university in the world. Started in 859 by a woman, this was where the Arabs taught students the concept of zero, algebra, literature, and the sciences. The story over, and the smoke continuing to choke us, we moved on to the carpet section. The shop showcasing the carpets was a former private residence that had been beautifully restored and converted. It was our first look at the fine homes hidden behind the small, nondescript doors in the market. The carpets were magnificent, but we didn't need a carpet not having a house. We did come a whisker away from spending five thousand dollars on a carpet. We came to our senses and moved on. Truth be told, if they chased after us with a better deal, we might have been sold. It seemed that five thousand was a little too high for something our dogs might pee on. Thirty-five hundred? Who knew? Then it might have been worth it.

Moving on, we found ourselves in a section that sold nothing but underwear. I was surprised to see fancy-colored bras and panties displayed out in the street. We have heard so much in the news about how modest Muslim women were in Arab countries, and here in the view of everyone who passed were polka-dot bras and colorful, striped panties. The stereotypical Muslim was not in Morocco.

I have already told you about lunch, so let's move on. After we left the market behind, our car was waiting to take us to the old Jewish quarter of Fez. This was interesting. The Jewish quarter was established during the 1400s when Spain was expelling Jews who refused to convert to Catholicism. The Jews knew they could find a safe haven in Morocco, because their ancestors had occupied the area centuries before and had always gotten along with the Muslims in the area.

The Muslims were also more accepting of the Jews than the European nations to the north. You have to ask yourself what the hell happened. The Jewish section was very interesting. We could see the Spanish influence with wooden second-story balconies. Inside the market court—surprise, surprise—lots of gold jewelry was for sale. Only today, Moroccans were selling it, not Jews. There were only sixty-three Jews left in Fez. Most of the others left for Israel in the 1940s.

Our next stop, just outside the Jewish quarter, was another chance to spend some money. This was a mosaic factory—same spiel: "Look at our craftsman; see our ovens; have a cup of tea. Now that we disarmed you, it would be nice if you bought something." Interestingly enough, we were looking for a new table for the lake house. After giving them the dimensions and being offered a price of $8,600, we decided to let Marc, our friend and caretaker up at the lake, make it. I got out of there by the skin of my teeth before Leanne took home a Moroccan fountain as a consolation prize.

Before heading back to the hotel, we made one last stop in the old city. This time we entered through the main gate, which was built in 1912 by the French when they occupied Morocco. This was our last chance to bring a souvenir home from Fez. Over two thousand shops and we couldn't find a thing to buy. Our last stop was a shop that sold handmade trays made of silver and bronze. Here we broke down and left a few—well, more than a few—American dollars. You can always find a place for silver. When we were leaving, our guide had another surprise in store. Entering a small door off the entrance to the shop, we found ourselves in a magnificent villa. It is one of over a thousand that supposedly existed throughout the market. Many have been turned into shops, restaurants, or apartments. This was still a private residence. At over ten thousand square feet, it must have been something to behold in days past. Now, unfortunately, it was in poor repair and under restoration by the billionaire son of the previous occupant. I was told the restoration would cost $3 million and that it would be a private weekend getaway. We have come to see that Morocco is not cheap.

Off to dinner—I won't bore you with the details of this meal. Let's just say that now that I have found my pastilla, it feels more like Morocco.

ROAD TO MOROCCO: DAY FIVE

We drove south out of Fez today through one of the nicer sections of the new city. I found the architecture very interesting for Morocco. It had a distinctive art deco feel to it. Many of the homes looked like they would fit in nicely on the shores of South Beach. This wasn't our destination, though. We were headed south, traveling nine hours into and over the Atlas Mountains to the Sahara.

Traveling up the northern slope of the Atlas Mountains, we saw most of what we had seen in Morocco so far—lush green plains, dense trees, and farmhouses dotting the landscape. We made our first stop off the highway at a beautiful tree-encircled lake with a modern resort and camp area. Here we saw kids from the city learning to ride horses. Most of the children from the city have never had an opportunity to ride a horse. It was cute watching them hold on tight to the saddle as a Moroccan guide ran as fast he could, holding a lead rope, hopefully reassuring the half-elated, half-terrified rider that everything was going to be safe.

Back on the road, our next stop was the little mountain town of Ifren. You would have thought we had driven up into the Swiss Alps as opposed to the Moroccan Atlas Mountains. It was a charming little village with wonderful stone homes in a Swiss or Bavarian style. The French built this town as a vacation getaway from the large cities. Apparently, during the summer, the heat can reach over 120 degrees, so these summer retreats, where it is cooler, are a must for most families. The altitude was perfect for the wealthy French to escape the hot cities in the summer and for the more adventuresome who had missed their winter skiing in Europe. Only miles away, you could still find Moroccan snow skiing. This was evident as we drove further south and could see the snowcapped mountains in the distance on both sides of the road.

As we progressed, we saw the landscape change dramatically. Outside our little Swiss oasis, you would have thought they were storing rocks on the plains. For miles it almost looked like topsoil was nonexistent in the mountains. A little further were lush grass plains where Atlas lions once roamed. Due to trapping by zoos, poaching, and hunting, the last Atlas lion disappeared years ago. It certainly wasn't due to loss of habitat; there wasn't much development here.

Continuing higher up, we passed many small villages, mostly goat farms with the occasional nomad tent camp. We were now in Berber country. The Berbers were the barbarians who came from the East into the southern part of Morocco. The Berbers were the biggest challenge for the French when they occupied Morocco. The Romans and the Arabs both tried to colonize the Berber people. The French had no better luck.

As we continued our travels, we could almost see why. We were slowly climbing into some of the most inhospitable land we had seen during our trip: vast stretches of nothing—no grass, no trees, no water. You would have thought you were traveling through the deserts of Arizona or New Mexico minus the cactus. There were miles of high desert plains, high plateaus, and buttes. A few pinnacles coming off the desert floor, and John Ford could have shot his many Westerns here instead of the Monument Valley.

When we thought it couldn't get drier, we turned the corner and found ourselves surrounded by stratified dry granite mountains. For a while we could see an occasional bush growing from a crevice between the granite, then the scenery returned to absolutely nothing. Then, after just a few miles more, through a tunnel carved into an outcropping of granite, we saw our first oasis. Suddenly there were dense palms, lush green trees, and what appeared as manicured lawn. It was so dense and green.

The oasis stretched through the valley. Clear away a few palms and this would have made a great golf course. Here, an underwater river flows to the surface, bringing life to the valley. Berber mud huts surround the lush green date palms. No thought would be given to building in the oasis and destroying a life-sustaining date crop.

Our trip to today's destination took nine hours. We arrived in Arfoud, a caravan hotel used for stopovers to the Sahara. Tomorrow we would start our adventure riding a camel into the sand dunes to our tent in the desert, where we were to spend the night. Our hotel appeared to be in the middle of nowhere. We looked forward to discovering where we were. As we stepped from our car, a Moroccan band started to play their drums and horns to signal our arrival. It was very romantic and exotic until we were followed into the lobby, where it became deafening and annoying. Picture six drums and a high-pitched horn better suited for charming a cobra then serenading our arrival. We couldn't tame the Berbers, either.

ROAD TO MOROCCO: DAY SIX

Psst, guess where I wrote this? No really, try. Naw, that ain't it. Shhh, come sit a little bit closer, and I will tell you. We were sitting in a Bedouin tent in the middle of the Sahara. There was not a sound, except for the sound of my thumbs typing on my iPhone. Miles and miles and miles and miles and more miles of nothing and more miles and miles and miles and miles and more miles of sand surrounded us. At least in the Serengeti there was an occasional elephant that wondered by, or we might have heard a lion roar, announcing its latest kill. Here there was *nothing*. I can now understand why the Arabs had multiple wives. When surrounded with so much nothing, having a dozen half-naked women dancing in front of you is one way to stop you from going out of your mind.

Seriously, it was beautiful. Our whole adventure here was magical. Midafternoon we arrived to our tent site, riding on the backs of three camels like Carrie, Miranda, and Samantha from *Sex and the City 2*—minus the Jimmy Choo pumps, of course. But, like every good story, let me go back and tell you how we got to this paradise in the desert.

Our route this morning took us to the town of Razzani. We were here to visit the tomb of another famous dead founder and the ksar next door that was built some two hundred years ago. Whoever uttered the words "Take me to the casbah" most likely actually lived in a ksar. A ksar is somewhat like a primitive apartment building. Construction would start with fortified mud and straw walls on the perimeter, and the walls then extended inside in a labyrinth of hallways that divided up the individual apartments. The halls were covered with thin beams cut from date palm trunks covered with mud and straw. All this made for a dark passage home. With only an occasional opening in the roof providing light, we ventured in, walking tight to the wall so as to not step into the muddy drainage running down the center. Passing pitch-dark side passages that led to homes, we continued on to see the well and primitive bread ovens before turning around to be on our way.

This ksar was definitely in the low-rent district. There were others more upscale.

Our next stop was a casbah, built with same type of fortified walls—only these walls housed a royal or other important family and their servant staff only. Although the building was in great need of repair, we could see the opulence that once stood in the desert. Like in many of the homes built in Morocco, there was a center courtyard garden with a mazen overlooking it all. I am going to take a guess here and say this is probably where the word *mezzanine* comes from. Each palace or large home also contains a riad, which is a courtyard garden. Riads are usually very green and plush and often filled with the sounds of hundreds of birds. The riad represents their little piece of paradise here on earth.

Other than sand, the Sahara is rich with fossils. About four hundred million years ago this part of the Sahara was an ocean. Now we stood on sand covering ancient sea life that was trapped and frozen in time when Africa split from Europe. Now squid, crustaceans, and a multitude of other sea creatures are being unearthed, polished, and displayed in shops that dot the road leading to the desert.

We visited several factories that use Italian-made marble-cutting machines to cut massive stones into multiple slabs like slicing a loaf of bread. The slabs are then used for furniture. Each piece is unique, showcasing a surprise view of ancient sea life. Walking through the door of a second factory we were struck by a five-by-eleven-foot fossil table that we knew would look great at the lake house. What did we do, you ask? Let me put it this way: come visit us at the lake, and we will share our piece of history.

Now back to our Arabian night. As we dismounted our camels, the gracious staff greeted us warmly with the traditional Moroccan mint tea, taken in our dining tent. This was just the beginning of a special evening. Before the sun was ready to set, we again mounted our camels to ride west over the sand dunes to reach a high point, where we could view a spectacular sunset in the distance. Here in our own special place in the Sahara, the staff set up a low table and chairs, where we sipped wine and ate olives and almonds while watching the orange sun drop below the horizon, our camels resting on the ground before us. It was amazing how much more comfortable a camel ride was after a few glasses of wine. On the ride out, we held the saddle tightly, but the way back, Leanne had her arms out stretched like she was on the bow of the *Titanic*. It was a breathtaking experience. We thanked Allah for providing such a gorgeous sunset. We were very lucky, because for the ten days before our arrival, it had been stormy with lots of rain and windstorms.

Night was quickly falling, so we again mounted our ground transportation and headed east back to camp. Climbing up dunes and sliding down the other side, we could see the lights on in our tents. With a row of twenty lanterns to lead our way, we arrived in time for drinks around a small campfire. The peaceful silence of the evening was broken as we watched our guide, Rami, start brushing and slapping his legs, at first lightly. We laughed hysterically as the swatting built to a fever pitch. We laughed so hard tears ran down our faces. It reminded us of a similar incident with our guide in the Serengeti, but he had been attacked by a huge swarm of no-see-ums. It seemed Rami had set his chair directly on an ant swarm. When they started on to our carpet and began to attack us, it became a little less funny. It was a good idea when someone suggested going into the dining tent for dinner.

Entering our Moroccan tent gave us the impression of entering a small version of one from a circus. Wide red, yellow, and while walls and a swooping ceiling put us in the mood for the feast to come. After a dinner of beef and couscous, we retired to our private bedroom tent, complete with king-size bed and wash vanity. The bathroom facility was in an adjacent tent with its own portable toilet and hot shower. It was truly a unique, special, and magical experience we will never forget. Good night!

ROAD TO MOROCCO: DAY SEVEN

We awoke this morning just as the sun was beginning to rise. After emerging from our tent, we walked on the soft, red sand of the Sahara, looking east as the sun started to peek over the horizon. There was nothing in front of us except our footprints from the previous evening in the soft sand.

Once we were up, the staff sensed it was time to emerge from their tents to provide the luxurious service we had come to expect. Back in our tent, I started to put my socks on. I instinctively brushed my feet to remove the sand, only to find none—the sand was so soft, it had the consistency of dust. By eight thirty, we were to continue our journey south out of what they call the white sand desert. We left camp not by camel, but by modern, four-wheel drive jeep. With all the excitement the previous day, I hadn't realized how far we had driven to get into the desert. It must have been fifteen miles judging from our bumpy, forty-five-minute drive out.

Once on the highway, we passed through many villages of all sizes. This was a very tribal area. Each tribe inhabited and developed its own town and culture. We stopped at one of the larger ones to tour yet another ksar. This one was much nicer than the one visited yesterday and much better cared for, with a paved drain running down the center of the halls. When we passed the rustic, uneven doors to the individual apartments, some still with primitive wood bolt locks for security, we had no idea the beauty that may lie behind them. So as not to flaunt wealth, Moroccans put more effort into the inside detail of their homes than the outside. The better condition of this ksar may have to do with the fact that part of it had been developed into a hotel. There was also a three-story house that once belonged to the town mayor and was turned into a museum. Again, it was interesting to see the history of the cohabitation that existed centuries ago between the Muslims and Jews.

Further down the highway, we passed an oasis. Circular piles of dirt dotted the landscape along the road, making the earth look more like the moon. Rows and rows of what must have been thousands of mounds stretched for miles. Stopping to explore, we found ourselves at one of several *khettaras*, or irrigation tunnels. One thousand years ago the Berbers dug holes up to forty-five feet deep every one hundred feet connecting them for over twenty-seven miles to bring water from the mountains to their oasis. Each hole was topped with a hoist and bucket for drawing water so homes and farms could freely get water. The holes had a secondary purpose as well: allowing someone to climb down to make repairs should a collapse or blockage occur. We descended into a tunnel through a newly built observation stairway. As we emerged from underground we ascended to one of the many mounds that were created from the Berber digs. It was here we counted five different rows spaced maybe three hundred feet apart leading from the mountains to the oasis. The Berbers hadn't dug one twenty-seven-mile tunnel, but five. I was not quite sure why they didn't put it twenty miles closer to the mountain.

Back in our Mercedes van, we continued onward and upward, literally. We were headed toward the mountains. At the top of the mountains, we stopped to look at and photograph one of the many mud, straw, and brick villages below built around an oasis. Past the homes and oasis, the landscape looked like the Arizona desert. The view was of a sweeping, flat desert dotted with mesas—and not much else. Even the mountains we were going through were barren of vegetation.

A few miles up a narrow mountain road, our driver stopped to let us out again for a view and a walk. For about a quarter mile, we traced the oasis and village as it continued into a canyon. I am sure we would be ticketed for that in the United States.

Back in our car, we were off to further explore the canyon. After we traveled a few miles more, the road ended at the beginning of a narrow canyon with towering cliffs. Much like the Grand Canyon, these high cliffs were possibly carved by a river running through the middle, or maybe it was created by an earthquake—or both? The gorge was a spectacular site. Mountain climbers, like our son-in-law John, would have salivated at the sight.

Going out the same way we came in, we headed to our last stop of the day. We were on the march, passing many villages without stopping. In one village, kids were selling strings of roses at the edge of the highway. Apparently the roses were grown here to produce rosewater for hand baths and French perfume. I thought to myself, *I wonder if anyone stops to smell the roses.* Cymbal, please!

After an hour and a half travel time, we pulled into a gas station where we were transferred to a four-wheel vehicle for our next stop: paradise.

ROAD TO MOROCCO: DAY EIGHT

Our driver turned off the highway and headed into the narrow, unpaved mud-wall-lined streets of Skoura. We twisted and turned until we reached the palm grove at the end of the village. Our driver put our four-runner into four-wheel drive as he navigated the small dirt road lined with olive trees and fan palms. Four-wheel drive seemed to me somewhat overkill for a road of this condition. I understood once we emerged from the grove at the bank of a riverbed that was the width of the Mississippi. Today it was dry and rocky. On other days, when the floods come in from the Atlas Mountains, it isn't passable.

Having made our crossing, we were now continuing our trip through the palm grove on the other side. As we approached our destination, the driver made one quick toot of his horn before coming to a stop in the driveway. Moments later, our host emerged like Ricardo Montalban from his casbah, hidden behind the trees to greet us as his guest.

Our host led us through a low, wide wooden door to the guest door of the dimly lit hallways of the casbah. Our host informed us there was no front desk, no credit card we needed to present, and nothing we needed to sign. Everything in and around the casbah was included for our enjoyment during our stay, including wine, food, drinks, aperitifs, and excursions. Even getting our laundry done was included. (We took advantage of that.) They were expecting us, and we were their guests. Welcome to Dar Ahlam, the house of dreams.

There was no menu here, no dining room, no fixed times to eat, and no social bar scene. They also didn't have clocks, telephones, televisions, room numbers, or Internet service. The only gathering area was the lovely and quiet salon, which was sprinkled with rose petals on every table and in every nook. The salon opened to a swooping canvas-covered patio with a view of a fifty-foot-long pool and adjacent gardens. Here our host explained some of the many excursions offered:

hiking, biking, guided garden strolls, camel rides, car tours of the mountains or city, horseback riding—*bingo*. Did someone say horses? We were set for tomorrow.

After enjoying a glass of wine—maybe more like two or three—in the salon, we were ready to be shown to our room. Our room was on the second floor, the second door on the left of the original casbah built in 1927. It was built as a farmhouse for a wealthy family and later updated into our accommodations. Don't call this a hotel. It is a mere twelve rooms where you stay as their guest. As we reached our room, our host pulled on the large metal ring of a massive Moroccan-style wood door, and it opened with ease. Moroccan doors are mounted on the outside of the wall and are a foot or two wider than the door opening. The door is mounted on wooden hinges affixed to the wall at top and bottom and locked only by a wood bar or metal latch inside. Guests did not need to worry about keys here at the casbah. To close, one simply needed to pull on the decretive rope hanging from the top of the inside and latch for privacy. Our suite was made up of three large rooms: an entry foyer, a bedroom to the left, and a bathroom with a massive tub that looked like it had been carved from a single block of stone. After little rest, we were up and ready for dinner at eight-thirty.

Descending our stairs, almost like magic, one of the staff dressed in black appeared from one of the many alcoves to ask if we were ready for dinner. We responded with a surprised yes and were led through several dimly lit passages to our own private dining room. Our host chose a new private area for each of his guests to dine in private. Now this was where the saying "take me to the casbah" came from. Romantic candlelight shimmering off the walls warmly lit our dining room for the evening. The only choice we needed to make was which cocktail we preferred.

With no alarm clocks sounding or pesky maids opening our door, we awoke at ten. As we made our way downstairs again, someone emerged to say our breakfast was set in the garden. We were escorted past the pool and down a narrow manicured garden path to a large patio lined with privacy bushes where our table for two was set. Not a soul or other table was in sight, only the warm sun and the sound of birds singing in the trees.

It was now time for our ride. In the front driveway of our casbah were our driver and a member of the staff who would accompany us to the stable. No rush. They would work on our schedule, not theirs. Good thing too—when we arrived, we had been so awestruck with the casbah we didn't pay attention to how to get out. Like a mouse's maze, each hallway and passage led to one of the many seating rooms, which were converted to dining rooms or led out to the gardens. Round and round we went until we gave up and asked for help.

As we expected, our car driver and staff member ran to greet us as we emerged from the doorway. Our travels would take us twenty minutes to reach the stable on the opposite end of the palm grove. Stepping out of the car, we were greeted by our trail guide and led to the stable, where twenty stunning Arabian horses were waiting for our visit. Here I received the some shocking news: they only rode English here, and I had to hang up my Stetson for one of those English riding helmets. Aw, shucks, ma'am.

Three Arabians were pulled from the string for our ride, two stallions and one mare. Guess who got the two stallions. I had never ridden an Arab before, let alone a stallion with an English saddle. I must say I looked mighty fine atop a jet-black Arabian stallion. Leanne, too, looked stunning mounted on her white and gray Arab.

We rode out over the rocky plains in the direction of the snowcapped Atlas Mountains. We would not be crossing them today; we were headed into the dense palm and olive grove up ahead to the left. The grove surrounded many small villages and homes, where children would run out and say *bonjour* as we passed and women washed clothes in the maze of cement irrigation ditches. Riding horses was the only way to experience the local life and landscape. Riding high in the saddle, we viewed the world from the trees. The path wound through the palms and into alleys lined with mud walls protecting homes, tent camps, and crops. We would not have been able to see the culture that lay behind these walls at eye level. Riding high gave us a chance to see beyond the walls, giving us a peek into their true lives. We loved the whole experience, including listening to the myriad of birds, a bellow from a laden donkey, the call from roosters to their chickens, and even the gobble from a gaggle of turkeys. Our favorite sounds, though, were the giggles of the many children who ran to greet us. The Berber children were just gorgeous.

As we got more comfortable on our English saddles, our guide suggested that we canter. A little apprehensive, we picked up the pace. I was a bit tense, expecting my black Arab stallion to go into overdrive. I don't think *whoa* is an Arab word, but that was all I had.

We shared these paths with motorbikes, children riding bicycles, and carts pulled by donkeys delivering the crops from the field. Things got very exciting when a motorbike behind me backfired at the moment a black cat jumped from a ledge. I don't know who was comforted more by me yelling *whoa*, my horse or me. Experience calmed us both down and we moved on. Back at the stable, I donned my Stetson, and Leanne and I bid farewell to another memorable event in our lives.

Back at the casbah, we were ready for a shower and lunch. Our table was set in another section of the garden reserved only for us. Turning a corner off the pool area, we found at the end of a manicured lawn a table for two under an umbrella strategically placed to shade us from the sun. The only person in sight was our waiter, who was bringing drinks, and the only noise was that of a soft serenade of birds in the trees.

We retired to the patio to relax before our spa treatment, having second thoughts about continuing on to Marrakech tomorrow. This was what the Koran calls paradise on earth. It was going to be harder to leave the house of dreams.

ROAD TO MOROCCO: DAY NINE

From all dreams, eventually, just like little Alice's, we all must wake up. After breakfast in our private garden, we too awoke and found ourselves back at the petrol station greeted by our guide, Rami, and driver, Mahjoub, standing in front of our Mercedes.

Our travels today will continue south up and over the snowcapped Atlas Mountains. We did make two interesting stops along the way. Our first was to a Glaoui Kasbah once belonging to the Glaoui brothers, the most powerful tribal leaders in Morocco. It is considered one of the most beautiful casbahs in Morocco. Most recently it served as the home of the *pasha*, or mayor, of Marrakech. The second was to the city of Ouarzazate, the film capital of Morocco. It's a relatively new city, having been built and financed in 1975 by the United Arab Emirates for falcon hunting. Not long after its creation, the first movie studio was built to film the Michael Douglas's film *Jewel of the Nile*. As we drove out of downtown the road became a straight boulevard lined with palm trees and a perfectly straight row of high streetlights with curved tops holding decorative copper lanterns. It wouldn't have looked out of place in Beverly Hills. This was Hollywood, Morocco style, with the filming of a historical movie on the left side of the road and movie studios and sets on the right. Just like Hollywood, the Atlas Studio offers behind the scene tours to visitors. Our guide for the next hours was a young Moroccan Berber who loved to hum movie themes. The Atlas back lot with its many ancient sets made of wood and plaster has been used for many epic films over the years. *Gladiator*, *The Mummy Returns*, the remake of *Ben Hur*, *Cleopatra*, and most recently *The Way Back*, a film produced by friends of ours.

Our last stop before we headed over the mountains was a twelfth-century Kasbah Ait Benhaddou, the best-preserved casbah in the region. It was built into the hillside and was more of a ksar then a casbah. (Remember the difference?) This casbah is most famously remembered for the filming of the epic *Lawrence of Arabia*. To reach the casbah, we took a stone road down through the village to the river's edge. This must have been the same river we crossed in Skoura to get to the house of dreams. The river was similar in width to the Mississippi, only this one ran with water from the mountains. No four-wheel drive here. To cross we must navigate sandbags and the occasional rock in the river, placed strategically to create two paths for visitors to reach the other side. Once on solid ground, we climbed the many stairs weaving through the fortified village. There were still several families living within the walls who may have run the restaurants or shops that filled some of the doorways. I would imagine there were also a few old holdouts who refused to leave for the other side of the river, where a new town and shops have been built. At the top of the ksar, one found oneself within the walls of the granary, which was placed high over the city so it would be easier to protect in the event of an attack.

The joy of traveling is getting to see some magnificent historical sites, experience the culture, and meet people in distant lands. At lunch today we had the opportunity to meet and talk with some very interesting women. Sitting next to us were five married Moroccan Berber women who lived and worked in Holland. Three of them wore the traditional headscarves and two did not. In Leanne's natural way, we struck up a conversation with them and learned they were very modern, emancipated ladies who worked for a nonprofit in Rotterdam that helps Moroccan immigrants settle and learn the culture in Europe. With Leanne in the room, I knew the conversation would eventually get around to Islamic terrorism. It was interesting to hear their perspective. They too were afraid of terrorism. They were just tired of being asked to explain what was happening and defending Islam as if the attacks were their fault. They said that when people of other ethnic or religious groups were in a conversation, they never got the same grilling as they did. Of course, they were against terrorism. The issue I saw for them and for the average Muslim was that they didn't want to believe a Muslim could carry out such repugnant acts. Until the good and peaceful Muslims come to terms with the fact there are bad Muslims out there trying to destroy Western life as well as their own, we will have a difficult time eliminating radical Muslim terrorism.

Listening to their views on how Americans were portrayed in the Middle East and explaining how we saw them in the West was a wonderful experience. We both agreed the media was to blame for fanning the fire. There is nothing worse than half-truths. Little truths are sometimes more damaging then big lies. All media have a habit of taking a little bit of truth and blowing it into big wars. William Randolph Hearst, after receiving a telegram from his reporter in Cuba saying, "There will not be a war here," responded, "You furnish the pictures. I'll furnish the war." We used to call this yellow journalism; now we call it Fox News.

Not two hours after our experience of friendship and brotherhood, Morocco was rocked by the tragic bombing of a popular café in the main square in Marrakech. This senseless act not only did damage to the lives of people and families lost or injured, but it also damaged the peaceful lives and livelihoods of the majority of Muslims around the world. This was a cowardly act that the news media must report on. The talking heads will look for any analyst or radical to interview to fan the flame of ignorance and hatred of a people they know nothing about.

We heard this news as we were driving away from our lunch. Our guide at first couldn't believe this was possible. As many times as we read the story, he refused to believe something like this could happen in Morocco. He kept repeating that they had no terrorists here. It was not until he called a guide in Marrakech and heard firsthand what was happening that he came to terms with this horrendous event. Our drive through the mountains became a bit more solemn as we wound our way to Marrakech.

The drive through this part of the Atlas Mountains was as diverse as Morocco itself. It seemed like the landscape changed every few miles, leaving us swearing we were someplace else. First, it was the southern Rocky Mountains, and next the Continental Divide. Twisting and turning and winding and turning, we drove for hours, eventually reaching 7,500 feet to the Toubkal Pass. We were still two or three thousand feet below the snow line, but that didn't make it any warmer. As we started to descend, we saw beautiful, lush valleys, terraced farms reminiscent of what we had seen in Machu Picchu, and small villages tucked into the hillside.

We were not due into Marrakech for another two days. It was just as well, given the turmoil that must have been happening there. The last things they needed were more tourists while they sorted this criminal event out. Our next two days would be spent at Kasbah Tamadot, the Moroccan hotel owned by Sir Richard Branson. Next you will read about what it's like to live like a billionaire.

ROAD TO MOROCCO: DAY TEN

Finally at the base of the high Atlas Mountains, our Mercedes turned left and headed back up, this time 3,500 feet into one of its many fertile valleys. This part of southern Morocco looks much the same as its northern sister: lush and green. We were only up a thousand feet when we had to come to a stop where a construction crew was clearing away a rockslide and installing a drainage pipe at Moroccan speed (i.e., not much faster than our Cal-trans crews in California).

Forty-five minutes later, we were again on our way, passing large valleys filled with olive and fruit trees. Then, in the distance, we could see the majestic Kasbah Tamadot, Sir Richard Branson's home away from home. He had just left the premises two days earlier after checking to see that everything was all set for our arrival. [It could happen!] Originally, Branson bought the casbah for a vacation home to entertain his family and many friends. At some point he decided to turn it into a hotel for his new friends (like Steve and Leanne).

The hotel was stunningly beautiful and very Moroccan. Passing the small reservation area, we climbed the stairs to a courtyard with a shallow square pool in the center brimming with floating white, red, and pink roses. A Moroccan trio played as we were shown to our room just off the courtyard, bright and airy with what appeared to be an elaborately painted nineteenth-century ceiling. Our bed and bath were also sprinkled with rose petals.

The casbah had two different accommodations: the twenty-four rooms of the old Kasbah, and five permanent Moroccan tents in the outer gardens. We had an opportunity to visit the tents, and they were just lovely and unique. They were very spacious, with modern bathrooms, televisions, and Internet connections and wonderful draped ceilings. If you are going to take the time to go out of your way to get here, this is the place to stay.

After freshening up from our nine-hour trek over the Atlas Mountains, we joined other guests having drinks around the rose pool. We have to say, for as peaceful and quiet Dah Ahlam was, this place was loud. One can only take Moroccan drums banging for so long.

Our excursion the next day was a 9.5-mile hike up 2,500 vertical feet to view the entire valley. Whose idea was this? Forgetting first my vest, then Leanne's jacket, and finally my diet peach Snapple to go, I was finally ready for a rest after climbing up and down the stairs three separate times.

After meeting our guide, Rachid, in the lobby, we walked to the road, where we were met by another guide with his donkey carrying our lunches and supplies for the day. The journey of a thousand miles, they say, starts with the first step. Our step was on the steep red soil leading to the six-thousand-foot peak of the mountain across from our hotel. The steepness was tempered a little by the terracing of the rocky trail we were traveling. It wasn't long before the cold weather gave way to heat and sweat. The three layers we had put on were slowly coming off.

About a quarter of the way up, I couldn't help but admire the ass in front of me and want to get on top of it. Get your mind out of the gutter—I am talking about the donkey. There stacked with carpets, stools, and our picnic lunch and topped off by one of our guides was a beautifully efficient animal that could whisk us up to the top with ease. We must have both been wondering what my best friend, Jason Balaban, would do—so neither of us dared hop on, even when offered.

A little ways farther and it started to sprinkle. Thank goodness it stopped quickly enough so we could persevere onward. Then, at about seven-eighths of the way to the top, the sky opened up with a torrential downpour. It was becoming obvious we wouldn't make it to the top. Without proper rain gear—not even an umbrella—our only option was to go back down to where our guide knew of a Berber village that would take us in to dry ourselves out. As we walked down the steep, rocky terrain, the water started to pool and run beneath our feet. Fifteen minutes back down the way we had come up, we turned off the trail onto a dirt road on the other side. Just then, we heard the crack of lightning and the roll of thunder filling the sky.

The dirt road was slowly turning to mud as the rain continued to fall and streams began to wind down the road as we walked. We were now looking for the rocks we had carefully tried to avoid hours earlier to help us gain our footing and keep our shoes out of the running water. Along the way, the hills gave way to waterfalls flooding the path before us. Two flowed so quickly we were forced to abandon our muddy trail and make for a shortcut through the rocky hillside. We had been traveling forty-five minutes from where we turned around, and the Berber village was still nowhere in sight. My vest, though warm, did little to protect my hands in my pockets. The material forming the pockets was so thin that the water just soaked through. This combined with the water dripping now from my sweater started to turn my pockets into little pools. Close behind me was Leanne, her hands turning blue, drenched and freezing in her capri jeans.

Fifteen minutes later we were at the backside of the small Berber village we were so desperately seeking. We were soaked to the bone, and our wet, muddy shoes needed to still navigate the rocky and muddy streets. I was surprised when our guide started to climb rocks in and around a steep rock stream of flowing water. Following along with Leanne and our donkey, I tried to balance on the rocks holding branches, only to slip and slide several times into the rushing water. Straddling rushing water, we slipped in the mud until we finally reached a home whose inhabitants could take us in. The woman of the home welcomed us, leading us upstairs to the mezan where she passed out warm blankets and poured us cups of sugar with a little tea. At that point anything hot was welcome.

Sitting looking out over the village at the local mosque, we could see an old woman kneeling in the rain, trying to start a fire. The fire would warm the water for which she and her husband could take their traditional Friday shower before visiting the mosque. Looking toward the mosque, we then heard the sounds of the call to prayer.

Trying to dry off, we ate the lunch our donkey had dutifully carried for us. We suggested that our guide call the hotel and send a car to pick us up. There were no roads to this remote village, so we were forced to put our wet jackets back on and walk through the village to the main road below. The half hour or so we spent on the patio didn't help the condition of the village streets, where torrents were now rushing. We tried to grip the mud walls in an attempt to stay on higher ground as the water continued to wash past our feet. Mud was now caked up to the knees of my wet jeans.

When we finely reached the road, our hotel car was nowhere to be found. Our guide called on his cell phone only to be informed that the driver had stopped to pray at the mosque. We had no choice but to walk the next two miles on the highway while the rain continued to fall and the muddy hillside gave way, showering mud in our path. Within sight of the hotel, our driver finally showed up with a smile.

This was definitely not something Liz Taylor would have done. If this was how the billionaires live, I wanted nothing to do with it. Then again, I am sure Sir Richard Branson's staff would have checked the weather report before he decided to go on a hike. It turned out we did hike the full 11.5 miles—we just did it a little differently than we had planned (two-thirds of it up, and one-third of it in rain and mud). Jason B. would be proud of us. And you thought this was just going to be another one of those boring nature stories, didn't you?

Now back at the hotel, we were warm and dry in our room, and the sun started to break through the clouds. Looking at the magnificent view from our picture window facing the mountains, we could see that the green peaks we viewed this morning when we left were now covered in snow. It was a gentle reminder of the hail we were being hit with at the upper elevations of our hike.

This day would fit nicely into my new travel book, *Don't Forget to Pack Your Sense of Humor*. Like the Alan Sherman song "Camp Granada" says, "Wait a minute, it's stopped hailing, guys are swimming, guys are sailing.... Gee that's betta! Muddah, Faddah, kindly, please, disregard this letter."

ROAD TO MOROCCO: DAY ELEVEN

We are just past the halfway mark on our Morocco expedition. We started in Casablanca, traveled north to Rabat and Fez, and then circled south. It's now time to head east to Marrakech and then north to complete a full circle of Morocco.

Our car and driver arrived to pick us up at the Kasbah Tamadot almost an hour late. Yesterday's heavy rains had caused slides on the road, making the drive that much slower and more treacherous. Our guide Rami wisely made the suggestion that we take an alternative route through the hills to reach Marrakech. It was a delightful suggestion. I have not been to Ireland yet, but I can't imagine their rolling hills are any greener or more pastoral then these.

The residents of the small stone towns we passed through were mostly sheep, goat, and cattle herders. As we entered the narrow main road of one town, there were so many black goats coming at us I thought we were in Pamplona, Spain, at the running of the bulls. As we began our descent we had a panoramic view of the vast plains and a dammed river that led us to the city of Marrakech far in the distance. The name Marrakech is believed derived from two Berber words. With many caravans passing through the region, robbers used to lay in wait for them to arrive. When the caravans reached the area they would say *"Mar kush,"* meaning go fast. At one time the whole of Morocco was known as Marrakech. Morocco is a relatively new name for the country.

As we approached the outer suburbs of Marrakech the farms gave way to modern large, Moroccan-style villas and condo developments. Marrakech is a very modern town. Pulling into the city, with cars, scooters, and bikes crisscrossing in every direction, we made our first stop at the famous square. We arrived not to explore, but to board our morning transportation. At the entrance to the square there must have been a hundred open carriages waiting to take visitors for a ride. Things got somewhat hectic when police officers on motorcycles started ordering all one hundred carriages to move. The king was here to survey Thursday's damage and to visit the wounded. Security was paramount this day. As it happened, one hundred horse-drawn carriages started to move as we boarded the one reserved for us.

Our open-air carriage made a U-turn and proceeded out of the square, heading down a wide boulevard lined with hotels and flowering gardens. We meandered through the street and at one point passed the hotel that Winston Churchill came to vacation and paint—in room thirty-three, they tell me. We turned down roads where modern apartment buildings lined both sides of the street in Moroccan-influenced modern style. We made one stop at the Menara gardens. The large irrigation pond was once used to teach Moroccan soldiers to swim. It is now overflowing with carp. Throwing a few pieces of bread in the water created a feeding frenzy so dense on the surface that one would have been able to stand. As we walked back down the promenade, our carriage was still waiting to take us to our next stop, the Majorelle Garden. Once the home of French painter Jacques Majorelle from 1924 until his death in 1962, the house and garden were purchased and restored by French designer Yves Saint Laurent in 1980. Laurent was so enamored with the house and gardens he set up a special trust to ensure that the home and gardens would remain undeveloped and cared for in perpetuity. Yves Saint Laurent died in 2008, dictating in his will that his wish was to be laid to rest in the gardens at his home in Morocco, not his native France.

Turning down rue Yves Saint Laurent Street, our carriage came to rest in front of the main gate of the gardens. As we entered, I was surprised to see the majority of the low-planted landscape was made up of different varieties of cactus, many of them in spring bloom. The low-lying cactus were accented by low palms and shaded by the many types of tall palms found in Morocco. The contrast between the desert cactus and the lush, dense palm made this one of the most gorgeous landscapes to meander through. As we walked toward the rear of the garden to a back wall separating the garden from the home, we came upon the meditation area and resting place of the famous designer who once dressed Jacqueline Kennedy Onassis.

Leaving the garden, our carriage again was replaced by our Mercedes, which would take us to lunch at a very fashionable French colonial–style café. The decor was what one would expect of a North African French bistro of the 1920s.

Back in our car we were off to the old city and the souk. This market was not as organized as the souks in Fez. Actually, at times it could be quite dangerous. Crowded with people going down the narrow streets, we had to share the walkways with motor scooters, bicycles, and the occasional donkey pulling a cart. The only thing saving our bodies from certain injury was the piercing sound of the horns as the scooters flew by at speeds exceeding fifteen miles an hour. Scooters at times would be coming at you from different directions; it's a miracle that no one has stepped in front of one trying to avoid another.

We walked for what seemed miles, passing stalls selling everything imaginable and negotiating hard for gifts to take home. Our guide, Rami, proved very helpful in most cases, negotiating the prices and making sure we were buying only authentic Moroccan goods. If one merchant tried to show us a Chinese knockoff, Rami would quickly usher us away.

Laden with bags, we exited the market and found ourselves in the Jemaa el Fna square. This was the sight of the tragic bombing last Thursday. If the object of the bombers was to keep people away, they hardly succeeded. I had never witnessed a scene so active, so alive, than this square. Looking like a gigantic street fair, the square was packed with people. The scooters finally had to slow down and inch through the crowds, honking and trying to part the crowd the way Moses parted the Red Sea.

On the perimeter of the square were snake charmers, fire-eaters, men with monkeys, and any other oddity you were willing to pay twenty dirhams to be photographed with. In the center of it all was a food market where fine fruits, vegetables, hog's heads, and lamb brains were piled high. Barbecues belched smoke, cooking or grilling every imaginable edible. Should you choose, you could also indulge in a delicious snail soup. It appeared to be bowls filled with boiling water packed with snails still in the shell—a simple recipe you can easily make at home with snails from your own backyard!

As we got to the middle of the square, we could see the devastation done to the second floor of the restaurant Argana. Although cordoned off, that didn't stop a large crowd gathered to take pictures. It was easy to see why this had been the target. Sitting directly on the square with second- and third-floor terraces, it was easily visible from everywhere. Strangely, it was in direct sight if the minaret of the mosque on the opposite side of the street. Before we left the square, we sat down to rest and have a drink. I have to say, I did feel a little apprehensive sitting by the window in a café only yards from where that unspeakable act had occurred.

At seven we left the square, which was still teeming with people, to drive to our hotel. It turned out we were within walking distance from the square. I was surprised when our driver made a U-turn and pulled up next to a tire store. That's right. The entrance to our five-star hotel was next to a little Moroccan Wheel Works. Just like souks, the true beauty of Morocco is sometimes hidden from public view. The Villa des Orangers is one of those hidden treasures. Liz Taylor would certainly stay here.

Once a private residence, the hotel now houses twenty-four villas that are centered around a Moroccan courtyard, including a newer section with a pool and dining room. After a quick tour, we were shown to our own private paradise: a one-bedroom, two-story villa with an entry hall, large study, and living room with fireplace downstairs, and a large bedroom suite upstairs with a balcony overlooking the black-bottom pool below.

With all this luxury at our feet, what was Leanne excited about? Free laundry service! We put all the muddy clothes from our previous adventure in for a proper cleaning. Yeah!

ROAD TO MOROCCO: DAY TWELVE

Last night we ordered breakfast and requested that it be delivered to the villa so we could enjoy the beautiful patio overlooking the pool. When we awoke, we realized those plans were shattered. It was raining cats and dogs.

The nice thing about having our own villa was that there were always other options. Our morning instead started in the living room.

Not wanting to waste a day in Marrakech, we decided to spend the day shopping. This too ran into complications, being that it was May Day, a holiday like Labor Day celebrated in parts of the Americas, Europe, Africa, and Asia. The rain wasn't the only impediment to walking. The temperature had also dropped. I had my utilitarian vest; Leanne, on the other hand, had sent her jacket to the free laundry. Rami yelled, "Are you going to go out like this?" as Leanne emerged from the hotel entrance wearing the hooded hotel bathrobe. She answered, "Of course." It might sound funny, but two people stopped Leanne to ask where she got her warm terry *jellaba*.

Rami suggested a large fixed-price store in the newer part of the city. This place was massive. Think Bed Bath & Beyond meets Pier 1 Imports all rolled into a Macy's. Goods were piled high, with racks and shelves so tightly stacked together we had to turn sideways to get through. Rainy days and shopping are not a good combination when you are on vacation. Two budget-busting hours later we had bought more then we could possibly carry home. We had packed light coming, but we would look like pack mules going home.

When we left the store, the rain had slowed enough that we could continue with our itinerary and sightseeing. It helped that this time at least someone was smart enough to bring an umbrella.

Our first stop was the tomb of Saadian, a king who ruled the last half of the sixteenth century. His tomb was made of a center mosaic tile outer yard reserved for his servants and other surrounding buildings for his relatives, princes, children, and wives. Small, rectangular tiles within the total mosaic marked the graves. Some of these were topped with a long, narrow, triangular slab of marble.

To access the tomb, we walked through a maze with twenty-foot-high walls. We needed to wind through a narrow passage barely wide enough for one person to pass. This wall didn't exist when the tomb was built in the sixteenth century. The wall was actually built by Ismail, one of the succeeding conquering rulers, who also filled the tomb with sand to bury the existence of his predecessor. It wasn't until hundreds of years later, in 1917 that a Frenchman uncovered Marrakech's treasured past.

Our next stop was the palace of Ahmed al-Mansur Ad Dahbi, or Ahmed the Golden. It was once the most beautiful palace in the world. Unfortunately for the world, this too was ransacked and destroyed by Ismail. What remains are its massive walls, large pools, and interior overgrown gardens. Climbing to the rooftop we had a commanding view of Middle Eastern democracy. Hundreds of satellite dishes dotted the rooftops. It is this access to information that is helping to change the Middle East.

Our last visit before lunch was to one of the most beautiful casbahs we have visited. Constructed in the beginning of the twentieth century, the casbah was built for a minister to the last king who ruled before French colonization. This casbah was used by the French during their rule and is now a government museum. It has a beautiful, ornate riad, or courtyard, planted with tall, ornamental orange trees and palms. The canopy would not only have shaded visitors in the 120-degree summer heat, but also helped protect us from the rain.

After lunch at our villa, we decided to go back to the square. Rami suggested a detour to La Mamounia, the favorite Morocco accommodation of Winston Churchill. After we drove through a security checkpoint fit for an American embassy, we continued down the manicured drive and pulled up to the entrance. La Mamounia was once a prince's palace similar to the one we had stayed at in Fez. This palace was much grander. Liz would approve. As we walked up the entry stairs, two uniformed doormen dressed in traditional red opened the double doors in unison. A few paces farther, another two interior doormen opened the second set of double doors to welcome us. We could feel the rich history of La Mamounia as we entered the dark, stately lobby.

We couldn't help but explore this wonderful hotel. Stepping into the dark wood and red-armchaired bar, we could imagine Churchill, a cigar in one hand and a scotch in the other, holding a high-level discussion. At the end of the bar were colorful Frank Lloyd Wright doors leading out to the most fabulous gardens. East, west, north, and south, it was worthy of a picture.

Back inside, we started to explore the colonnade. Here were all of Churchill's favorite shops: Dior, Gucci, Fendi—okay, maybe not Churchill's favorites, but most certainly the favorites of his mistresses. In any case, this was where visitors of Marrakech could find the city's designer shops. Before we departed, we passed through the magnificent spa. The spa looked like something one would find in Las Vegas, and I am sure Churchill had many massages and steams here. We couldn't help but compare it with our five-star accommodations. As spectacular as it was here, we would only have a hotel room. It was a toss-up. Both had different things to offer. Then again, having our own villa in a beautiful, romantic setting in the middle of Marrakech couldn't be beat.

Our four uniformed doormen again opened both pairs of doors in fine synchronization. Our car was waiting for us in the drive with the doors open. We were now off to the square. The square really didn't get going until six in the evening. We arrived just as the food vendors had just set up for the dinner crowd. As we passed the food stalls, barkers tried to pull the passing crowd in for a snack. They didn't even try to entice us, knowing that Americans wouldn't be drawn to grilled lamb brains or pig testicles. We continued past, walking into the souks. We passed the fragrant smell of the many olive stands; it was a welcome reprieve from the smell of tanneries. The rain hadn't dampened the crowds who were still gathered in the square as the rain stopped and the sun was starting to break through. April just might finally be arriving in Morocco.

ROAD TO MOROCCO: DAY THIRTEEN

Our last night in Marrakech was spent having dinner at the home of a dear friend of our son-in-law's mother, Patricia Ardigo. Patricia, like us, fell in love with Morocco and just insisted that we contact her dear friend Mustapha. Leanne and I love meeting new people when we travel, and this was a special treat. Mustapha and his wife live in the more fashionable section of Marrakech in a very modern high-rise condo. Any time we can sit down with a local resident to discuss the culture, economics, religion, and politics of a host country, we jump at the chance. It helps us get a balanced perspective of the local life. Mustapha is a more modern, progressive Moroccan, spending half his time in Morocco and the other half, wisely the summer half, in Belgium. After he and his wife hosted us for a wonderful Moroccan dinner of tajine chicken, we were driven back to our hotel, where we shortly received the news we were grandparents. I want to give a special thank-you and congratulations to Nana Trisha for introducing us to her wonderful son, John and to Mustapha.

May 1, 2011, would be a memorable day for the Troy's. Today a despicable terrorist left this earth unceremoniously and a little angel arrived in the form of Aideyn Ardigo. The world was celebrating with us on this joyous day.

It was now time to bid Marrakech adieu and travel east toward the Atlantic coast. Today was mostly a transfer day to the coastal city of Essaouira.

It was still raining when we left Marrakech—and what do we do when it's raining? Shop, of course. I hate to say this, but that carpet in Fez was still on our minds. Since this was our last chance to spend a buck or two in Morocco, our guide recommended we stop along the way at a carpet wholesaler. Everyone in the Middle East claimed to wholesale carpets. About an hour into the drive, we pulled up to an old, unmarked casbah to take a look. We looked and looked and couldn't find a carpet similar to the one in Fez. They pulled dozens of carpets—still no Fez. Eventually Leanne settled on one she liked. It was nothing like Fez, but she was not leaving empty-handed. Now it was price. It took us getting in the car, driving off, and then backing up with a final offer before we had a deal. When bargaining for a carpet, it all comes down to how badly you are willing to get screwed. Oh well, it was vacation.

Our next stop was a plantation of argan. Argan is a fruit with a large nut for oil and cosmetics. Leanne has used products in the States with argan oil, or Moroccan oil, for hair. What could be better than buying it at the source to get a deal? We watched three women on the floor with rocks stripping skins, cracking shells, and grinding nuts with stones to create argan paste. Like at Disneyland, the tour ended in the gift shop. Elizabeth Arden wishes she could get these prices. A hundred dollars later, we emerged with two small bottles, and we didn't even get our free gift.

Back on the road, we finally pulled into Essaouira, a little poorer than when we left Marrakech. Essaouira is a beach town. Restaurants dot the shoreline, and people walk the wide sandy shore. The rain had just let up here, and like in another city at sea level, Miami, the streets flooded easily. Driving along the coast, we turned off the main road and pulled into our next five-star hotel, the Heure Bleue Palace. Walking through the doors, we stood in the middle of the riad and had the distinct feeling we had just walked into a scene from *Our Man in Havana*. We found lush green trees reaching high up the colonial style balconies with white-cushioned rattan chairs circling the veranda. This was going to be a nice place to spend a couple of restful nights before leaving for Casablanca.

ROAD TO MOROCCO: DAY FOURTEEN

We awoke his morning with blue, sunny skies. Seagulls were again filling the skies over the Atlantic Ocean looking for food. Essaouira is a fishing village once used as an ancient port for the Phoenicians, Romans, and Corinthians. The Portuguese fortified the medina on a rocky coast a bit over a century ago. The sea has washed most evidence of these early settlements away.

We started today's tour going to the seaside docks. These were working docks. You wouldn't find a marina with large pleasure yachts in slips in a harbor. Here you would find fishing boats of all sizes. We saw dozens of small (about twenty-five feet long with high bows and low draft, or low sides for you landlubbers), bright-blue fishing boats packed close together next to large, weathered, deep-sea trawlers. These boats were working boats. The midst of it all, we saw fifty, sixty and seventy-foot boats in dry dock being refurbished for a new life at sea. Some boats had been taken down to their skeletal frames, and others are being re-clad in steel to protect their bows and side rails from nets, ropes, and crashing waves.

We arrived just a few hours after the boats got back from sea, bringing their bounty. This was why the seagulls were filling the skies. The smell of fish permeated the air. Just off the docks there was a circle of tents, composing a sort of food court of restaurants. The restaurants are about twenty feet wide and are separated by canvases where they display the catch of the day. Leanne noticed not a one had their fish displayed on ice. It didn't matter how fresh they claimed it to be. We decided to go someplace else for lunch.

In the 1800s, the king of Morocco developed the town by building a fort off the rocky shore with the city behind it for protection. The city was once known as Mela. The name is derived from the word for salt or for beauty, depending on the legend you believe. This city was once home to a large population of Jewish traders who traded in not only gold, but also in the precious commodity of salt. Although it has since broken down and mostly been abandoned now, we saw the large Jewish quarter that once supported sixty-three synagogues. Today we visited the only one still open and active, built in the 1400s when Jews from Spain immigrated here.

Walking from the port, we went through the city walls into the open-air market. This market was different from the souks we visited in the other cities because it was not covered. Only about 10 percent of the shops were here for tourists. Our first view of the market was while walking through the meat and poultry section. Seeing plucked chickens in boxes and severed goat heads staked on butcher-block tables was … interesting.

On such a beautiful, sunny day, what would we have done in a beach town? Shop, of course! Turning the corner, we were in the chukkas areas. Essaouira is known for its unique wood and inlays. Rows and rows of shops displayed a variety of designs and quality. Shoppers could buy burl (wood from the root of the tree) boxes, tables, chairs, and carved animals. Some were plain; others were inlayed with mother-of-pearl, black walnut, or other exotic woods.

Weighed down with packages, gifts, and a Moroccan wardrobe for Aideyn, we headed back to the hotel in the late afternoon. Tonight we were in for a treat most Americans don't experience: we were going to watch the sunset west over the Atlantic Ocean from the roof deck pool of our hotel. We have been fortunate to see the sunset in the Pacific Ocean, the Indian Ocean in Zanzibar, the Aegean Sea, and now the Atlantic.

This is my last Morocco travelogue. Tomorrow we would travel up the coast to Casablanca, and, barring any extraordinary occurrence that I would need to write about, this is it. We have circled Morocco, traveling three thousand kilometers (over eighteen hundred miles) and walking countless steps in fourteen days. It has been a great and exciting adventure seeing new sights, smelling new aromas, and meeting wonderful people. We left holding a warm spot in our hearts for Morocco. Next stop: Paris!

CREDITS

Head Writer: Stephen Troy
Writer & Editor: Leanne Troy
Travel coordinator: Jan Morris of Peak Travel
Moroccan arrangements: Abercrombie and Kent
Hotel accommodations: Relais & Châteaux
Moroccan guide for the Troys: Rami
Driver for the Troys: Mahjoud
Air transportation: Air France
Ground transportation: Mercedes Benz
Limo transportation to and from airport: Jan Morris
Mr. Troy's Diet Peach Tea Snapple fix: Diet Peach Tea Snapple to go
Communication: Skype
Moroccan sunsets: Allah
We would like to thank the Moroccan, Arab, and Berber people for their graciousness.

Riding a camel in the Sahara Desert Morocco

Camping in the Sahara Desert, Morocco

Sir Richard Branson's hotel Kasbah Tamadot, Morocco

Sunset Cocktails in the Sahara Desert, Morocco

One of the few Roman ruins in Morocco

THE OTHER AMERICA: SOUTH AMERICA
JUNE 2010

NATURAL BEAUTY OF RIO: DAY ONE

Well, we arrived in Rio de Janeiro. We left San Francisco on July 6, and except for our connection having mechanical problems at midnight and the flight almost being canceled and the Nathan's Hot Dog stand next to the Admiral's Club closing right before I got there, the trip was pretty uneventful. After flying all night, we did arrive safely in Brazil around eleven on the seventh. As we flew over the outlying city, there seemed to be a lot of old and poor parts. We also noticed a thick layer of smog hanging over the city. For a city that boasts the use of biofuels for cars, I was surprised. Either they were burning too much sugar cane to make the stuff, or they were still far from seeing the benefits of alternative energy. It looked like LA in the seventies.

Driving in from the city, we were surprised at the level of poverty we passed—mile after mile of shanties and deserted buildings and factories. Brazil is one of the most successful exporters of resources and products in the world; it just doesn't seem to be from this place. This is the eighth-largest world economy and the largest of South America. We mentioned this to our driver and guide and were told that a full 20 percent of the city lives in poverty and that the middle class was just now emerging. The infrastructure was also very old and crumbling. We were told Brazil didn't even have a rail system—

twenty-six states and none were connected by rail. Mass transit might be a better idea than burning sugar cane for fuel for cars, which there were plenty of.

We were staying at the Copacabana Palace on Copacabana Beach, Tom Cruz and Carmen Diaz were staying here while promoting Tom's latest movie, Mission Impossible IV. We just missed them. They checked out yesterday. The hotel was built in 1923 and stands in stark contrast to the rest of the area. This hotel, along with all of the other hotels and apartments, sits across a large, busy boulevard from the beach. Stretching from one end of the long beach, which is sandwiched between two granite outcroppings, to the other are apartments, none of them modern or new. It appears that from 1923 to around 1950, nothing else was on the beach except our hotel—a beautiful, majestic, colonial-style building. Then, in the fifties, row after row of nondescript buildings must have appeared. As far as the eye could see there were 1950s to 1970s plain-Jane boring buildings.

But you don't come to Rio for the buildings. You come for the beaches. Across the street was one of the most fabulous beaches in the world, where the sand beneath our feet felt and looked like powdered sugar. I had never felt anything quite like it. Turning our backs to the water and facing the city, we could see the boring apartments. Turning 180 degrees, looking east to the water, we saw the white sand beach, blue water, and thong bikini backsides of the Brazilian girls lying face down getting a tan. Now that was Rio.

The other thing we noticed about the beaches was that they were devoid of the T-shirt shops and souvenir stands common to other tourist beach towns. The beach here was more a sanctuary than a tourist trap. We saw a few small cafés to sit at, and they were spaced so far apart that they didn't obstruct our view. Even the other side of the street, on the bottom floor of the hotels and apartment buildings, we only saw stylish cafés. Not one retail shop. If you love beaches, these are some of the best. I'm not sure I would recommend traveling eighteen hours to get here, though, bare butts and all.

We quickly discovered that Rio didn't cater to tourists. As we walked into the center of town, we saw it as a working city—no lures for tourists. Very few people even spoke English. The city is old, somewhat dirty from pollution, and in need of repair and modernization. This was not a city with quaint colonial buildings to save and cherish. It looked like they started building quickly in the forties and stopped in the seventies. Outside investment has passed this place by for years. I didn't see the usual imports evident in other big cities. It might be in San Paulo, but it wasn't here. The whole city could be leveled and you wouldn't miss a single bit of architecture.

We had heard that the city was dangerous, so we inquired whether it was safe to walk the streets. We were told it's as safe as any big city you might visit. Most big cities I have visited didn't have large, tubular steel gates enclosing the apartment buildings and shops or guards at every store and police officers on every corner. We were told it was safe to walk—just not with rings, watches, or passports, and with a hand on your wallet at all times. Other than that, Rio was ours to enjoy. If someone had given me that advice in New York I would have been scared to death there as well. Then again, you can walk into most any bank in New York without having to pass your valuables and camera through a window and be buzzed in by a guard.

Later in the day, we traveled to Ipanema Beach, which we did notice was newer and more affluent. It looked like they started building there into the 1970s after they stopped in Copacabana, and then stopped building here in the eighties. We are not talking different cities here. Ipanema was just over the granite rock on the right. There were newer and modern neighborhoods there. As the sun set at six, the streets became charming and tropical. The buildings didn't look so old or dirty. We stopped at a nice seafood restaurant that was recommended to us and had a large lobster dinner for two before we headed back to the hotel. Brazil is expected to become one of the world's largest economies over the next few decades. If they are on that track, they sure are not investing their newfound wealth here. Tomorrow we would be with the guide all day, and we would find out more about why things were like they were here—and act like tourists.

NATURAL BEAUTY OF RIO: DAY TWO

Our second day was devoted to seeing the natural beauty of Rio. The city is built between, under, over, and on top of large granite rocks. Our first stop was to the Tijuca National Park. The park takes up over 7 percent of Rio and is home to the most famous sight in Brazil: Christ the Redeemer. The statue sits high above the city, up a long, winding, and steep granite rock in the heart of the city, separating the northern and southern sections. The climb to the top was through a dense tropical forest. It was interesting to find out that at one time there were plantations on the rock. They were made to move in the late 1800s. The rock was reforested, and between planting and natural growth, it was now dense with trees, plants, and bushes. It was hard to believe something could grow on such a steep, solid surface.

When we reached the top, we were right in front of this imposing statue carved out of cement and covered with small soapstones in a mosaic. As impressive as this statue was, it was even more impressive that they could create it on the top of this very narrow granite rock. From one cliff to the other couldn't be more than one hundred feet; then it seemed like straight down on all sides.

From the top we saw the entire city. Here we saw Rio's natural beauty. Tall, narrow granite rocks rise from the flat land and cascade into the ocean, creating small hump islands that fade out into the Atlantic. One of the most stunning is one they call Sugar Loaf. It looks like a bullet stood straight up. It's not unusual to see people climbing or rappelling off the sides. (For our visit to that we took the tram.) We could also see the many stunning beaches. We discovered, to our surprise, that they were not natural. With the exception of a couple, they were all man-made by a Dutch engineer. The Dutch are good at reclaiming land, and they excelled here.

From Christ the Redeemer we went straight to Sugar Loaf for another view of the city. In 1912 a family built a tram to the top and another across to another peak one-quarter mile away. Both of these peaks were narrower than the one with the statue, and the only way up was by tram or mountain climbing. The tram was fine with us. Why someone would build this in 1912 I am not sure. They have improved the tramcars since then. After sixty years, in 1972 the old cars were replaced. As I mentioned before, nothing in this city changed after the seventies, and these trams were no exception.

At the top of Sugar Loaf was a heliport where for an extra charge one can take a quick ride around the city, something we definitely wanted to do. It was well worth the cost. Zooming down the mountain, we cruised the beaches, the city, and the cliffs back toward Christ the Redeemer. After a quick buzz around the statue, down the cliffs, and up the coast of the Copacabana and Ipanema beaches, we were back on the peak of Sugar Loaf. One thing that really struck us was that as we buzzed the tops of the peaks we didn't see large, beautiful houses taking in the view. We saw shanties and slums filled with lots of rusty, corrugated roofs. The poor who moved there when being on top of a mountain was not desirable control the best view lots. How different it was today. Our ticket allowed us to go across to the second peak, where we could view the forts the Portuguese built to protect the bay. That's when we found out why this is called Rio de Janeiro. It seems the Portuguese thought they were protecting the mouth of a river, so they called the area Rio de Janeiro, "River of January." Turns out it wasn't a river, but a bay. Baia de Janeiro, "Bay of January," doesn't have the same ring to it.

By the time we left Sugar Loaf we were ready for lunch. Our guide took us to a restaurant in the downtown area. We were told it was built in 1898 and had been owned by the same family since. With the condition of everything here, I didn't expect much, but this was a gem! Large, magnificent mirrors lined the walls, and a large oval stained-glass ceiling made us feel as if we had left Brazil and entered a Paris bistro, expecting to see Toulouse-Lautrec. It was a spectacular place that shouldn't be missed.

Traveling the downtown area, I finally did see old colonial architecture. Unfortunately, it was in disrepair and covered in graffiti. It is such a shame—no historical preservation or pride in the past. Some of these buildings could be saved. There was no interest, it seemed, in attracting tourism. Passing through the city we went to the old presidential palace that was turned into a museum, mostly to Brazil's political past. What we found was that their present is much like their past: corruption, corruption, corruption. I could see why things didn't get done here. Anything they spent would be less than the politicians and mobsters would be able to divide amongst themselves. As late as 1964 Brazil was a dictatorship. When the last dictator left, he pretty much handed the keys to the bandits. It's a shame. If Brazil expects to be one of the most important economies in the world, something will have to change politically.

The 2016 Olympic Games and the 2014 FIFA World Cup are both coming to Rio. These two events might just do the trick for Rio. The Olympic committee demands state-of-the-art facilities and infrastructure. Rio has neither. Already they have approved a bullet train to San Paolo. They have six years to pull it all together. A little infrastructure, a restored historic district, and tight butts in tiny bikinis on the beach, and this will be someplace you will want to travel eighteen hours to visit.

NATURAL BEAUTY OF RIO: DAY THREE

I first want to correct an error. I was wrong when I said most of the beaches were man-made. In fact, only three are, including Copacabana Beach, the one right outside our door. The three that are man-made are very long and wide. The other one hundred or so beaches are natural.

Leanne and I were warming up to Rio—not for what it was, but for what it could—and I am sure will, with the coming Olympic Games—be. Today we traveled south out of the city to a more affluent area. We passed through Ipanema along a beautiful picturesque lagoon that had much newer apartment buildings along the shore—not that these are modern by our standards. We were now getting into the eighties and nineties construction, a wonderful setting nevertheless.

Farther south, Rio opened up to a beautiful landscape with still more high-rise apartments. There was a hodgepodge of sixties, seventies, eighties, and nineties buildings. They didn't get rid of window air conditioners here until the nineties, so all the buildings appeared to have pegs all over. One architect managed to incorporate the window machines in the design. This was the area where the Olympics will take place. Like the rest of Rio, it needed some TLC. For the life of me I couldn't figure out why they bid for the games. They didn't seem to be interested in tourism here. It must have had something to do with someone lining their pockets.

Passing through the city, we turned up the coast and headed back to the center of Rio, driving along the white beaches. Even though this was winter and a workday, they were still busy. Each one was more beautiful than the last. Again, nothing has been or could be built on the beach side. All apartments were on the opposite side of the street. The southern beach apartments were of a better and newer quality, but nothing that would knock your socks off. The views, though, would be spectacular if you lived there. We stopped a few times just to stroll along the promenade and people-watch. The weather has been fantastic while we have been here: mid-seventies and very blue skies—perfect for a stroll.

In the later morning, we were taken back north toward the downtown area, where we were shown a few historical sites. One was a Seventeenth-Century baroque-style church—not much to look at from the outside, but typically dark, heavy, and ornate on the inside. Built in 1637, it was one of the most ornate interiors I had ever seen. What was more interesting was the very modern thirty-story office building next door, though not for its architecture: this modern skyscraper is owned by and sits next to the original church. Apparently the church owns the hill and all that sits on it.

From there we went to a much more modern church. This one, built, of course, in the seventies, was made to look like a cross between a cone and a Mayan pyramid—very interesting, with four stained glass panels, one on each side, maybe 120 feet tall. It is near this church we saw some of the finest restored architecture in the city, the opera house and library. Both buildings were in pristine condition and brought us back to the nineteenth century, European colonial style. I am now sorry we didn't stop to take a peek inside. Traveling Rio, we couldn't help but think what this city, with its natural beauty, could become.

It was now time for lunch. We decided on a typical Brazilian barbecue, which are now starting to pop up in the States. The one we went to was supposed to be one of the best in Brazil. Judging by the line of cars, the crowds, and the need for a reservation, I think it's true. The food lived up to the reputation. There, fifteen styles of meat on skewers and sizzling platters descended on us once we turned our table card to green—green for "Feed me," red for "I am exploding! *Please stop* and get help." Suffice it to say we skipped dinner. The restaurant is situated near the harbor with an unobstructed view of the bay and Sugar Loaf, and we couldn't help but stare at that natural wonder that we visited yesterday. When we saw the tall, pointed granite rock shaped like a bullet, it was hard to believe we had been on the top. From the ground it looks like a very small, rounded peak capable of holding a few people if they huddled close, trying not to fall off the edges. The tram platform appears to take up the complete top.

Finishing lunch at three thirty, we were now at the end of our Rio tour. We headed back to the hotel, miles of beach laid out before us, and on to the water to relax, people-watch, and enjoy the unique view that the Rio beaches had to offer—and of course the nice views of the water and rocks.

Leanne was pleasantly surprised that the beaches were filled with "normal-looking" bodies. All were still wearing the thong up the buttocks, but she seemed to be pleased they didn't all resemble the girl from Ipanema! I, on the other hand, only seemed to notice the one girl from Ipanema. Go figure!

BRAZIL: DAY FOUR

We got up this morning for an action-packed day. We were leaving Rio, heading south to visit Iguaçu Falls, which shares a border with Argentina. When we left Rio, we could see the clouds coming in. Rain was coming to Rio. The forecast for Iguaçu this day called for rain and thunderstorms.

As we approached the Iguaçu airport, flying over the Iguaçu River, the sky was still blue. It was one of the most spectacular sights I had seen from an airplane window. The river is a labyrinth of tributaries that seem to have a border about a quarter mile wide, lining the river, which separates the water from the many manicured farmlands set in the center. Picture the blue water twisting and turning wildly with trees lining the shore and multicolored farmland on the other side. Van Gogh couldn't have painted it better.

We landed at noon, and before we knew it, our guide and driver had us up again in our own private helicopter circling the famous falls. As we left the ground, we could experience the vastness of the forest. In every direction we looked we only saw green trees and blue skies. Then out in the distance like a puff of smoke, we saw not a forest fire, but the pounding of one of the largest waterfalls in the world.

As we approached the forest it opened to a massive river a mile wide, with multiple falls all along the plateau crashing below. It was breathtaking. We could feel the power of the falls dwarfing that of our helicopter. We circled the falls from several directions before we headed back across the vastness of the rain forest to land.

Once we were down, our driver drove us into Iguaçu National Park for a closer look at the falls from the Brazil side. They say Argentina has the falls and Brazil has the view—and what a view it was. A one mile trail led us down a canyon. As we descended, we could see the falls on the opposite side. With each step we wanted to stop and take a picture of this natural wonder. As we went lower there were many photo stops to get a great picture. It all culminated when we found ourselves midway down the Brazilian side of the falls, where the upper falls landed on a small plateau and continued down again to another fall to the bottom. There was a walkway at this point where we could walk out to the middle of the falls, ten feet from the edge of the falling water and one hundred feet from the falling water above. We were standing right in the middle of one of nature's greatest forces of power. We were soaked with water spray from top to bottom but it was worth every drop.

When we had had enough of the pounding noise and the drenching, we arrived at a landing where we took an elevator up the side of the falls to the top, so close we could touch the water. The Brazilian side of the falls is the only place visitors can descend by foot to the bottom. The saying is right—Argentina has the falls. The Troy's are now immortalized in one hundred pictures of the falls, or something like that.

At the top, our car was waiting to whisk us off on our next adventure. Before we left the park I had to stop at the Hotel das Cataratas. This hotel was built in 1958 in the colonial style and is located right across from the falls on the Brazilian side. It was one of two hotels we were thinking about staying at. This hotel was just redone and is owned by the Orient Express group. The renovation was terrific. I decided against it for a number of reasons. First being that the renovations might not have been done by the time we got there; second, it was very isolated in the middle of the park, and supposedly the rooms are a very old style and small. It was beautiful hotel, and I was worried whether I had made the right choice—more about our hotel in Argentina later. Our next stop was not on our itinerary. Our guide in Rio had told us not to miss the bird sanctuary. Boy was he right! The sanctuary was a twenty-acre park where we could see and even be among all kinds of tropical birds from around the world. The birds of South America were so colorful I think we took more pictures of the birds then we did of the falls. Everywhere were colorful tropical birds: toucans, parrots, macaws, flamingos, and so many different species I don't have time to mention them all.

We left the bird park at six as the sun was setting and headed to the Argentine border. As we approached, the line of cars was backed up and resembled a traffic jam at the Tijuana border. This was where our private tour connections come in. We followed a private lane and were ushered through two border crossings within minutes. Thank you, A&K—and thank you, Tom Cruise. (Leanne thinks our tour guide looks like Tom Cruise.) I'm guessing other girls must have thought so too by all the "extra help" we seemed to get from them. When we got to the other side we saw why so many cars were waiting to get to Argentina. Right when we crossed the border there was a big, lighted sign: "Casino." It wasn't all about the falls here after all.

After a few minutes we turned down a dirt road and then a paved road to our hotel. When we approached the entrance we knew this would be special. The Loi Suites, where we were staying, were spectacular. We drove up to a lodge entrance that would make the Ahwahanee in Yosemite green with envy. The lobby is large with high-beamed ceilings, exotic woods, and stone walls. A big picture window at one end and a pond in the middle completed the natural feeling of the forest.

We were taken by a golf cart through the grounds, past a large, magnificent pool that was lined in a natural stone, and to our cabin in the forest. It was large and furnished in exotic woods, stone, and rattan. We felt more "out of Africa" than Argentina. To top it off, there was a hot tub under the trees right outside our door.

Not having had lunch we headed straight to the mini bar. There on the table was an Argentine Cantera Malbec (thank you, Jason, for introducing us to this one). We just had to open it. Being cautious and thrifty, we first checked the price: eighty-five pesos, or twenty-one dollars. Damn, we could have bought out the whole mini bar for forty dollars—and that was what we did. I see why people like Argentina. We popped the cork, sat in two rattan chairs, stared out into the dense forest, and thought about how wonderful life was. The Hotel Cataratas was so fifties. Cheers.

DAY FIVE

Today was devoted to exploring the Argentine side of the falls. As we left our room to be driven back to the main lodge for breakfast, Leanne saw a monkey climbing on a tree above our cabin—just one more reminder that we were deep in the jungle. I can't say enough about how nice this hotel was. Now that it was light we could see that there were more traditional-style hotel rooms here. The different buildings were connected by cable bridges going over the walkways and treetops, reminiscent of the walkways in the rainforest of Costa Rica.

Our guide picked us up at eight thirty, getting us to the falls before the crowds descended upon them. We drove deep into the rain forest to the visitor center, where we lined up to board a narrow gauge railroad to travel closer to the falls. Seems we weren't the only ones who wanted to get an early start. The ride lasted about fifteen minutes and passed through the thick jungle of the rain forest.

To get to our first stop we needed to take two trains. The organization of the park was amazing. Leaving the station, we hiked along a mile-long bridge over the river that leads to Devil's Throat. Devil's Throat is a narrow, horseshoe-shaped part of the falls where massive amounts of water fall on three sides, crashing to the bottom in a thunderous roar. We were only a few hundred feet from the edge, watching as the water cascaded over the side in slow motion, picking up speed until it crashed in the pool below. The resulting spray was so large we couldn't see the bottom, an experience we would be up close and personal with a little bit later in the day.

Our next stop was the upper trail. The upper trail winds through the rain forest and then over the river and provides different vistas of the many falls, each with its own volume of water and plant life growing off its cliffs. Some falls flow in a foaming thunder, while some cascade gently, reminiscent of the falls that spill off the cliffs in Hawaii. The moss and foliage around the rocks reminded me of the peaceful opening scenes of *Jurassic Park*, minus the dinosaurs. In truth, this was actually used in a scene from one of the Indiana Jones movies. Each trail leads you closer to the falls. It's hard to explain how walking a trail can feel like a thrill ride. Argentina has its own share of natural beauty.

As we were walking back off the upper trail, the sky opened up with a light sprinkle of rain. Hey, this was the rain forest, so it was okay. We were headed to the rafts downriver to see the falls up close and personal from the river bottom. As we walked we reminded ourselves that the rain was important to keep the leaves green and make the plants grow—and, let's not forget, to fill the river and create these magnificent falls. Unfortunately, the sprinkle turned into rain along with thunder and lightning. Even the birds, insects, and animals knew to take shelter. Not us—we marched on. This became the second day of touring where we wound up drenched.

We arrived at the station, where we were to board a truck that would take us downstream to our rafts. I couldn't help but observe that twenty-five people were all in the back of a metal flatbed truck in the pouring rain, with lightning striking around us. The crew didn't seem concerned even though they were holding long metal microphones.

We started our journey downriver through the rain forest, stopping to be shown different plants and in one case a pack of monkeys that were dumber than we were—out in the rain. We had an opportunity to see one monkey jump from one tree to the other spread-eagled. It was pretty cute.

Arriving at the river's edge we boarded our large, motorized, numbered raft, pulled out, and headed upstream. The raft must have had at least five hundred horsepower pushing it upriver. The granite cliffs on both sides were awe-inspiring. Small falls dotted the way to the main falls. As we approached the main falls, our raft, which was traveling at about thirty miles per hour, slowed to a crawl as the engines at full throttle struggled to break free. We could feel the power of the river trying to push us back downriver and our engines fighting back. Soon our skipper won the battle, and we found ourselves right at the bottom of Devil's Throat—at a good distance, of course. The crew allowed for a short time of picture taking before turning the boat to another section of the falls. The skipper proceeded to position the boat within fifteen feet of the falls. We were up close and personal. At one point I could have reached out and touched the falls. The force of the water might have ripped my hand right off. We were close enough that we all got soaked, something the skipper ensured by turning the boat so each passenger did, no matter which side they sat on.

As we turned back, Leanne noticed that some of the rafts were venturing very close to the bottom of Devil's Throat. At that moment the skipper turned the raft and he too headed straight to the main body of falling water. As we got closer we were sure he was going to stop. But he didn't. The skipper drove the nose of the boat straight into the falls—not once, not twice, but three times. Each time we were engulfed in a plume of water so large it was capable of taking out a small city. For moments we were in a whiteout, wondering whether the captain was smart enough to reverse the engines and save his passengers. Needless to say we were soaked after experiencing one of the greatest thrill rides we have ever been on.

Brazil might have the view, but Argentina has the power and the energy—and the views are not too shabby either. Tomorrow we would be up early to catch a flight to Buenos Aires. Hopefully we would have a chance to dry out there!

COSMOPOLITAN BUENOS AIRES: DAY SIX

Before I tell you about our first day in Buenos Aires, I just have to tell you about my last evening in Iguazu Falls. Arriving back at our room soaking wet, we decided to strip down and partake in that wonderful spa outside our door in the rain forest. Sometimes it's possible to have just a little bit too much luxury in life. Walking out the door butt-naked to join Leanne in the hot tub, I had to cross that magnificent, beautiful, shining, slick, frickin' slippery exotic wood. Then *shit!*, three steps out the door, my feet slipped out from under me on that beautiful frickin' deck, and *bam!*, I was down like a brick, bare-assed on the ground. Leanne was in hysterics. Slapstick is always amusing, I guess. Only thing is, I might have broken my toe. Next was of the comical view of me crawling bare-butt to a safe surface to stand on. Well, you had to be there. Hopefully, I would be okay for our hike in Machu Picchu.

Getting out of the Iguazu Falls area proved to be a lot harder than getting in. When we arrived at the airport another of our planes had mechanical problems and was delayed. After three hours in the airport I decided to play it safe and buy a ticket on another airline. Wouldn't you know it? Both flights left at the same time. We chose to follow our bags on one and waved good-bye to my money on the other.

We flew over what we thought looked like a very muddy ocean only to realize that it was a river running the water from Iguazu Falls. This is one big river—almost 150 miles wide at its widest. Even though we landed six hours late, Leanne, our tour guide, and I were game to head out on a short walking tour of the city. We'd only been here and hour and we both had fallen in love with Buenos Aires. At times we felt like we were strolling Paris, other times New York City. Brazil boasts that between it and Argentina, it is the richer country. That may be true. I don't know where all that wealth went in Brazil, but here they spent it on beautiful parks, streets, infrastructure, and preservation of history. I would rather be the poorer country any day.

Our walk was in the more fashionable part of town. There were magnificent art galleries, shops, and mansions a city block long. The shop windows seemed to be a magnet drawing us in. Polo is a big sport here, so we passed a number of shops selling equestrian gear. Those were the ones I would visit soon. I risked coming back a gaucho.

Many of the buildings are in the French château style—strange when you consider that the Spanish founded this city. It seems the wealthy Argentineans saw France as the center of style and culture, so they imported it here. Many of the hotels, shops, and even streets were named after ones in Paris. There are parks throughout the area, and they are all very well lit. Even the streets are like Paris. Every fourth street is a very large, open boulevard lined with trees, modern apartments, and château-style buildings. This is a lovely city.

We passed many private mansions built in the early part of this and the last century. Each had been meticulously restored or maintained. Most, if not all, no longer belonged to the wealthy families who built them. Many were now private residences of ambassadors, embassies, foreign ministers' houses, or shops. The love and care of these building is in stark contrast to Rio. Leanne and I came back, looked at each other, and said, "I love this place." And had only been here a couple of hours.

I have to mention our hotel. We are staying in the Park Hyatt, one of the five-star hotels in the city. The Hyatt bought one of the block-long mansions built in the previous century and combined it with a brand-new hotel on the other side of the street. The resulting hotel is almost a city block in size with a large courtyard in the center. We'd had a little difficulty with our guide in Iguazu that we informed A&K about. As a result we had a magnificent suite overlooking the courtyard and the old palace, as well as a very nice bottle of Malbec, a popular wine from Argentina. Thank you, A&K!

Our dinner plans were prearranged at a tango club. All I knew about tango was what I'd seen on *Dancing with the Stars*. Argentinians take their tango as seriously as they take their polo. Why shouldn't they? They invented the game.

At eight thirty we set out for dinner. We traveled down boulevards wide enough to land two 747s side by side—very Parisian. Our destination was the Faena Hotel, a Philippe Starck creation. Philippe Starck creates some of the most incredible, over-the-top, and expensive hotels in the world. He is the Picasso of hotels. The Faena Hotel was in new Buenos Aires and was very over the top in design. I love over the top. The hotel had very small cabaret with an incredible tango floor show. The show room was very intimate, very red, and very sensual.

We had a table that Eva Perón would have enjoyed, right up front and center. The show started with the tango as it was performed in the bordellos of Argentina and then moves to the cafés of Paris. The tango then traveled back to Argentina, first to the dock and finally to proper society. This was not your run-of-the-mill *Dancing with the Stars*. It was very sensual. This was Argentinian tango. Len Goodman gave a ten. Leanne Troy gave a ten. Steve Troy gave a ten. That's a thirty for Buenos Aires. It's not to be missed. As we were driving back, Leanne and I both had the same thought: *Let's buy a place in Buenos Aires.* Who would spend the winter in Palm Springs when they could winter in the summer in Buenos Aires? Anybody up to sharing a place here?

Well, it was now midnight. My stomach was full of wonderful wine and excellent food and my head was full of sensual tango—and we had to wake early for our polo lessons tomorrow. So good night!

COSMOPOLITAN BUENOS AIRES: DAY SEVEN

Walking out of the hotel we were met by the crisp, cold air we'd experienced in New York City. Remember, it was winter here. We started our first full day in Buenos Aires walking to, of all places, a cemetery. We didn't get very far when one of the polo stores (not Ralph Lauren, a real polo store) called my name. I couldn't get out of here without buying something. The prices were very good for our American dollar. The goods were also of the finest quality. The finest dinner for two with wine is less than one hundred dollars.

Weighed down now with shopping bags, we proceeded to our first destination. The cemeteries in Buenos Aires featured strictly mausoleums. At first I thought it kind of a strange idea. When I got there, though, I felt like I was strolling down fashionable streets lined with shops. The architecture of the mausoleums ranged from old to new, and from classic to modern. Granite and marble walls and intricate sculpture were everywhere. The crypts went underground for three floors, and many had the resting places of one hundred to two hundred family members. This was also where Eva Perón was buried. Her mausoleum was not as large or elaborate as some of the others. Black granite lined the walls, and brass plaques were affixed to the fronts, listing the names of relatives inside. On Eva's crypt there were also plaques commemorating the play and musical, which I found kind of strange.

After our visit with Buenos Aires's previous residents, we headed south out of the city to the town of Monte. We were there to visit Estancia los Patos and its owner, Ángel de Estrada, a world-famous polo horse trainer. Angel's ancestors founded the town in the 1800s on their modest three-thousand-acre cattle ranch in what was then the southern frontier of Buenos Aires. Over the years the ranch had been divided up and given to various family members. There were still dozens of fathers, mother, brothers, sisters, cousins, and other relatives living on the land. It was one of the top breeding areas of polo ponies in Argentina. Angel was an amazing man, so gracious and smart. Ángel and his polo ponies were the highlight of today's adventure.

The province of Buenos Aires is flat, flat, flat. It makes Kansas look like the Himalayas. When Spanish settlers discovered this place, sailing up the river, they noticed several things. One was the good winds, thus the name Buenos Aires. Our other observation was that there were no trees at all and no rocks. It proved to be great for farming—terrible for building shelters or blocking those strong winds, but excellent for growing crops. To this day the people were protective of their trees, all of which were planted in the past two hundred years.

Our visit to Ángel's house brought us down a dirt road lined with several hundred poplar trees all in perfect rows. Ángel had planted those fifteen years ago for firewood and then didn't have the heart to cut them down. That said a lot about his personality and why he was so good with the horses.

After a very, very warm greeting, Ángel invited us into his beautiful classic adobe home for the noon happy hour. After a lively conversation about horses, we all retreated to the dining room. With the ring of the bell at his side, two household staff members came to serve the lunch. After we finished each course Ángel would ring the bell, and someone would quickly appear to clear the course and serve the next. The food was just delicious and would be welcome in any top restaurant in the city.

After lunch we stepped out to the stables, where we were shown some of the ranch's top polo pony prospects while trading stories about training and riding. I think Angel was very impressed with our knowledge of and love for horses and animals in general. In the corral one of the gauchos was already saddling our horses for a ride through the ranch. (*Gaucho* was originally an insult for the "half-breeds" that roamed the plains. Fencing stopped them, forcing them to find work at ranches. The negative connotation of the word switched when the ranchers got to know these hard-working, friendly, and quiet men.) The Argentine saddles are not western. The traditional gaucho saddles were nine layers of blankets, leather, and ponchos topped with sheepskin. Our saddles were English riding saddles layered with three blankets topped with a thick sheepskin. It was like riding on a couch. It was made all the more comfortable when we ran through the ranch on well-gaited animals that were smooth as a carpet. At one point I carried on a comfortable conversation with our host for several minutes at a full canter. We rode for over an hour, and I think we ran through the ranch half of the time. On the way our host pointed out different points of interest.

One was the nest of the ovenbird. This bird builds a very unusual nest. It's round and made of mud and grass. These birds were the first builders of adobe houses. I say *houses* because they make them with a very narrow door and a narrow hallway that splits the nest into two "condos". One side is for the hatching and early development of the chicks and the other is for the proud momma and papa. There you have it: the first adobe two-bedroom home.

Arriving back at the corral Ángel showed us around his tack room. His gaucho even gave us a short demonstration of the art of intricate rawhide braiding. What a lot of work. While in the tack room Ángel picked out our polo equipment for our first lesson in polo. I was the first to mount. My first shot at a stand was pretty good. The ones after that went downhill. I accidentally hit my horse in the chin with my mallet. Next, it was Leanne's turn. Her first shot wasn't bad, but she got progressively better. I have to say, she outshined me in this one. You know what that means? Steve now had to go out and buy six polo ponies and take lessons. Nothing competitive about us!

After our embarrassing lesson, which was graciously encouraged and complimented by our host, we again went into his home for high tea. We have so many ideas for return trips here we just have to buy a place. We still have some partnerships in a condo available. Any takers? I have some prices. Or maybe some of you would be interested in flying to Ángel's ranch to take polo lessons?

We had a leisurely drive back to the city, and again its beauty enthralled us: wonderful old architecture combined with some stunning high-rise apartment condos and office condos. There wasn't much in the way of rentals here. Politics had hampered real estate ownership for investment.

Tonight we went to one of Argentina's best steak houses. For the two of us the bill came to $130. I know, I know—I told you, you could have a great meal here for two under a hundred! Well, let me explain. Leanne and I had three appetizers and a bottle of wine, she had the rib eye, and I had the filet and one side dish. We followed all that with dessert. After we ordered, I started to notice the steaks coming from the kitchen and got concerned.

I called the waiter and asked for the menu again. Leanne's steak was listed as four hundred grams and mine at a whopping six hundred. Not understanding the metric system, I plugged those numbers in to my iPhone. Do you know how big a six-hundred-gram filet is? Almost one and a half pounds! That's the size of a small roast. Leanne's wasn't much smaller. We could have served four people tonight. So it still holds—you can get a gourmet meal with wine here for under one hundred dollars. It was good, though. We finished it all. Our only saving grace was that if we were with my friend Jason we would have had three bottles of wine, six after-dinner drinks, and a selection of desserts. Oh, well, we all must settle.

COSMOPOLITAN BUENOS AIRES: DAY EIGHT

This was our last day in Buenos Aires, and boy did we pack a lot in. We started heading north, exploring the very fashionable residential district. It was amazing how many wide boulevards, parks, squares, and plazas there were. Some of these streets were laid out two hundred years ago, and they are wide enough to land a good-sized plane— something you don't find in most of Europe.

We twisted and turned through the residential side streets that were lined with large shade trees, making the neighborhoods very intimate. We passed row upon row of stately townhouses in the classical style, each and every one a treasure. On occasion we would find a newer home nestled in between homes built more than one hundred years ago, and sometimes we'd spot a home in need of repair, signaling that the owners might not have weathered the economic downturn like the others. Banks didn't give mortgages here, so everyone paid cash to own a home and cash to restore it. Many families have their whole net worth in these homes.

Something else we noticed was dogs—lots and lots of dogs. There were fourteen million people here in Buenos Aires, and I think each and every one had a dog. That also created a big service industry of dog walkers. As we passed homes and apartments, we saw dog walkers going in and out of houses, collecting dogs and tying them up until they had collected a dozen or more for a long walk. The dog walkers will take groups of dogs for two or three hours in the morning before repeating the job again in the evening. Some enterprising people collect dozens of dogs, loading them in vans and taking them to the park. You will pay twenty-five US dollars a month for this service.

Continuing through the neighborhood, we stopped for a stroll through a very lovely park with a rose garden. This park was meticulously maintained and had the most fascinating collection of busts on pedestals throughout the area. The busts were sculpted in many different artistic styles, making for a very interesting walk. The park was surrounded with several lakes where visitors could find boats to paddle, sharing the water with some beautiful white swans. We passed many plazas that surrounded the city. Going from place to place, we enjoyed the many magnificent pieces of art placed around the city. My favorite artist is Botero, and we found his work prominently placed throughout the city. (If you have been to the Grand Wailea in Hawaii, you have seen his work.)

My eye was drawn to an Italian patio and fountain. Our guide explained that this particular structure came from Seville. It seemed the mayor of Buenos Aires was visiting the mayor of Seville, Spain at the turn of the last century and commented that he loved the patio at his house. He mentioned that Argentina didn't have anything like it. With that the mayor packed up his whole balcony and sent it, bricks and all, to the good people of Buenos Aires. That story made me want to go to Seville.

Continuing on, we went to another park, which was more reminiscent of Central Park in New York. The difference here was the dogs—hundreds of them ... *several* hundreds of them. All the dog walkers either walked or vanned their charges to this park. Small dogs, medium dogs, every kind of dog you can imagine—all were getting along, some running off leash and some (I suppose the more unreliable) tethered to trees. Several of the dog walkers even grouped all the dogs together. There were so many dogs that I didn't know how they kept straight whose dog is whose. It was a very interesting sight.

Next we headed south toward the shopping area and a forty-block promenade lined with shops. It was interesting to see a very old, neglected building taking up three-quarters of a block with the name Harrods etched in the metal frame of the windows. Harrods closed this store thirty-five years ago, and it has been sitting since. I supposed it was because of the political atmosphere at the time. Our guide said she had just read they would be opening the store again soon. New owners bought Harrods in England for several billion dollars, so they must've had expansion plans.

Across the street from Harrods was an old railway station dating back to 1880 that was turned into a fashionable mall. It reminded me of Victoria Station in Sydney, also a transformed railway. Both were stunning in their turn-of-the-century designs. The one here had the oldest fresco in the city on an arched ceiling—just beautiful.

We, of course, weren't able to leave without buying something. Between the prices and the quality of the goods it was hard to leave here without several shopping bags. The service in the shops was some of the best I had experienced—no feeling of pressure. When we looked at something in a showcase, the clerk graciously pulled the tray, laying it on top of the glass for a closer look.

Loading our bags in the car, we went off to the government building area, one of the main tourist spots. We viewed the balcony Evita stood on to speak to the people on the plaza in that classic scene from the movie and play. The whole area was historic with terrific Italian, French, and Spanish architecture. The city was full of these marvelous and cared-for buildings. It was here that our guide told us about some of the political difficulties of the past.

Argentina has a very tumultuous political history. Dictatorships, socialists, corruption, and terrorist groups have made it hard for the country. She said that back in 1974, Buenos Aires was a very dangerous place to live. Terrorist groups roamed the city, and it wasn't uncommon to see people machine-gunned down in the streets. She described it as Chicago in the twenties, only a thousand times worse. Eventually the military took over. The citizens were relieved until they realized they had jumped from the frying pan into the fire. It wasn't until 1983—very recently—that Argentina had free elections and democracy. The fact that these people survived all this and their city was not a crumbling mess was a testament to their strength.

Argentina still wasn't out of the woods. The financial collapse from 1974 to the mid-1980s left the citizens shaken. During that period inflation was 1,000 percent a year. Many lost their life savings in the banking collapse and still didn't trust the banks. The cozy relationship the current president had with Chavez in Venezuela also made everyone very uneasy, and they worried that things could turn again at a moment's notice. Many of the young didn't want to chance their future here and chose to leave. It was also difficult for the young to get ahead. To buy a home or apartment here in Argentina it was most likely necessary to pay cash. The banks that stole money from their citizens wouldn't provide mortgages on real estate. That made it difficult to own a home here. The economy did start to stabilize in the 1980s when the peso was tied to the dollar. Banks had been gradually coming back into the market. The public, however, was still wary.

Let's get back to the good stuff. After taking our *turístico* pictures of Evita's balcony, we went to a great steakhouse on the harbor. This time I looked at the grams. One of the filets was eight hundred grams. That's twenty-eight ounces. A large filet in the United States is eight ounces. I ordered one that didn't have grams. It was 106 pesos, or about twenty-seven dollars. I could swear that this was the same size as last night. They love their beef here, as well as their French fries.

Are you getting tired yet? Well, continuing on. After lunch, we went to old Buenos Aires. A few buildings dated back to the 1600s. The streets were filled with charming antique shops. I have to say, the area wasn't as interesting as the rest of the city. What was a treat was the Boca, an area next to the docks where the immigrants built houses and shops out of corrugated metal sheets. Most of the buildings were multistory and painted in a kaleidoscope of colors. Many of the walls were in blues, reds, and yellows. The immigrants used to bring back single cans of leftover paint they would find to paint their homes. Color wasn't important. The Boca was also the area where the sensual tango developed before it spread to Paris and eventually back to the proper society of Argentina. It was now a colorful tourist spot with street artists, shops, and restaurants. On the second-story balconies many of the owners have placed full-sized caricature figures recreating different scenes of Buenos Aires's past. This was very fun. Think of it as a cross between Montmartre in Paris and Bourbon Street, but just a bit bawdier.

They say Buenos Aires is the Paris of South America. I say it's Paris on steroids with welcoming arms. This was definitely a place we would return to. We are already thinking about stopping here on our way to Patagonia in the south and the Galapagos in the west.

THE MANY RICHES OF PERU: DAY NINE

We were delayed at the airport for six hours for the third time in as many flights. I was thinking, *Boy, do they need Mussolini here!* If the government was going to be corrupt, it might as well have the trains—or in this case the planes—run on time. Our flight didn't leave Buenos Aires until midnight. The flight to Lima, Peru, was five hours. We arrived early in the morning and were able to get only two and a half hours of sleep before we were off to the Peruvian Amazon.

Tragedy did hit me here. I lost my iPhone. Being without it was like coming down from crack. I've never experienced that, but I think this had to have been worse. While I was searching everywhere I even slammed face-first into a wall. I almost had a breakdown. I was now one of three people in South America who didn't have a cell phone.

Let's get back to the trip. We flew over the Andes Mountains arriving at our final destination, Puerto Maldonado, in the middle of the Amazon. The airport there was exactly what one would expect in the middle of a jungle. Joining our guide, we drove through town, heading to the river's edge to take a canoe south to our ecolodge. Passing through the town, I felt like I was in a movie. You know the ones—the Americans or the Englishmen coming to the jungle to meet the natives. It was very rustic, very much the jungle town, very local, and surprisingly clean. It has a colorful, Mexican-village feel without the dirt, broken down cars, T-shirts, and advertising. The vehicle of choice was a motorbike. If one needed more room or a taxi, one was in a three-wheel scooter. In Bangkok I think they call them tuk-tuks. There were very few cars.

Arriving at the river's edge, we were ready to board our motorized canoe for the trip southeast down a tributary of the Amazon to our five-star ecolodge. I didn't think I had ever been anyplace so remote. On the two hundred miles of river, there were only eight lodges. Occasionally we would see a thatched hut that served as the home of one of the local family farmers. There was no telephone, no electricity, no Internet, and no TV. Farming from sunup to sundown was the daily recreation. As we left the little dock we saw rafts like in *Huck Finn* transporting a couple of people and cars from one side of the river to the other. The town was between two rivers with no bridge. A bridge was just now being built. It was unfortunate that that would spell the end of these enterprising Vanderbilt's.

Our canoe, which was around twenty-five feet long and five feet wide, made the thirty-mile journey in forty-five minutes. The trip back upriver against the swift current would take a while longer. As we approached our landing dock, a bell sounded, signaling our arrival to the staff, who, unlike in the movies, had not greeted us at the airport. Jumping off the boat, we carefully followed the wooden stairs to the top and were greeted by the general manager and four staff members.

The resort is five-star, just not what one might think of as five-star. We had electricity only part of the day. There was no heat or air-conditioning (it wouldn't do much good, since there are no solid walls or glass for windows, only screens to keep out the bugs). On the other hand, the main lodge is spectacular, and the cabins in the jungle are comfortable and exotic—pure jungle living. There was a spa where guests could get rubbed down with ingredients from the jungle. The service was amazing, and there were plenty of activities and hikes (more about them later). The only way in or out of here is by canoe—no roads, helipads or landing strips.

After a quick orientation and lunch, we joined our guide for our first eco-walk. A nonprofit group that owned twenty thousand acres of jungle owned the lodge. Tourism was only one part of the nonprofit's work. The money raised went to research and to finding ways to protect the rain forest. The farmers were the ones clearing the land. The process they used was a very inefficient use of the land and caused the most destruction. The nonprofit's researchers were able to come up with alternative practices that would allow farmers to use less land more efficiently, reducing the need for clear-cutting the jungle. It was all very impressive.

Joining our guide, we entered a narrow trail to the deeper part of the jungle. Every few steps he stopped to explain the many plants and roots the natives had used over the centuries. We both joined him in scooping up termites from a tree, crushing them between our hands, and using the scent at a natural insect repellant. He also demonstrated how fire ants and their venomous sting were used for the treatment of arthritis. I will spare you the use of beetle larva.

We didn't see manicured, maintained trails here. These were trails forged by the guests before us. When trees go down or branches pass through, we just went around or over. No one moved, cut, or touched anything in the ecosystem. We were constantly tripping on roots or falling into holes—pretty interesting and demanding.

This was all I could write today. We were heading out for a late-night trek into the jungle with our flashlights to see the nocturnal creatures of the Amazon. This was a true *National Geographic*-esque experience.

THE MANY RICHES OF PERU: DAY TEN

Last night we went on our nature walk through the rain forest to spot some of the native animals that hid in daylight. Unfortunately, it was very cold and overcast, and any mammal, insect, bird, or reptile seemed to have burrowed in out of the cold. The only things moving were a few mammals walking through the woods with flashlights. Oh, that was us. We only found a small frog after an hour. A few birds rustled the trees but didn't make a sound. At one point we turned off our lights to try to attract something with no luck. It was so black I couldn't see Leanne or the guide standing right next to me. The night was especially cold. It was a three-dog night, but there were only two old dogs under the covers sharing a couple of hot water bottles. By midmorning the rains came and the wind howled. Luckily it stopped before we needed to go out for our morning adventure.

This morning we boarded the longboat heading upriver to visit a native family. The resort we were staying at, as I mentioned, was on twenty thousand acres, or thirty-one square miles, and owned much of the land here. The company that owned it was Inkaterra (check out www.inhaterra.com). The family we were visiting was given land to live on and farm so long as they use the methods developed by Inkaterra. After a short introduction we were smeared with a red paint made from a local fruit and oil to signify we were welcomed into the family. By the end of the day I still couldn't get the stuff off.

Our longboat beached on the shore in front of a thirty-foot cliff towering overhead. At times this was the high water of the river. To ascend to the top we followed a set of mud steps that had been carved into the riverbank. We then did the welcoming dance, running in wild circles around papaya trees and banging drums, boys one way the girls the other. It seemed to last forever. Once they tired us out, it was off to our native archery lesson, shooting wooden parrots out of trees. The arrows they used were very primitive— no flint tips like one would find in other parts of the world. To create the arrows they used a narrow sugar cane stalk to which they tie long, sharpened pieces of palm wood, carved into a serrated pattern for optimal damage.

We then joined them for a native game. They had cleverly created toys using nuts that they inserted the strong, thin palm wood through to create tops. Winding string, which they dipped in water, we all launched our tops onto a stretched deer hide that had a slight bowl shape. The object of the game was to be the last top standing. The winner would get to take something from the loser—women included, they said, but somehow I doubted that.

We ended our visit with a very candid Q & A. I asked about religion, education, missionaries, hunting, and construction. Leanne asked about their sex lives—how they make babies and how they prevent them—among other personal topics. I was surprised at how open they were with both. That's my Leanne. They talked about these topics in the present and in the ways of their ancestors. All the topics were very enlightening. We touched upon every topic we could think of before heading back down the mud steps to the canoe and back to the resort.

After lunch we took our canoe and headed back into the jungle to the canopy walk. After climbing the mud of the riverbank we found ourselves in the dense wetlands of the jungle. I didn't think I had ever been in forest so thick and tropical. As we got deeper in, we found a bridge that Inkaterra had built to cross the vast marsh and ended at the canopy walk. Inkaterra built seven towers linked with cable bridges over the rain forest. The towers rise ninety-plus feet from the forest floor, with some bridges 150 feet long and about two feet wide. I have to say, it was one of the scariest things I had ever done. It was nothing compared with what was coming next. We ascended to the last tower, again ninety-plus feet from the ground below, where drinks and snacks waited for us. This was a prelude to what was coming next. Off the last tower, ninety feet above the forest and one hundred feet across a cable bridge that swayed with every step, were our accommodations for the night. This was the only access to our room for the night. We had reserved the only tree house in the rain forest. It sat on top of a tree that broke into a Y shape at around eighty feet and then passed straight through our nine-by-twelve-foot room, complete with a portable toilet. The sides of the building were made of screens, so we were exposed to the world. If we sat down to go to the bathroom, ours would be the only moon shinning over the treetops. We didn't plan to shower since there was no hot water or electricity. This was man-against-wild, with a nice Cabernet thrown in.

THE MANY RICHES OF PERU: DAY ELEVEN

Before we settled into our tree house, we hiked to the river, taking our boat back to the lodge to get some things for the morning and an iPod Touch with movies and an extra battery in case we got bored sitting high in a tree like two lovebirds. After we left the lodge and were heading back to our jungle accommodations, it started to rain. We thought about calling the whole thing off, but were encouraged by our guide to go for it, so we soldiered on. Covered in rain gear, we took our boat downriver into the night and then trekked through the jungle with flashlights to our new room. Climbing the stairs of the ninety-foot tower in the black of darkness, we took turns crossing the two-foot-wide, slippery bridge to our cabin perched in the treetop. Then it really started to pour. This was going to be one interesting night. I remember thinking, *Didn't Indiana Jones fight the bad guys on this bridge high in the sky?* I had a hard time just walking on it.

The room looked smaller than before with our guide and Juan the canopy manager crammed in with us serving us our dinner. Normally if it was not raining we would be eating outside on top of the tower. The rain made for a cozy time. The tree house had two beds that were separated by a very large and thankfully sturdy tree trunk—almost like a two-bedroom condo. The beds were small, so there would be no mile-high fun tonight.

We woke in the morning to our guide signaling that breakfast was ready on the upper floor of the tower. Crossing the walkway one by one, we reached the top of the tower, and there was a table set with a large breakfast, attended by our trusty canopy manager, Juan.

After breakfast we joined our guide to the river's edge, going downriver another thirty minutes to a new section of the Amazon. Our first stop was a native family farm to see firsthand the new sustainable methods they were using to cultivate crops here in the jungle. Surprisingly there was very little edible food here in the wild. We passed through the farm, heading deeper into the primary heart of the jungle. Our guide pointed out the different roots, bark, sap, and plants that the natives had been using for centuries as medicine. We learned how to use the dragon's blood sap from one tree to heal wounds, and roots, which help with ulcers and indigestion. I have to mention that our guide was fabulous. He was born on the banks of this river here in the Amazon and had never been more than three hundred miles from this area; three hundred miles didn't get you far here.

Hiking deeper into the jungle, we could hear the wild birdcalls and photographed the birds and flowers as we walked. The weather still hadn't cleared here, and a light mist was still coming down upon us between the trees, also hitting the lower vegetarian and large palm fronds, which struggled to find sunlight. The good news was that it wasn't humid and there were no pesky bugs. The bad news was that we were cold and wet. It was definitely an adventure.

The end of our trail was at a narrow tributary that fed the main river. Our boat driver towed a small canoe up this passage so we could board with our guide and paddle to float in the quiet solitude of the river and search for and photograph birds as we drifted. The night rains had raised the river by six feet, so the trees and foliage were now to the river's edge, where birds could sit in the trees by the banks. This was very Indiana Jones.

After lunch we went to the eco center to be fitted with rubber boots. We were heading upriver to the other bank to venture into a two-and-a-half-million-acre national reserve. Our one-hour hike was taking us to Lake Sandovale. This hike was the most challenging of all. The park had cleared the trail of vegetation. Between erosion and the latest rains, the trail was a mishmash of mud, craters, branches, and water holes—a very tough and messy hike. Halfway through, our guide heard something in the trees, so we followed him off the trail into the jungle, where we found a clearing with a good view of three macaws. We photographed them until they were chased away by another larger, angrier group, and we ventured on.

Our trail ended at a canal, where there was a canoe waiting for us to paddle through the Amazon into the main lake. The canal was amazing, just wide enough for our canoe to pass along the snaking shoreline. Mangrove-like vegetation grew into the water. Along the way our guide pointed out the many shore birds and a caiman that hid just below the surface of the water with his eyes poking through.

The canal opened into a large, beautiful lake lined with thousands of tall palms hugging the shore. The soil had eroded over many years, so now only the fibrous roots of the palms and vegetation kept the water back. The lake was quiet and tranquil, with only the slight sounds of the birds rustling the trees. Paddling close to the shore, we spotted parrots, macaws, herons, and water bats that we got so close to we could touch them if we'd wished. One seemed to tremble with its eyes open as if we might. When we passed through a field of water lilies and came out the other side, we were in a swarm of a dozen small baby blue-and-white birds skimming the water looking for bugs. The sun was setting, and it was dinnertime in the jungle.

As the sun set we too headed back up the canal for the hour-long hike home. When we exited our canoe, we found ourselves under a troop of squirrel monkeys jumping from tree to tree so fast it was difficult to get a shot. As they moved on, so did we, down this horrible trail that was no better than when we'd come. It did become more interesting, though. Feeding time brought out the macaws and monkeys as we hiked back. I never thought of myself as a bird-watcher before—I am a meat-and-potatoes kind of guy usually—but this was a lot of fun.

By the time we reached the river's edge, night had fallen, and we were now dependent on flashlights. We were headed back to the lodge and the end of our Amazon adventure. This had to be the most interesting and unique five-star experience Leanne and I have ever had.

THE MANY RICHES OF PERU: DAY TWELVE

We left the Amazon the way we found it: *cold*. The weather didn't clear the whole time we were there. It was interesting, though, and adventuresome. We saw parrots, macaws, anteaters, monkeys, a sloth, and various bugs and land mammals. I was sure that when the weather finally cleared many more would come out to find food.

Our motorized canoe traveled back up the river to Puerto Maldonado, where we were departing for Lima. We passed through town, and I had the same thoughts about it the second time as I'd had the first. It was local color at its finest, with motorcycles and tuk-tuks buzzing around colorful, weather-beaten streets with hardly a car in sight.

On the way to the airport we passed a festive open air market. Parked out front in the field were hundreds of multicolored tuk-tuks packed so close together it looked like a Costco parking lot on a Sunday afternoon. This was where all the local farmers and craftsman came by boat along the river to bring their goods to sell.

When we landed in Lima we were surprised that there was no one there to meet us. This leg of the trip we changed tour operators, and there was obviously a mix-up. It turns out I gave them the wrong flight info; it was flight seventy-four, not seventy-six. It was my mistake, but they should have checked when they noticed there was no flight seventy-six on the schedule. A&K would have never made that mistake.

We had come up with a plan B and make our own way. The only problem was where we were going. I never wrote down the hotel info, assuming we were going to be picked up. It was surprising how many people didn't speak English in Lima. I did eventually manage to find the hotel info in my e-mail in a hotel lobby at the airport, using their Wi-Fi, and we caught a taxi.

Our first impression of Lima was that it ain't no Buenos Aires. Not even Rio. Getting to our hotel, the taxi seemed to be making endless U-turns and passing through the most horrible neighborhoods I had ever seen going to a five-star hotel. Leanne and I looked at each other and at the same time said, "Who would want to put a five-star in this place?" We did manage to get to the ocean, where our hotel was—only to be turned back on a number of occasions by the police officers who blocked the streets. Again with the U-turns. The ride to our beachside hotel took almost forty minutes, and for that it was fifty Nuevos Soles, about eighteen US dollars with tip.

We drove up the coast for a ways, and I have to say, it was one of the most unattractive coastlines we had seen: large, eroded cliffs on one side and red clay dirt beaches on the other. Every few blocks there were signs pointing to Waikiki Playa, Makah Playa, and a number of other different Hawaiian beaches. Someone had a sense of humor here for sure.

We did manage to make it to our hotel at about the same time our tour director did. It was somewhat awkward. The hotel was very nice and it did have a commanding view of the ocean. It was nice to have a window that closed and heat. It's the simple things!

At dinner we saw a few of the couples we had met in the Amazon. We found out we were famous for our bravery in the tree house. It seemed everyone was talking about the crazy couple who braved it in the storm. Most said they would have never ventured out that night, and one couple said we sure picked the worst possible time to live in the canopy of the Amazon. We were now Amazonian legends. Maybe they would name the tree house after us.

We were leaving in the morning for the Sacred Valley, so we wouldn't have time to see much of Lima. We would be back in seven days, and we were hoping the rest of Lima wasn't like what we saw on the way from the airport. I would hold judgment until the twenty-fifth.

THE MANY RICHES OF PERU: DAY THIRTEEN

This would be our last week in South America, and most all of it would be spent in Peru visiting Machu Picchu. Our guide met us this morning to take us back to the airport for our trip over the Andes to the town of Cusco, situated on a plateau eleven thousand feet in the Peruvian mountains. This would be our third trip over the Andes in five days. How many people could say that?

On our way to the airport our guide gave us some great information about Lima and Peru in general. Apparently, the coastline was so unattractive here in Lima because the climate was very arid, with no rain—not ever. This was the winter, and the sky is gray. Our guide informed us that it was pretty common for it to be gray and overcast due to the cold Pacific. During the year, there was only a mist, but no rain. With no evaporation there can be no rain.

Peru had just started doing well economically, and only now did they have the money to improve infrastructure and beautify the city. One of the areas they were concentrating on was the coastal community where we were staying.

We could see, as we were leaving, tractors clearing the coastline so they could get ready to build resorts, restaurants, shops, and beaches. The cliffs on the opposite side were being planted to stop erosion and beautify the hillside. It could work for them.

Rising prices and demand for minerals, including gold, silver, and copper, have helped the economic climate here and lowered the poverty rate by 15 percent. It was still over 40 percent. A new, more progressive president, concentrating on macroeconomics, had helped the growth of Peru as well. This was a developing nation on the move. They had a long way to go from what I saw.

As I mentioned, we had traveled over the Andes three times in five days and landed in Cusco three times. On this trip we would finally get to deplane and see the city. This was the gateway of the Incas. Our first stop would be the Sacred Valley. We were traveling from the airport through town on the longest drive I had ever experienced. Our journey takes us to 12,500 feet over the mountains, and then descends to nine thousand feet into the valley below.

The scenery on the way was breathtaking, with rolling hills of farmland dropping off to deep, dark valleys. Just beyond the hills we could see the contrast of the jagged, snowcapped peaks of the rugged Andes Mountains, making the contrasts of the different topography stunning.

You might wonder why on earth anyone would choose to farm up here. Well, we had just left the damp, gray arid desert of Lima, which was sixty degrees; up here at twelve thousand feet, it was green, clear, and seventy-five degrees in the middle of winter. Which place would you settle? Due to an inversion, the high mountain region here had warm, pleasant weather. The access to mountain rivers, which feed the Amazon, and the rich soil, made it ideal for growing crops. I for one was happy to see the sun shining.

One of the interesting facts we learned was that potatoes grew naturally here in the Andes and were discovered and brought back to Europe by the Spanish. They weren't native to any place else. The Peruvians say the higher up the potato is grown, the better the taste. The potato isn't Irish or French (French fries—get it?).

As we drove through the mountains, we could see the many farms and farming plots dotting the cliffs. I wondered how farmers even accessed these areas, which seemed to be on very high hillsides;

it looked almost impossible to stand. Truth was, farmers walked up the hillsides and tilled the land by hand.

After an eighty-minute drive, we finally descended into the narrow and picturesque Sacred Valley. Our first stop was lunch at a farmhouse nestled partway up the hillside at one end of the valley. There were two homes on the property, one from the 1800s and a newer one built in the 1950s. Both were charming. The garden and grounds were just spectacular, and everywhere we turned was a Kodak picture moment.

Lunch was set in one of the salons off a large sort of reception hall, decorated with a fine collection of artifacts from the many civilizations that have occupied the area for hundreds of years.

We were in for a treat. The lunch was of course very good, with the traditional Peruvian food prepared using all local ingredients. For an added treat, we had the honor of hearing from a gentleman named Peter Frost, who had studied the Inca here for forty years and wrote for *National Geographic*. It is not often one has an opportunity to ask questions of and listen to a world-renowned authority on the subject of the Incas. After lunch we were treated to a traditional shaman ceremony to the gods, welcoming us to the area.

After lunch we crossed to the other end of the valley to check into our room. For an area so remote I was surprised at our accommodations. Driving through the gates we saw a wonder of class and culture. This had to be one of the most beautiful mountain resorts I had been to— magnificent stone architecture. The resort was made up of a number of casitas stretching back to the hillside.

Our room is huge with a dark, wooden-beamed ceiling and a stone and stucco wall decorated in rich red desert colors. The architects and designers of this place are world-class. I have to say, I was very pleased. After being in the Amazon, even a window would have pleased us at this point.

Today we started our exploration into the life of the Inca. We drove down the main street in the valley for about forty-five minutes, passing through three separate towns to get to the archeological site.

The road travels straight down the middle of the valley. All the towns we passed looked pretty much the same with their stucco and adobe shops, restaurants, and hotels.

Our guide told us the main street was the ugly part of town—her words, not mine. She said if we went farther back near the hills, there were some very nice communities. In fact this had become a very popular place to retire for the residents of Peru. Land prices have been steadily rising here. Five years ago you could buy land for seventy-five cents a square foot. Today you would have to pay eight dollars for the same land—still a bargain for our part of the world, but a very high jump in price here.

Our car brought us up the mountain to eleven thousand feet, where we were going to hike in the footsteps of the Inca farmers. The Inca have terraced these hills to grow a variety of crops. As we drove up the steep roads, we could see the terraces starting as high as thirteen thousand feet, some descending to the valley floor at nine thousand, while others stopped at ten thousand, where they would end at a cliff with a straight drop down the other one thousand. Between the terraced areas, the Inca had built lookouts as well as farm houses and homes for royalty.

The rows of the terrace are separated by stone walls, each contouring the hillside. We followed these two- or three-foot-wide paths along the side of the hillside and stopped at each lookout or home to get a majestic view of the mountains and the valley below. From one vantage point, we could see the straight river going through the valley for miles. Before the Inca, the river meandered through the valley. The Inca chose to straighten it six hundred years ago to reclaim more farmland on the valley floor.

As we walked along, the path narrowed and widened. Sometimes the path was just a couple of feet wide, with a soaring cliff on one side and a sheer drop of a couple thousand feet on the other. We didn't want to stumble there. When the trail ended, up a few steps was a tunnel the Inca had dug in the side of the cliff, wide enough to allow a crouching body through. Coming out the other side was somewhat scary, as you had to descend a few steps back to the continuation of the trail, which was, again, at the edge of a deadly drop.

The Inca had built a very sophisticated aqueduct system to move water from the glacier lakes above to the different terraces below. Cutting channels in large flat stones, they lined the hillsides for miles, and as high as 14,000 feet, to divert water to the lower parts of the mountain and homes. Some of the aqueducts were still filled with running mountain water even as we passed them. When the water was not needed for the crops it could be diverted to create dramatic manmade waterfalls coming out of the rocky hillsides.

We hiked these hillsides for about two hours, visiting many of the different housing and storage areas. The construction of the homes varied with the importance of the occupants. The royal homes were made of three-foot block stones that had been chiseled into perfect squares using stone tools. The edges of buildings were finished with a perfect curved radius. The laborers' homes were made of loose stone covered in stucco, which has long disappeared. It was an interesting hike but a tough one at eleven thousand feet. It was hard to breathe.

It was now on to the market, which here was split into a market for the locals, selling fruits, vegetables, and meat, and, of course, one that catered to the tourists. We chose to turn right into the local market, where shopkeepers were selling llama meat, fruits, potatoes, beans, and other local crops. There was also beef and chicken, as well as chicken feet, all for sale. One of the more disturbing things for us was the sale of live guinea pigs, a delicacy here. We even found a bakery and barbecue where roasted guinea pig was displayed for sale. Having raised guinea pigs with the girls, it was not our favorite, and we didn't buy one. I understand it tastes like chicken.

Coming back to the resort hotel, we had lunch at the stables. The hotel had a beautiful stable with a large, green lawn where performers gave a wonderful horse show using the Peruvian Paso horses. Folk dancers danced on the ground while riders on horseback followed them.

The Peruvian Paso is a gaited horse that is a cross between an Arab and a gaited Andalusia horse. It makes for a smooth riding. They are a fast and hardy horse that can take the thin air of the Andes. Wonderful animals—we just had to try. The best way to see the countryside has got to be on horseback. We rode along with two other guests who had also decided to go on a two-hour ride through the villages and farms here in the valley.

The horses were brought out one at a time, the first two going to the other guests and then the third to Leanne. All of theirs were older geldings. Mine was brought out stomping and kicking. I got the six-year-old stallion. They had to run him awhile before he calmed down enough for me to mount. I think it was because I was wearing my cowboy hat. The saddles they provided were magnificent authentic Spanish saddles with stirrups so large they looked like giant bells hanging off the side. This was truly a special experience.

We started the ride crossing the street in a very, very fast gaited walk. If you have never ridden a gaited horse, they move very quickly and are very smooth. Riding that fast in a jog or trot for any time on a regular quarter horse would just wear you out. On one of these horses you could do it for miles.

We traveled through the adobe villages and farms along the hillside, following the train tracks that led to Machu Picchu. We were now off the main road, and I still didn't notice those nicer houses the guide was talking about. It was very pretty countryside where occasionally we would come upon an adobe farmhouse. These were definitely the working people, not those retirees from Lima.

Crossing over the road we went to the opposite, glacial side of the valley. We followed the trail back, sharing the trail with cows, dogs, roosters, and bulls. The horses were rock solid. We were also following an aqueduct that was bringing the freshwater from the mountain to the farmers and residents of the town. At times it rushed down the hillside in tremendous volumes. Again, I didn't see any of those retiree homes on this side of the tracks either. As we were coming back to the stable, our horses picked up their speed and gait. I was sitting tall in my Spanish saddle. I couldn't help but feel like a Spanish duke returning from town.

This evening ended with a cooking demonstration by a French-trained Peruvian chef. All of the dishes were typical of the cuisine of Peru, and each was presented with style. Everyone totally enjoyed the meal and demonstration. The owner of the hotel was also on hand to give her insight about the area and the building of her hotel. We came to find out that she was the wonderful decorator here, and her husband was the architect and builder. Then it was time to pack; we were leaving for Machu Picchu by train very early in the morning.

I can't finish my writings about the Sacred Valley without saying more about this hotel. We were at the Sol y Luna Resort. A French woman who has been planning the hotel for fourteen years owned it. The hotel had only opened a year ago, and as I mentioned, the rooms, or should I say casitas, were big—850-square-feet big. That's double a standard hotel room. The rooms were decorated with lots of Peruvian art and deep, rich, colorful fabrics. They didn't skimp on modern amenities either. The casitas were arranged through a beautiful flowering garden. When we'd walk around, every guest would be talking about how wonderful this place was. It was a little slice of heaven in the Sacred Valley. We knew Liz would have enjoyed this piece of paradise.

THE MANY RICHES OF PERU: DAY FIFTEEN

There were three ways to get to Machu Picchu. We could take the twenty-eight-mile Inca trail, which takes four days. We could take the train part of the way and hike the last seven miles, which takes around five hours, going up the mountain, down the mountain, up the mountain, and then down the mountain, finally arriving at Machu Picchu through the Gate of the Sun. *Or* we could take the train all of the way to the base of the mountain and then take the bus up two thousand feet to the top. Since I never heard that Liz Taylor had hiked the Inca trail, we stayed on the train.

There are several trains going to Machu Picchu, one being the luxurious Orient Express, with salons and dining service. The others are basic standard-service trains with windows in the roof so you can see the towering canyons we would be passing. I was a little disappointed that we were not booked on the top-of-the line train. My philosophy is this: "You are going already, so you might as well go all the way. Damn the torpedoes—full speed ahead." Liz would have taken the Orient.

Don't get me wrong; the train we were on was very comfortable and very smooth. Not being distracted by the opulence onboard, we might have paid more attention to the scenery outside. The two-hour-or-so trip wound through the mountain canyon following the river. This particular river was the second-longest tributary of the Amazon. Jacques Cousteau himself once came here to map it. The ride took us past some of the ruins, bridges, and lookouts from the time of the Inca. It's important to mention here that when people talk about the Inca, it's a general term. The true Inca only ruled this area and developed an empire around the Thirteenth Century. Other tribes, I believe, called the Andes Indians inhabited this area for centuries before. The Inca ruled for less than one hundred years before they abandoned the city, and no one knows why, exactly.

The river we were following was the one that overflowed last February, eroding the banks and collapsing the train tracks we were traveling. I think Peruvians did a quickie repair of the damage, because we seemed to slow many times going over the new sections. It's hard to imagine the amount of water that must have come down the river. The level was now more normal. With the many large rocks in the path of the flowing water, we saw and experienced white water and rocky falls for miles at a time. Many of the sections where the river narrows created picture moments not to be missed. The train makes two stops, one to let the group of crazy hikers off for their five-hour trek to hell and gone, and the last for us Liz Taylor devotees.

We were staying at the bottom of the mountain at the Inkaterra hotel here in Machu Picchu. Machu Picchu is set in the beginning edge of the Peruvian Amazon jungle, and Inkaterra was king of the jungle. Our hotel was situated at a ten-minute walk from the train station—an odd location, since it was right next to the tracks. The tracks at one point went straight through the resorts for a very short way. Walking up to the hotel, though, was memorable. We first crossed a bridge (Inkaterra was fond of bridges) and then walked up steps that led to the lobby.

Walking up the steps, with ancient stone walls covered with ferns and moss growing from the crevasses, coupled with the overhead canopy of jungle foliage and the constant flow of water rushing down an aqueduct on the sides along the steps, we felt like we were in an Indiana Jones movie. The gardens leading to the rooms were also lush and tropical. The rooms, on the other hand, didn't live up to the quality the landscape portrays. We were here, nevertheless, for the ruins, not the hotel. Unfortunately, Leanne had gotten a touch of food poisoning, and since she was laid up today, she couldn't make the first visit to the archeological site. I, then, had to venture out alone with our guide. The road up the mountain was amazing as it zigzagged along the rugged cliffs. When I reached the ruins I was in awe. I have seen many pictures of Machu Picchu, and none did justice to what I saw before me with my own eyes. The two hundred or so pictures I took couldn't describe it.

It wasn't so much the construction of the buildings that caught my imagination; the Romans and Egyptians had greater craftsmanship three thousand years earlier. It was the setting of the city. This sprawling village of temples, homes, and terrace farms is perched nine thousand feet high on rocky cliffs with majestic views of the young Andes Mountains that surround it. Even on the surrounding sheer cliffs, which are covered in green foliage, the Inca managed to cut trails to the tops, building lookouts, terraces, or astrological sites. The terraces here made the ones we had seen a couple of days earlier look amateurish. These terraces seem to hang from the cliffs. The stone structures lining the green grass of the ground make this place majestic.

I had heard Liz walked the last part of the Inca Trail, so I just had to do it. The Inca Trail starts in Cusco and ends at the city gate in the middle of Machu Picchu. My guide and I ventured forth to conquer the last part of the famous Inca Trail, going in reverse to greet the crazies who had started out four hours earlier. The last two miles of the trail is the most spectacular, since that's the section that descends into the city. We set our sights for the Gate of the Sun, which rises two thousand feet above the city on a ridge top, two miles straight up.

The trail was challenging with its high stone steps and uneven surface. With every step we got a magnificent view of the terraces cascading down the steep cliffs and the buildings that seemed to rise from the granite rock looking as if they were one. The builders followed the uneven cliffs, using some of the huge granite stone that lay in their path as a foundation when necessary.

When we reached the mountaintop and the entrance of the Gate of the Sun, we got a spectacular view of the city below. This is the gate the Inca would have passed to approach the city walls below. Machu Picchu was a special place for the Inca. Our fellow travelers, a little tired from their journey, appeared one by one through the gate while my guide and I welcomed them to Machu Picchu.

Usually I would get to the top of these hikes, turn around, and go back. Just as I turned, the sun was setting low, and we just had to stay. I sat down on a step with my guide for a half hour and just watched as the sunlight moved across the city below.

As the sun started to approach the ridge tops, we realized the park was closing and started our descent down the two-mile trail we had just climbed, stopping every one hundred feet or so to take another picture of the rugged mountains as the light shifted along the deep canyons. It was an amazing place. Making it more amazing was that the Inca built this city in a mere eighty years. It must have taken thousands of people and thousands of man-hours to create this place in such a short time with crude tools.

When we got back down, we entered the city exactly the same way the Inca would have entered five hundred years earlier. With a little time left, we continued our exploration of the many terraces and buildings around the area. The buildings the Inca constructed were still intact, minus their wood and thatched roofs. Wood pegs hammered into the blocks, which held down the wood support beams, were still visible on many of the houses. Several houses had been restored, so visitors could get an idea of how the city would have looked during the time of the Inca.

I had walked the Roman ruins, Turkish cities, and Egyptian palaces, and this was every bit as amazing, given its location high in the Andes—well worth the trip, and a surprise I wasn't expecting. In total figure, I hiked around six miles up and down the cliffs and terraces at nine thousand feet, all without a drop of water—not because I was tough, but because Leanne wasn't there to remind me to bring it. Boy, was I thirsty when I returned! I hoped Leanne would be up and going to enjoy our second visit to the city.

THE MANY RICHES OF PERU: DAY SIXTEEN

I visited Machu Picchu for the second time, and thankfully, Leanne was feeling well enough to go with me. When we went through the gates I felt as excited as the day before. I wasn't sure whether it was simply because I was there or because Leanne still wasn't 100 percent and I didn't have to make the four-mile hike to the Gate of the Sun. I think it was the former. The place was just majestic—the soaring cliffs with lush tropical trees falling sharply to the valley floor and the terraced cliffs manicured into the rock! I didn't know which was more inspiring. Today we followed our guide into the urban section of Machu Picchu. This was where the families lived, gathered, and worshipped at their temples. It was also where the workshops were that turned out megatons of blocks that were moved around the different peaks.

The urban area was made up of finer-cut stone blocks, cut to such a perfect tolerance that one couldn't even seep water through the seams. An earthquake, splitting the blocks just enough that one could look between them, had moved one of the walls. In these cracks we could see that the blocks were not only carved to a perfect fit, but they were also carved on the inside so as to interlock and not move out of place laterally. This was a lot of work and no one is sure why the Inca even built it.

A Swiss engineer visiting the site said what we saw here was only 30 percent of Machu Picchu. The other 70 percent was underground: the work that had gone into the clearing of the terraces, the backfilling of the land, and the drainage system and foundation support to make all above stand for the rest of time.

Looking around all the area, I was amazed by just how many large stones had been used to build the walls, foundations, and buildings. I mentioned the trail I walked but not the stone walls that supported the walkway below me, the walkway itself, or the wall holding back the cliff next to me. This went for miles and miles and miles. Isn't there a song like that?

Most of what we know of this area is guesswork and theory. When the Inca abandoned this place they took everything of importance and set fire to the rest. The Spaniards also contributed to the loss of Inca history by burning the ciphers that could have decoded some of the remaining mathematical and engineering material that has been found in burial chambers. The writings of the Spanish who came to the area also contradict themselves in the stories they tell.

It is incredible that the Inca could move so many enormous stones and place them precariously off a cliff to create a terrace. It has been determined that the Inca had rollers used to move large stones, but that doesn't explain how they moved them to the different levels and across canyons. Surprisingly, the Inca didn't have or ever invent the wheel. With such rugged terrain, they just hadn't seen a need. They must have known about pulleys and levers. To get off the sides of the cliff, they also must have used scaffolding. Just what kind of scaffolding could support the placing of a three-ton stone, I am not sure.

Leanne was a sport. After all, only twenty-four hours before she was praying to her own porcelain gods. Moving up and down, even the urban area could wear you out. We started at nine thirty in the morning, and by one Leanne was winding down, so we headed to lunch. I, on the other hand, was still ready to explore. Leanne stayed back at the Orient Hotel, which was situated at the entry gate of the site, and I went with the guide for one last hike. This time it was the Inca Trail to the bridge. This trail is about one and a quarter miles one way, and it seemed the first half is up, up, up. When we finally got to level ground, it was a two- or three-foot-wide walkway built with stone off the side of a sheer cliff. The cliff side soars a thousand feet straight up, and the down side is two thousand feet straight down. As we wound along the side of the cliff, we could see how the Inca started on ledges twenty to one hundred feet lower and built the sides up with rocks, creating a level path. What held the rock to the side of the cliff, I wasn't sure.

I have to say—and I think I wrote this before—I don't like heights. Chelsea can attest to that if she remembers when we floated over Prague harnessed to a rubber balloon. It isn't so much the height that bothered me as the lack of railings to hold onto. Someone did, in his or her wisdom, attach a rope off the upper hillside to hold onto, and I did. I seemed to be the only one. It was a little embarrassing.

The bridge trail ended at the bridge. We are not talking the Golden Gate here. The bridge ended where the Inca ended it and then continued twenty or thirty feet on, creating a sort of break in the road. The builders then could lay logs across the gap that they could remove at any time. I think the Peruvian government was wise in not letting people cross it. It was straight, straight down a long, long way.

I took another hundred pictures today, and I don't think I got one that can describe this place. It is said that a picture's worth a thousand words. Whoever said that was never in Machu Picchu. After almost twenty miles of hiking this past week, we were now headed for a nice long massage.

THE MANY RICHES OF PERU: DAY SEVENTEEN

We left the natural beauty of Machu Picchu and drove over the Andes heading for the town of Cusco. Cusco was the capital city of the Inca and was at one time rich with gold and silver. It was the Spanish conquistadors that raped the city of all its treasures. In the early 1500s, 168 Spaniards landed in Peru and, thanks to conflict between warring tribes, managed to capture the Inca emperor. The Spaniards demanded a king's ransom of gold and silver for his release.

With some Inca soldiers' help, the Spaniards helped themselves to 5,200 pounds of gold and twice as much in silver. The conquistadors didn't keep to their part of the deal, eventually killing the Inca emperor. That's a short version of a long story of the demise of the Inca.

Much of the gold and palaces were in the town of Cusco, where the conquistadors came to strip the golden walls of the Inca palaces and temples, melting the treasures down into ingots to ship back to Spain.

After securing Cusco for Spain, the Spaniards built many churches on top of the walls of the palaces of the Inca nobility and also on their temple. Today visitors can walk through the city and see the huge blocks used to build these massive palaces, which dwarf the buildings that were built on the hilltop of Machu Picchu.

After lunch, we visited the main plaza of Cusco, which is flanked by two ornate Spanish churches. Around the plaza, we could see the Inca walls that were used to support the Spanish architecture that was built on top of and all around what were once the Inca palaces. I think there were five churches in this small area, all built to convert the Indians to the world of Jesus Christ.

Our first stop was a visit to a church built by the Inca with adobe and stucco and painted inside to look like marble. The altar and chapels were of baroque style, made of cedar covered in twenty-two-karat gold, something they had much of. There were two items we found of particular interest. One was the life-sized figure of a black Jesus on a cross. We had seen the black Madonna, but we had never seen or heard of a black Jesus. We came to find out that he didn't start out black; he was originally white. Four hundred years of candle smoke turned him completely black. During restoration six years ago, there was a plan to clean him up to his original condition. A strike by the people demanding that they leave the black Jesus alone changed the minds of the restorers, so there he hung.

The second item stopped us in our tracks. The Spanish brought art and painting to the Inca as a means of converting them to Catholicism. The painting they taught the Indians had its own style to Cusco, much of it copied from famous Renaissance works they had heard about. One of the paintings they heard about and chose to copy was Leonardo da Vinci's *The Last Supper.* They had heard that the Last Supper was something special. Weren't we surprised when we came around the corner to view the painting, and there was Jesus, sitting with his disciples around a tray of roasted guinea pig! You read it right. The table is set with the Peruvian delicacy of roasted guinea pig in their copy of Leonardo's *The Last Supper.* We pretty much lost it. Leanne almost peed in her pants, and if I wasn't struck down by lightning at that moment, then—let's just say we almost had to leave the church. The Inca, forced to believe a new religion, interpreted what they were told to fit into what they actually still believed. They made all the statues and paintings of the Madonna in the form of a mountain with her dress forming into a sort of triangle. To the Christians it was the Madonna, but secretly to the Inca, it was Pachimama, the spirit of the earth, whom they worshiped.

Our next stop in the church was down some stairs to a tomb where the ashes of a royal Inca lay at rest. We had lost all sense of time by that point, and as our guide was translating the plaque on the wall and explaining who begat whom, the lights went out. Maybe I *was* being struck by lightning. Three people never screamed so loud. The tomb was pitch-black. As we turned, we could no longer see the stairs we had come down. Thank goodness someone heard our cries and turned the lights back on. Never have three people left a church so fast.

Leaving the church, we took an evening stroll down the narrow streets of Cusco, passing the softly illuminated massive stone walls built by the Inca elite five hundred years ago. This city must have been some sight when the Spaniards came upon it: large stone palaces encircling the large central plaza, some with walls covered in gold.

Our walk took us through the bohemian section of Cusco as we headed back to our hotel. The town was very charming and very much a surprise. We were staying at the Hotel Monasterio, another Orient Express hotel. The hotel was an old seminary some four hundred years ago, so it had a great historic charm. It had been very well restored and converted. I loved the piped sounds of the chanting monks as we walked the lobby and the magnificent courtyard. There were wonderful old paintings in ornate frames all throughout the hotel and even in the rooms. I felt I was transported to another time.

Right next door were shops and restaurants in a building of the same age that once housed the nuns. My understanding is there is a tunnel connecting the two buildings. You can draw your own conclusion. I have caused too much trouble as it is.

THE MANY RICHES OF PERU: DAY EIGHTEEN

Cusco is a charming city. It was the center of the Inca Empire, and its most important city. The word *cusco* means *navel* or "center of the universe." Cusco today has a Florence feel to it: very clean with very narrow stone streets and even narrower sidewalks. There are several plazas around the city, all with a nice park in the center.

The first part of the day we spent high on a hill overlooking the city, where the Inca had one of their astronomical sites. We arrived in a large, park-like setting, which the Inca probably used for festivals, gatherings, and play areas for children. The area had a large, rocky hill on one side that the Inca used for some type of monitoring of the sun, and on the other side, they built one of their famous walls. The walls were not the straight blocks they used in Machu Picchu, but rather a free form of massive blocks all fitted together as perfectly as any puzzle one would put together.

The length of the wall was built in a zigzag pattern going in and out of the hill, and the walls rose from the level ground and staggered back to what must have been a sacred site of the Inca. The free form of the blocks really was amazing when we saw how tightly they fit together. Some of these blocks weigh 150 tons with one stacked on the other so a piece of paper couldn't be slipped between them.

This is the site where the Inca started their revolution against the Spanish invaders. Unfortunately, they started it three years too late, and most of the Inca blood was spilled on the gathering lawn below. The Inca retreated to the mountains, but with the influx of the foreigners, it was too late for their society.

Our next stop was a silver jewelry factory. For some reason guides love to take tourists to these places. Of course, this one was wholesale—you know, the ones that cut out the middleman so they can charge twice the price of retail while offering a 10 percent discount for cash. Unfortunately, we fell for it and walked out with a few boxes to bring home—so much for reason and willpower.

Our last tour in Cusco was of the one and only Inca temple in the city. Today the foundation and some of the walls support a Dominican church. It was interesting to see the perfect professional work of the Inca walls contrasted with the stonework and mortar joints of the Spaniards. The Spaniards couldn't even make a straight line. Outside the church was the Lawn of Gold. Today there was nothing there except grass, a small fountain, and some scattered stones. During the Inca days it was filled with re-creations of animals, flowers, and plants found around the area, all made of solid gold and silver. This was where Inca emperor sent the Spaniards to pick up their ransom. These treasures all disappeared, melted down and shipped back to Spain.

I for one couldn't help but be a bit angry to see what these murdering thugs did to the Inca. What it comes down to is that the 168 Spaniards who came here were no better than common thieves and kidnappers. They weren't here for food, water, more land for expansion, colonization, or friendship—none of that. They wanted gold, and they were willing to kill and steal for it. It was only after they kidnapped, murdered, and stole that they sent for and received a royal decree, making their plunder legal. History is filled with these injustices.

For the last night here in Cusco, we had a farewell dinner with all of the people we met on this wonderful trip. They took us to a wonderful private home up on the hill by the Inca fortress. When we arrived, we were presented with colorful Peruvian clothes to put on for cocktails and dancing out on the patio, which had a commanding view of the lighted city below. As the music played and we danced a Peruvian version of "Hava Nagila" (seems like every country has one), fireworks started to explode in the sky. What a wonderful way to end the trip! This was something Leanne and I never experience, because we normally travel alone. There are benefits to traveling alone, and there are some traveling with a group. The group benefit is you get to meet some very, very nice people, and we did. One more day in Lima and we were heading home.

THE MANY RICHES OF PERU: DAY NINETEEN

On our last day in South America, we thought we would give Lima a second chance. When we landed in Lima, it was as gray as the day we left. We came to find out that it was not only the foggy weather creating the gray sky, but also pollution. I asked if they had blue skies in the summer, and the answer was yes. It was followed with the comment that the blue sky came with 80 to 100 percent humidity. Oh, yum!

Our first stop was to a very nice restaurant in the middle of a second-century pre-Inca temple. It was very interesting and very much a contrast to the Inca stonework. Here the builders used small adobe bricks, which they stood upright and spaced ever so slightly with the idea of absorbing the damage from an earthquake. The temple construction was very primitive. The temple took up over an acre and stood about twenty-five feet to the top. Today the stucco looked worn off on the side. This step-style temple with its tens of thousands of bricks slightly spaced looked more like an abstract view of the New York skyline than a temple.

After lunch we took a city tour to find the real Lima. It was hard to find. The gray sky made the city very depressing. Our first stop brought us to the old historic section of the city. The whole city was a mishmash of construction. Some old buildings that once featured marvelous neocolonial architecture with beautiful wooden balconies were in disrepair and mixed in with mid-twentieth-century worn-out junk.

Lima's location on an earthquake fault has worked against it. The frequent earthquakes here have taken down many of the old historic buildings. I imagine that it was difficult financially for owners to rebuild the older ornate structures. The owners who could afford to rebuild grand structures did so in the style of the day. So there were Sixteenth, Seventeenth, Eighteenth, Nineteenth, and Twentieth Century structures all somewhat decaying together. The Twentieth Century structures were in such a basic and boring style that they deserved the wrecking ball.

Many of the older historic buildings still standing were in need of restoration or had had minimal restoration work. There were a few that had been lovingly redone, but they were few and far between. The nicest area we found was a beautiful central plaza where a festival was in progress as we walked through. Some very nice Spanish architecture lined the streets, where horses and carriages gave rides around the plaza to tourists. Again, the gray sky again didn't make it very inviting.

One of our most interesting stops was to the Church of Saint Francis of Assisi right outside this central plaza. It was in a Moorish style and wasn't as gold-laden as the churches we had visited in Cusco. The fascinating part was the catacombs below. We descended a narrow staircase into the basement. There we found large, rectangular plots filled with bones of the dead. One estimate has it that twenty thousand bodies were buried here during the two hundred years it was used.

The method of burial was to stack bodies one on top of the other, covering them with lime so they would decompose quickly. Once they decomposed, more bodies would be stacked in the grave on top of the existing bones. Room after room was filled with stacks of bones in uncovered graves that were fifteen feet deep. Most of the bones were femurs. The femur, having the most calcium, survived total decomposition. There were also plots where skulls and other scattered hip bones and ribs had survived. Many of the bones had been arranged to make it more interesting for the gawking tourists that visited. There were thousands of bones stuffed all over the place. It looked like a scene from *Pirates of the Caribbean*.

Leaving the old section, we drove to the nicer sections of Lima. We weren't impressed. It wasn't until we left at night that the city looked its best. The colorful lights of the many restaurants and shops and the floodlights shining upon the fountains, churches, and artwork made the gray city come alive. Then there were the neon lights lighting the sky from the many casinos around town, with names like New York, New York; Hello Hollywood; and Atlantic City. Still, from what we saw—and I know we didn't see everything—this wasn't a place we would care to come back to. It was no Buenos Aires. There we want to go back.

This was my last travel log for this trip. I hope you enjoyed traveling along with us. For some of you who have been to the places I wrote about, I hope it brought back memories. For those of you looking to travel here, maybe it can help with your planning.

Adios.

Rope Bridge the Amazon, Peru

Eva Peron famous balcony, Buenos Aires, Argentina

Iguazu Falls

Machu Picchu, Peru

Leaving our Tree House, The Amazon, Peru

View of the beaches of Rio, Brazil

Bird Sanctuary, Iguazu Falls, Brazil

The Plaza de Armas, Cusco, Peru

MIDDLE EAST: THE NEW AND ANCIENT

2010

DAY ONE

After twenty-two hours of flying, we landed in Dubai at midnight Sunday. Walking out of the plane reminded us we were in the Middle East in July: ninety degrees! We hurried to the terminal where we were greeted by a VIP staff of three who whisked us through immigration. I had paid for the extra service. What I didn't know was it included a city tour before we went to the hotel. After an hour, we made it to the Royal Mirage Place at one thirty. The tour would have been perfect if we had landed at noon.

Monday, we still got an early start. At ten we were picked up for a historical and city tour. One of the things we noticed was the air quality. We couldn't see a blue sky. The buildings in the distance were also hard to see. We were told this was normal eight months out of the year; the high humidity mixed with sand, construction dust, and sea salt makes for murky sky. December, January, February, and March are the good months. It was cooler today, around ninety degrees. Don't expect it to be bearable. The humidity rises to 60 percent.

Our guide proceeded to tell us that the freshwater in Dubai comes from a desalinization plant. We asked were the salt went and was told it was put back into the ocean. She said it's eventually going to be an ecological disaster. The ocean salt level has been rising. Going down the highway, we saw construction everywhere—building after building going up. The buildings that had been finished didn't appear to be occupied. I asked about that and was told that most of the condos had been sold to speculators. The office buildings were just sitting, waiting for tenants. I have to say, some of the skyscrapers were incredible. I was not sure about the quality. The hotels and buildings we went into or were near didn't appear to be of the highest caliber workmanship.

Some of the buildings would have been impressive and magnificent in New York or Chicago. Here, they look like they were sitting waiting for someone to buy them and move them to a real town. Other buildings were tall and narrow and placed side by side down the street; all were for rent. In the evening the many dark windows were noticeable. I think the sheik saw the Kevin Costner picture *Field of Dreams*: "If you build it they will come." Time would tell.

Dubai is famous for their extravagant buildings that touch the sky and the development of private islands for luxury housing. There are two island communities that have been created from reclaimed sand, Palm Island and The World. The World has sold 60 percent of the lots on the islands. I mention islands since there will be many in the World development. Together the islands will make up a map of, you guessed it, the world. Not one had a structure even started. To be fair, there was still much to be done in Dubai before it could truly become the destination Emirati dreamt of having. They are planning to build a new convention center, airport, and stadiums, as well as Dubai Land (like Disney World, Universal Studios, and Six Flags all rolled into one).

One thing we learned today was that only 20 percent of the citizens were native; the rest were workers from other countries. These workers could not become citizens unless they were born in an Arab country. Eighty percent had very little rights. Most of them are very poorly paid; five hundred to eight hundred dollars a month was a good salary, and their compensation usually included room and food. The conditions were questionable. The local citizens got paid much more, plus benefits, such as public schools, health care, housing, and much more. They got the best jobs even if they have less experience or education. The other 80 percent had to send their children to expensive public schools and rent their own housing, which seemed to double in price on a whim.

We went to the old city and toured the cultural center. Although people have been in Dubai since 3000 BC they didn't leave much in the way of culture—maybe because it was so blooming hot and sandy. The guide said it was because there were so few of them. I think the smart ones migrated to Italy. The earliest settlement known as Dubai town was in 1799. It went until the 1970s when the sheik figured he needed something other than sand. He used his new oil money to create tourism and imports and exports. I was still trying to figure out what they export here. They had very little oil and no trees or other natural resources. Any labor they had was being used to build mega resorts and office buildings. I got the import part. It seemed like it was everything.

Since Dubai was on a river, we took a water taxi to the gold market. Way too funny! We sat on a bench on a deck with no railings. Our water taxi backed out of the slip and didn't even look behind him. Bam! Right into another boat. It wasn't a problem. They were all hitting each other and pushing each other out of the way. The thick wood hulls of all the boats were gouged and splintered. That was the way it was done, and it seemed to work. In Italy they would be arguing for an hour.

Midday we stopped for lunch at that famous seven-star hotel. We were surprised and disappointed. Our driver said many people stay one day there at two thousand dollars a night and then move someplace else. This was a touristy, gimmicky hotel. Our lunch there holds the record for our most expensive lunch of all time: $425. We didn't have drinks or dessert. Before lunch we wanted to go to the sky bar and see the palm islands. Unfortunately we couldn't get in with sandals. But if you remember what I said about the air quality, it was a blessing. A glass of wine was forty dollars, and the air was so dark that the palm trees on the street were barely visible. I couldn't think of who would go there twice. We did walk around the place. We agreed that it wasn't very classy. It was also a small hotel. The lobby was smallish and not impressive. I think they need to hire Steve Wynn to class the place up.

We finished our $425 lunch in time to go back, change, and get picked up for our dinner adventure. We were driven into the desert to a one-hundred-thousand-acre desert reserve for dune jeep driving and a camel farm visit. The drive ended with watching the sun set into itself. What I mean by this is before the sun actually set, it disappeared behind the crappy air. All in all, it was not very impressive. When darkness did come, we went to a tent village for a barbecue and entertainment. Starting with a camel ride and pictures, the night moved to dinner and belly dancing. Think your first luau—fun, but you wouldn't do it again.

Please don't get the impression we were sorry we came. This was a very strange place, and it seemed it was going to get stranger. Tomorrow we would snow ski indoors here in Dubai and then drive to board an afternoon cruise on the bay in Abu Dhabi.

I was perplexed at how they were going to fill all these buildings.

DAY TWO

Today we left Dubai and headed to Abu Dhabi. As we drove out of town on the highway, we noticed that the roads of Dubai were jammed and packed to a standstill. These roads seemed to have been plowed through the barren desert. Everywhere we looked was sand topped with construction cranes. Most were working on Dubai's most ambitious project, Dubai Land. As we left Dubai and reached the outskirts of Abu Dhabi, we noticed a change: trees! Tens of thousands of trees lined the highway, all of them with individual drip irrigation. Abu Dhabi seemed more permanent from the start. Our first stop was a mosque—in fact, the third largest in the world. It was newly constructed of white marble with inlaid semiprecious stones. In the main prayer room were magnificent chandeliers as well as the largest handmade carpet in the world. Two thousand women worked seven years creating a masterpiece that weighs forty-seven tons.

I couldn't help noticing the sand. The white spires were thick with the desert sand, and the fountains and floors were constantly being swept of it, a brief reminder that the air isn't any better here than in

Dubai. It was three degrees cooler today—only 107. With the humidity at 80 percent, we didn't notice this cold snap.

After the mosque we went into the city. Here was the most striking difference with Dubai: Abu Dhabi appeared more permanent, with wider streets and more continuity of the buildings—and lots of trees. Driving up the streets, we also noticed Abu Dhabi's historic past—all forty years of it. In 1970 apartment buildings were built very quickly and poorly. As we looked down from the tall new high-rises, we saw these old, dilapidated buildings, a third world slum mixed with some of the finest architecture in the world.

I couldn't help but think that in some ways Dubai and Abu Dhabi were third world countries. They had managed to take all of their wealth and use it to import third world laborers to serve them. Low salaries, substandard living conditions, and no rights—it was a form of modern-day slavery. Dubai, being newer, was able to hide them outside the city. This was the contrast of this part of the world: all the wealth was for the few, and the rest were exploited.

For lunch we went back to the world Abu Dhabi wanted us to see, the opulent Emirates Palace Hotel. This hotel was in strict contrast to the one we were in yesterday: subdued and classy—more like a fine European hotel, only ten times the size. They like things big here.

After a wonderful lunch, we toured an exhibit of Abu Dhabi's new development of museums and performance halls. This was a stark difference with Dubai. Abu Dhabi was going cultural. Incredible architecture would house some of the finest art they would borrow from France. The performance center would welcome great artists. In contrast, Dubai was becoming Disneyland.

Abu Dhabi was desperate for culture, and Dubai was being Disneyfied. Both were like rich little children buying their favorite toys. At the hotel there was also an exhibition of works of Picasso. Leanne got to see it. Unfortunately, I couldn't go in—it was women's day, a reminder that we were in an Arab country, where there was still a separation of the sexes.

Abu Dhabi was to double its population over the next twenty years. The native population would drop to 10 or 12 percent. Almost

90 percent of the people here will be from somewhere else and serving the rich Arabs like slaves. As a matter of fact, Leanne and I don't think we met one native while we were here. Serving tourists was not becoming to them. My guess is at least half of the natives weren't even in the country during the summer months.

It was nighttime here, and that meant it was time to eat dinner and enjoy a little downhill skiing. Yes, before dinner, we took a few runs at the only indoor ski resort. It was a little fun and a little crazy.

As we were leaving Dubai I had a few final thoughts. This was a very interesting place. I hesitate to call it a country; there were no resources and one couldn't become a citizen. The military was made up of professional mercenaries from a host of other countries. Only the top brass are citizens. It was still a tribe—a very wealthy tribe. With oil slowly disappearing, they had to make a decision for the future. Tourism was the answer. The tribe owned everything. All this wealth wasn't going to waste. Vast amounts were being invested and consumed. In a consumer economy, the country was doing more than its part, creating a world-class resort in the most inhospitable part of the world. In 2015, when it would be finished, it would be a sight to see. Come around January, February, or March. The air will be clear and the water warm, and there will be much to do for the whole family. Maybe that saying was right: if you build it, they *will* come.

I don't want anyone to get the impression I didn't like Dubai. I think the difference between Dubai and the rest of the Middle East was most interesting. It was an experiment unfolding. As I mentioned, it was in a desert with no significant changes over the years. They were trying to create something out of nothing. They were bringing in third world workers at very low wages, but these workers seemed to all be happy. It was more money than they could have made where they were. Many send money home, and in those countries the money goes a long way. They are fed well and certainly trained very well in hospitality. All were very professional and very well dressed with well-tailored uniforms. In Jordan our guide was in jeans and a T-shirt and smoked when he got out of the car. Dubai was doing a lot for these people and for the economies of the world, spending all that wealth.

As our guide told us in Dubai, no one questioned anything in Dubai. It worked, so everyone was happy to be there. The speculation on property was going to be the test in ten years. They were hooking people in by letting them buy property so they would return to vacation and spend money. It might work. It's not any different than what Disney World did. Disney World is a good comparison for Dubai: an area of no significance, built only for vacationing and tourism, run by people brought in from other countries. You don't see Disney executives in Disney World, either.

DAY FOUR

On this day we woke up at four thirty to head to Jordan. Like everything else in Dubai that process was amazing. When the elevator opened into the lobby at five, we were greeted by an impeccably dressed hotel employee. Our bags were taken and we were whisked into a limo for the ride to the airport. On arrival at the airport there was a very professional and well-dressed representative waiting at the curb, expecting us. Our passports were taken and we followed. She bypassed the lines and checked us in efficiently. She proceeded to follow us through security and arrange for a golf cart on the other side. That was the last time we needed to walk in Dubai. After being dropped at the front door of the Emirates first-class lounge for a quick visit, which included a full breakfast buffet, we were paged to the desk. Again, our guide was there with another cart to take us to the gate for boarding. The service on the plane was equally impressive; two stewards waited on us hand and foot.

Landing in Amman, we saw the difference between oil money and no oil money. Jordan was an old civilization, crowded with people trying to make a living. Our guide even mentioned that coming from the airport. "They have oil. We have history." I asked which he preferred. He said, "History."

If he saw Dubai he might change his mind. As a traveler I think I like the history too. We were just smart enough not to want to live in it. There was a lot of history here to see. We hit the ground running with a tour of the old city and a visit to Roman ruins and local museums. When we got here we didn't expect to go back ten thousand years. This was old, old history. Amman ten thousand years ago was rich in fertile land and forests. By the second century BC the land had been cleared of its forest and the soil depleted from overplanting. The preserved writings on a wall of a building some two thousand years ago projected the end of the world because the citizens of the area were not taking care of the land and were overusing the resources. It seemed that global warming started way before us.

We were glad we went to Dubai. When people talk about the Middle East, they are talking about two different worlds. Dubai was an oasis, built in the desert, whose only reason for existence was that there was oil, unlike Jordan and the surrounding countries that were hilly and once were trade routes to the rest of the world. Even the ancient Romans and Greeks figured out Dubai and the desert had no importance. Since they hadn't discovered oil, there was no reason for them to conquer the desert. One world became rich in history and one rich with money. That changed a person's attitude. In Jordan they were fighting for traditions to preserve the past, for survival; in Dubai they were fighting to save traditions to have a past.

Today was a short day. Tomorrow we travel north and visit ten thousand years of our heritage.

DAY FIVE

We started out at nine for our first full day in Amman, Jordan. We headed north out of the city. After traveling thirty minutes we started to see why people settled here over the ages. The area was hilly and had a great climate and soil for agriculture. The hills were either dense with trees or planted with crops—mostly olive trees, lots of olive trees. The valley floor had farm after farm of various crops as well. In passing an excavation of a building we could see the difference in the very deep red fertile topsoil and the light beige drainage soil three to four feet below—perfect for growing. This is the Fertile Crescent students read about in history books in school.

We didn't drive north only to see olive trees. An hour and a half out of Amman was one of the oldest and best-preserved Greek and Roman cities: the city of Gerash, or Gerasa, as it was known, was first built by the Seleucids in 170 BC. Established in what became the south of the Roman city, it was centered on the mound of the temple of Zeus. But the city was not merely a Greek colony. Coins and inscriptions in both Greek and Nabataean show that these eastern traders had a considerable influence in the city. Jerash became a Roman city in 63 AD, and its expansion began. By the second century AD, one hundred hectares were contained within its city walls. The Greeks started the city, and the Romans built upon it. It had one of the most complete ancient theaters in the entire world. No restoration had been done to this theater. It was so complete it was still in use during our visit. The stone seats still have the carved seat numbers on every seat—all fourteen thousand, with assigned seating just like today. Attendees better know their Greek alphabet if they don't want trouble: it was the Greek letters that were carved in the stones.

The rest of the city was also very well preserved. There was a temple that still had the original columns standing where they were placed two thousand years ago. The Romans knew about the devastating effects of earthquakes, so they carved holes through the columns and poured lead down the center to stabilize them. It worked. Many earthquakes later, they were still standing today.

On our way out there was a reenactment of a Roman show in the still-intact Hippodrome. Leanne and I got to race in a chariot pulled by two Arabian horses around the original track used by the Romans, while "Roman guards" watched. These rickety chariots going at a gallop around the corners was, to say the least, interesting, if not downright scary. When these cities were built they must have been an awesome sight. There were roads for chariots and wagons and covered walkways for pedestrians alongside as we strolled the colonnade. The roads were built on top of a sewer and water system that was so well built it is still in use in Amman. The path we walked down in this ancient city still had the stone manhole covers in place, every fifty feet or so. I couldn't help but think that Caesar's Palace in Las Vegas wasn't very far off the mark in what it might have looked like.

We proceeded on our journey farther north. We were headed to a castle built at 4,500-foot elevation that was used to protect northern Jordan from the Crusaders. From high on this mountain we could see every entrance to the area. We could see all the way to the Jordan River and the mountains of Israel. The castle was very well preserved with its medieval arches keeping the rooms cool in the hot sun. The day finished with a great Arabic lunch (at $35 it tasted a lot better than our $425 lunch in Dubai). Before we got back to the hotel we stopped at a new museum that housed the car collection of King Hussein, who died in 1999, eighty great cars that told a story of the kingdom. Most of those stories seemed to end in assassination. Amman is well worth the trip if you have the extra time. Tomorrow, we would head south to Petra with stops along the way.

DAY SIX

Today we left Amman and drove south toward Petra and eventually the Israeli border. On the way we made a few interesting stops. The first was to, of all things, a Greek Orthodox church. The reason for this stop was that it was built over the floor of a mosaic—not just any mosaic, but the oldest known map of the Holy Land to exist, created in 560 AD. From the looks of it, they must have started in 640 AD. The map had all the names of the areas and the inhabitants of the time. We were told that when disputes of land happen, even now, everyone goes back to the map to see who really did inhabit the land. We were told that that very thing did occur in a dispute between Israel and Egypt over some godforsaken desert they seem to always fight about here.

The second stop was Mount Nebo, which had the monument of Moses. Supposedly—and I emphasize *supposedly*—this is where Moses came and saw the Promised Land right before he died. Let's forget that it was quite a hike up the mountain and that he was 120 years old at the time. Again, supposedly, he also had perfect sight at the time. He would have needed it. According to the Bible he saw Masada and several other places in Israel. Good thing his eyes were good. Masada is over 250 miles away. That's hard to see on a clear day. Today was anything but clear. He must have seen those places in March when the air was cleaner. Anyway, we did get a nice view of the Jordan Valley and the Jordan River—or should I say Jordan Creek. The Syrians and the Israelis had taken so much and dammed so much of the river that by the time it got to Jordan it was a creek. Do I see a fight over water once they stop fighting over religion? Their story was made all the more unbelievable by the lack of discovery of even one piece of evidence of Moses or anyone else of that time being there. With all the crap pottery they have found around this place someone must have broken a cup or a bowl when Moses was here.

Well, we left Moses's burial spot and headed south again to look for the Crusaders. They weren't around anymore but their castle and forts were. In approaching the Crusaders' castle we stopped to visit an old Jordanian who lived in a cave below the mountain. It was a real cave and decorated very nicely: couch, bed, television, and Internet—yes, TV and Internet. He told us that his father, grandfather, and great-grandfather all lived in the same cave, but they didn't have TV. It might be true. But like all other Jordanians living along the route to Petra he was selling authentic bead jewelry. Either the cave story was not true or the beads are from Taiwan. It could be it was both—interesting nonetheless.

Finally, we got to the castle without buying the Jordanian beaded necklace. What the hell were these Crusaders protecting? You could see nothing for miles. With all the walls, stone doors, and cannonballs I had to wonder why they had so many secret passages out of there. The castle was built in 1110 AD and left around 1180 AD. What a waste of work. We think they just plain ran out of water up there and went back home.

Before we got to our hotel in Petra, our guide asked if we were up for a little side trip since we seemed like the adventuresome type. Of course, he was right. We headed off the highway, and after going through a pass, we saw the mountains change. They went from dry, arid, flat shapes to sandstone mountains that looked like clouds as far as the eye could see. This was the northernmost part of Petra. We came to the end of a small road, walked through a four-foot opening in the stone, and we went back 2,500 years in time. This was a rest station run by the citizens of Petra for the travelers heading to Gaza. As we came through the four-foot crevice we saw buildings carved into the rocks. This was Little Petra—room after carved room as far as the eye could see. Here was a rest station where traders could spend a night and get a meal while they traveled through the desert on the Jordanian Silk Road.

We were in an exciting part of the city. It was here that they had the only surviving fresco in Petra. We chanced a daring walk to the second floor of one of the buildings, and there, clear as day, was the most intricate, colorful, and beautiful fresco, dating back two thousand years. This was a treat. I will talk more of the civilization that lived there and what they accomplished tomorrow. Today was about that fresco. If this was what the main part of Petra was going to be like, we were in for the treat of our lives. For now, it was late, and we needed a drink. A glass of wine, dinner, and sleep sounded good.

DAY SEVEN

Wow! Spectacular! That was the only way I could describe Petra. Think of the elegance of Ephesus for its architecture, the grandeur of the Grand Canyon for its scale and majesty, and the Anasazi cave Indians for their clever use of the hills. Combine all of those together and you have Petra!

We started early in the morning, leaving our hotel at nine. Our hotel was a fantastic five-star right in front of the gates of Petra. We were fresh and brave and forewent the horses that were there to bring us to the gorge that was the official entrance of Petra. After a short walk we reached the gorge, which at one time had a large gate and arch protecting the entrance. As we entered this narrow gorge we knew we were traveling a special road. It was majestic. The gorge was about twelve to twenty feet wide and traveled for a mile. It wound its way through the mountain with dazzling colors and shapes everywhere we looked. The Nabataean tribe that built Petra had created rest areas, carved relief statuary and niches, and built an amazing water system that fed the main city. One side of the gorge had a covered trough for irrigation, kitchen, and livestock water, and the opposite side had a terra cotta pipe system that traveled a zigzag line into the city. Along the way were dams, cisterns, and an ingenious filtering system for the water. The engineering was amazing, but it was the shapes and colors of the sandstone that dazzled us. Time had created something special in this gorge. Many of the reliefs had eroded away, but there was still enough to let our imaginations run wild.

As we came to the end of the gorge we came upon the view we have all seen in travel magazines: the well-preserved Treasury. Our guide proceeded to tell us that although it was called the Treasury, it never served as such. It was actually a tomb—a massive tomb. It must stand 130 feet high and one hundred feet across. Our guide explained that the building was built around two thousand years ago and was actually built on top of two tombs that date back 2,500 years. We could look down an excavation and see the older tombs. Although this building was the most famous, it is only one of seven hundred in Petra. Time had eroded hundreds of others.

As we turned and headed to the city center, we saw more of that fantastic water system and many more spectacular facades carved into the mountains. Turn after turn brought more surprises and awe. When we reached the city center the gorge opens up to a small valley. This was where they created a colonnade that was lined with shops and had a few freestanding buildings and temples on either side of a man-made river. Spinning around, we could see tombs carved into the hills and houses carved high into the mountain.

Still feeling fresh, we decided to climb to the top of a cliff to see close-up the tomb of an important minister. Again, these facades were strikingly perfect. As we entered the rooms we noticed the perfect chisel marks that were done to create a pattern on the walls and ceilings, the perfect ninety-degree corners, and the straightness of the walls and ceilings. Walking on the top of the ridge, we were able to look down on theater seating for seven thousand carved perfectly into the hillside. These were not blocks placed to create a theater, but seats and a stage and decorations carved right out of the hill.

As we descended the other side of the hill, we decided to go for the gold and take the hike up to the very top of Petra and see the monastery. It is a 4,500-foot ascent and would take an hour and a half of very hard climbing to reach the top. An executive decision was made to take donkeys two-thirds of the way up. Good choice. The trail has hundreds of steps carved into the rock, and the donkeys navigated it with precision. As each donkey fought for the front, there were times that one of us would be in danger of being pushed off the edge of a cliff and dropping several hundred feet. I don't know what impressed me more: the donkeys carrying us up, or the donkey guide following us on foot and making sure none of us took a wrong turn and plunged to our death.

We lost our donkey about a half mile from the top. As we climbed we were amazed to see more and more cave facades carved into the hillside and steps everywhere carved into the hills. We could tell there was much that has been erased by time. When we reached the top we saw the largest carved structure in Petra, the Monastery. Standing at what appears to be two hundred feet tall, it was overwhelming—just incredible that someone could design and carve the hillside so precisely. Since we climbed so far, we continued on to the back of the mountain to take in the view of the Jordan Valley and one of the many hidden springs that the citizens depended on. It was not hard to find. It was that small strip of green in the middle of sheer nothingness as far as the eye could see. After a short rest it was time to head down. Walking down was definitely better then walking up. On the way down on foot, we were even able to stop and take a detour off the trail and find even more carved tombs and houses.

When we got to the bottom, it was getting a bit hot, and some of us were getting a bit tired. It was three, and we still had more of Petra to cover. Donkeys to the rescue! Racing on donkeys, we traveled to a church built in the fifth century that had some beautifully preserved mosaic floors and then deeper into Petra to see the tombs of the kings, an imposing five-story structure. Going by foot again, we climbed to the top of the tomb and traveled along a path to what was once a government court. The court building was three stories high. The bottom floor was a jail, the second floor was the court, and the third was a tomb.

We covered a lot of ground today, and I wanted to leave Petra riding proudly on a camel like the Magi. Unfortunately, I didn't have enough dinars and had to take a donkey and ride out like Sancho Panza. Oh well! We kept our heads high and had the experience of a lifetime. Petra is high on our list of things you must do in your lifetime.

DAY EIGHT

Today we headed for the Gulf of Aqaba and crossed over to Israel. As we left Petra we climbed high over the mountains we had just explored. As we reached the top, we had an opportunity to stop and admire the Petra Valley below. The gorge of Petra actually stretches for over thirty miles. Much more was yet to be explored. As we drove back down, the sandstone cliffs that have been carved into exotic shapes over many millennia enchanted us. Lower and lower we descended until the sandstone gave way to the desert floor. The sandstone cliffs disappeared and were replaced with granite mountains. These weren't the gray granite of California, but the colored, veined granite that might have decorated your kitchen counters—rich veins of green, red, and black snaking through the hills.

As we traveled the desert floor, our guide decided to take us on a side trip to an area rarely visited by tour groups. This was the ancient settlement of the Hawara tribe. These people developed the area and controlled trade here from 80 BC to 200 AD. The city is on the ancient King's Highway that ran from Damascus to Cairo. As we reached the city we noticed there wasn't much left. Nevertheless, our guide was very excited to show us the water system, which was the major part of their civilization. The problem was we couldn't find it. They were so protective of their water system that they buried it, and no monument stood above the ground. The curator of the area was so excited to see visitors that he personally took us on a tour of the area and showed us the system. By building channels and aqueducts from the mountains some ten miles away, they collected rainwater, which was stored underground and hidden by using arches to support a roof that kept it out of sight from their enemies. Like Petra, every home in the city had running water right to the door. This system was so ingenious and well-made that it was in use from 80 BC until 1974, when the department of antiquities moved the last inhabitants out of the area to preserve the site. Unfortunately, these same inhabitants had two thousand years to dismantle many of the old buildings, including the old Roman garrison, to make new homes for themselves. Thousands of years of history and architecture have been lost for all time.

Continuing on our journey, we finally came to Aqaba with the Israeli resort town of Eilat in the distance on the other side of the Red Sea. We quickly noticed which town had money and which did not. The Israeli side has many large hotels, apartment buildings, and office buildings. Aqaba had fewer and smaller hotels and small apartment buildings—and, we would come to find, also much less tourism. It was interesting to note that with all the talk of the destruction of Israel, corporations and businessman had no problem investing vast sums in the country and wouldn't invest in Jordan for fear of its instability. Their proximity to the Red Sea, for all practical purposes, appeared to be exactly the same.

After a quick tour and lunch in Aqaba it was time to cross to the Israeli side. Our guide was only allowed to take us as far as the Jordanian checkpoint, and we had to bid farewell to him and Jordan. We grabbed a luggage cart and walked the five hundred or so yards through the desert past five checkpoints—one Jordanian and four Israeli—onto Israeli soil. Thoughts of Checkpoint Charlie in Berlin came to mind. As we crossed the desert in the 110-degree heat we made our first checkpoint. A *blaze'* Israeli soldier opened the door to his air-conditioned office and checked our passports. Passing the first test, we continued on to the next checkpoint, where we were stopped again. This time we were asked what we were doing in Israel. What did he think we were doing there? We were two American bumpkins pushing a luggage cart filled with bags through the 110-degree desert heat and snapping pictures of Welcome to Israel and Good-bye, Jordan signs. I thought of making a joke to make him smile but thought better of it. The last stop was passport check to get our passport stamped. Leanne and I felt there was bit of arrogance with the process that we have never felt in the rest of our travels through the Middle East. Finally, we made it through the last gate, and we were now in a parking lot with all our bags and not a person around. Something went wrong, and our guide and driver were not on the other side to greet us. After fifteen minutes in the heat, we grabbed a taxi.

As we arrived at our hotel, which was billed as one of the best in Eilat, it was bedlam. I could have sworn I was at the Fontainebleau Hotel in Miami Beach in the 1970s during Christmas break: kids running, tour groups checking in, and just general craziness. After a quick stop in the room we got into our bathing suits to hit the pool to escape the heat. My idea of fun was a Diet Coke and a good book while soaking in the water. My rest time was postponed when I was told that I couldn't take my Diet Coke near the pool. Running kids, strollers blocking the aisles, shoes thrown about, splashing, screaming, and general chaos was okay. My Diet coke was a danger to the pool. Go figure. After a quick dip we headed out to soak in the Red Sea. You have got to do that. Looking across the water, we couldn't help but see the Jordanian flag in the central plaza in Aqaba flying proudly, begging for guests. There was something sad about that. I hoped these two towns could one day share in the wealth of this area and exchange tourism as easily as the United States, Canada, and Mexico. This was an interesting place to visit, but I was happy we weren't spending too much time here. We were leaving tomorrow for the Dead Sea to continue our historical adventure.

DAY NINE

We had been in Israel for two days and I have to say, I was disappointed. We have stayed in a five-star resort hotel in Eilat and a five-star in the "resort area" of the Dead Sea. Both wouldn't qualify as three stars in the United States. Even a three-star is kept in better shape than the hotels here. The towns were hot and very dirty. Anyone looking to make some money might think of bringing a power washer to Israel. The streets were filthy with spilled, baked-on crap, and many things were broken or badly worn. Some of this would be tolerable if the service in the hotels was at least top rate. If there is a word for *service* in Hebrew I don't think they understand the meaning here. At least, no one here was trained in the art. People rarely smiled, and when we asked a question, we might get a finger pointed in the appropriate direction. Everyone looked at us like they didn't know why we were there.

The town of Eilat was a beach resort, and for the life of me I couldn't tell why people go there. It was hot, crowded, and dirty and had substandard accommodations and service. If anyone is interested in traveling eight thousand miles to go to the beach may I recommend the south of France? It's cleaner and has great service, and you won't see cargo ships out your window. The French even smile in the south.

We left Eilat for the Dead Sea this morning, starting with a two-hour drive going north through the desert. We spent the time discussing the political and historical problems of Israel—a crash course, you might say, on why there is no peace. By the time we got to the hotel at the Dead Sea we were convinced we couldn't fix the problems here and neither could anyone else. I will leave the politics at that.

As we approached the Dead Sea we saw what appeared to be icebergs. At 110 degrees that was obviously doubtful. What we were seeing were salt mounds all throughout the sea. The area we were staying in is the shallow part of the Dead Sea, so it was easier to see the salt come high out of the surface. When we arrived at our so-called five-star hotel our driver recommended that we do a spa treatment and then take a quick dip into the Dead Sea. Why not?

Like everything else in Israel it wasn't five-star service. (Liz would have been appalled.) When we got to the spa we saw that it consisted of a few communal pools right off the pool and lockers behind the reception desk that Leanne and I had to share. The place looked more like a cheap bowling alley to me than a spa. I don't know what happened in Leanne's room but I will give you a glimpse into my treatment. For some reason the big thing here was mud. Forget that we were in the desert and the mountains and the sea were both made of salt. When I got into the room for my mud treatment, I was still in my bathing suit. After a difficult hello since she didn't speak English, the masseuse took some mud and put a generous glob on the table. She proceeded to ask me to sit in it. After an awkward moment I had to ask her, "With my suit on or off?" I was surprised when she said, "On." I then proceeded to sit in my bathing suit but into the hot, dark mud. I have to admit it was a first. I had never had a spa treatment in my bathing suit, let alone been asked to sit in mud during one. This bizarre treat continued, but I will spare you the rest.

After the treatments, Leanne and I met up in the reception lobby to get dressed—no classy dressing rooms here. The next phase of this insane adventure had to be completed: a soak in the Dead Sea. Swimming in the Dead Sea, we noticed that we couldn't sink, it smelled awful, and, being in the desert, the water was a refreshing ninety-five degrees. We couldn't help but notice the Muslim women in their swimsuits: long, black tops with turtlenecks, pants, and headscarves. The bathing suits of the 1890s were sexy in comparison. I don't know why they didn't drop dead, dressed head to toe in black, swimming in 95-degree water in 110-degree heat. We took our pictures to remember the moment, and we were on our way.

No travelogue would be complete without a mention of the food; here, *five-star* must have meant "cattle call." At both hotels, the only restaurants were big halls crowded with side-by-side tables and long buffet lines. I felt like I was in the Israeli military. Other than matzo ball soup, potato pancakes and a giant pastrami sandwich from the Carnegie deli in New York, I don't find most Jewish kosher food very appealing. So there was not much to write about with regard to the cuisine.

We had three more days in Israel, and I was still hopeful that when we got to Jerusalem, the historic part of Israel would salvage the visit for me. As for the resort side, I would prefer Hawaii. So far this place was on my bottom five of places I would come back to.

DAY TEN

It was a very, very busy day. We left the Dead Sea Hotel and headed north along the coast. I have to say I was feeling better about Israel, seeing the tranquility of the sea and knowing that we were headed back on our historical tour, with our first stop being Masada. Masada was a mountain fortress and palace built by King Herod. Why King Herod wanted a palace in the godforsaken part of the desert no one really knows. Well, after Herod's death, Jewish rebels, in defiance of the Romans, used the fortress. The Israeli rebels tried to hold off the whole Roman army in the desert with nine hundred or so men, women, and children. When the fight became futile, so as not to be taken as slaves, they committed mass suicide on the top of the mountain. The rebellion seemed to start over some silly disputes with the Romans in Jerusalem and escalated into the loss of the Jewish state of Israel, the destruction of their temple, and the killing or suicide of many of the Jews in the area. There is a Hollywood movie that tells a great story if you want to know more.

After our tour of Masada we traveled up the coast toward Jerusalem. There were sinkholes dotting the coast because the sea was receding. I want to point out that the sea wasn't shrinking from evaporation but from the drainage of water upstream. The Dead Sea at the present rate would disappear completely in forty or fifty years. Israel, as well as Syria and Lebanon, was taking so much water from the Sea of Galilee upstream that there was none left to flow down the Jordan River to fill it—thus why I called it the Jordan Creek.

Continuing on took us past the caves where the Dead Sea Scrolls were found and then into the West Bank. Going through the West Bank, we were surprised to see it so quiet. From what we had seen on TV, we almost expected there to be riots around every turn and rocket launchers pointed at Israel from every hilltop. What we found was a desert with some very poor people and Bedouins living in tents. It seemed safe to us, but then again, we were in a Mercedes heading down the highway at eighty miles an hour. When we left the checkpoint on the other side, we could see Jerusalem in the distance, high on a hilltop. We made a quick stop at the David Citadel Hotel, a five-star hotel next to the Old City, and were ready to tackle Jerusalem. This hotel was much nicer and closer to a five-star ranking. I can't say that any hotel in Israel was up to US or European standards. We all agreed that the Israelis needed an attitude adjustment before the ranking could be higher.

Leaving the hotel, we tried to get two important destinations in: the Israel Museum, which houses some of the most complete Dead Sea Scrolls, and the Holocaust Museum. Although I had been in the Holocaust Museum in Washington, DC, taking a trip to this museum was an important part of an Israeli tour. Both were great. Seeing a two-thousand-year-old pen and paper document up close was exciting and worth the trip. Seeing the story of the Holocaust was something I couldn't deem exciting. It was emotional. It almost made me want to scream and dream of turning back the clock. There was a new children's memorial with a million lights, and the names of the children who were murdered were read one at a time, listing their ages and places of birth.

After we were finished with the museums, we went back to the hotel, where we met up with Mike and Diana Passcuzzi, two friends from home who would finish the trip with us. We arranged our first night together to be at the best—and some say the most expensive—restaurant in town. The "expensive" part was correct—the "best," not so much. The meal was one of those disasters that was so bad it would become a story to tell the grandchildren.

As we were walking back from dinner, almost in hysterics laughing about the meal, we all of a sudden got solemn. We were reminded this was Israel—not by a sign or building or street, but from tragedy. It seems that some Palestinian lunatic on a tractor murdered another twenty-six people right behind our hotel. In addition, two tourists in a Palestinian taxi were murdered and robbed by the driver. My guide was correct when he said the people of Israel were the way they were because of this hard, dangerous life. With all of this happening this afternoon, the young people of Israel were still flooding the streets and having fun. I guess one can get used to anything.

DAY ELEVEN

Today was a very busy day and maybe one of the most difficult to explain. It's hard to describe Israel and its history without including the current political climate, so bear with me. We started our day outside the Old City of Jerusalem on the Mount of Olives. This was where Jesus came to Jerusalem, met with his disciples, and supposedly ascended to heaven. (There was an actual footprint where he launched off a rock.)

From the mount we looked back at the Old City of Jerusalem and the Golden Gate. It was pointed out that this gate, which was closest to the temple base, was bricked closed. The story goes that Suleiman, an Ottoman sultan, was told that there was going to be a Second Coming of Christ. To prevent that, he bricked the gate closed and proclaimed, "Once was enough!" It's supposed to be a true story.

Traveling off the mount, we entered the Old City. The Old City is very hard to describe. It had been conquered and occupied by so many people over the centuries it was hard to know what period we were looking at. The city had different sections: Armenian, Palestinian, Christian, Jewish, Ethiopian, and more I just can't remember. Today we spent time trying to understand the Christian part of the city. We saw where Mary was supposedly born, where Jesus supposedly walked, and where he supposedly was crucified. I always say *supposedly* because they know it happened in the Old City but they don't know the exact locations. Emperor Constantine's mother chose the locations in the third century. She went through the city pointing her finger on a spot proclaiming, "It happened here." That seemed to be good enough, and so the tradition continued. She must have been a medium.

What we also realized around here was that no one seemed to care about the history they were trying to hold on to. Over the centuries, things were torn down, built over or around, or totally destroyed. Over twenty-five civilizations built over each other here. As I was looking at this mishmash of buildings, a car went by, and the driver threw a coke can out the window onto the streets of the Old City. That seemed to be the attitude of the people here from the beginning of time.

Again, this had been a living, working city for three thousand years. As we walked through, we noticed that the city had lots of contrasts. It was not unusual to see police officers with machine guns on every street. It was also not unusual to see men standing at doorways or walking down the street with their guns drawn and their fingers on the triggers, expecting trouble. Still, the city felt very safe, and everyone was very nice and friendly. Halfway through today we stopped in the Palestinian area to have lunch. We were in Jerusalem having lunch in a Palestinian restaurant. I think the guide brought us there because the Arab food was much better than the Jewish food. Just kidding. Okay, it's true.

After lunch we had one last stop. We were going to Bethlehem. Bethlehem, if you don't know, is controlled by the Palestinian Authority and not secured or controlled by Israel. Our Israeli guide was not allowed to go with us into the Palestinian Authority areas. He told us he was going to "stay in the parking lot like a schmuck."

Since he couldn't take us, it was arranged for us to be hosted by a Palestinian family. They would pick us up outside the walls and take us on a tour of the area. Passports in hand, we made an important trip in our quest to understand the incomprehensible situation here. When we went into the town we were surprised at how new it was. Again, we expected poverty, burning tires, and danger on every street. What we saw were kids at play and new hotels and apartment buildings. These buildings were being built with oil money from the Gulf.

Our first and only stop was the Church of the Nativity. This was where Jesus was supposedly born in a stable and put in a manger. The place where the church stood now was the location of the inn that Mary and Joseph went to before going into the back stable to have Jesus.

Please, let's not forget that I don't believe a word of any of this. I was surprised when my Jewish guide said this was an important site, for it was where a nice Jewish boy was born. He always reminded me that Jesus never set foot in a church and never met a good Christian or a bad Christian. The long and short of this is that most everyone in this area, like every other part of the world, wanted to live in peace. It was the government authorities that didn't seem to want it. Pride would eventually kill the lot of them here. My guide made a good point about Israel. With a Jewish population that has had minimal worldwide growth for the past sixty years and an Arab population growing by the day, the Jewish population of Israel is actually shrinking. The danger to the Jews of Israel was not Iran, but the growing Arab population getting a majority control of Israel without firing a shot. Our guide spoke for many Israelis when he said he didn't understand why they were fighting for this crap piece of land—no oil, no water, no gold, no nothing. The water situation might eventually do all of them in.

I know this is all very complicated. It is not simple. At the Greek or Roman sites we had visited, we could take a few pictures, learn about the people of the time, and check it off our list. This was living history that had been evolving and changing for three thousand years or more. Don't think for a moment that Leanne wasn't trying to find a solution for these people from the moment she arrived. Our guide was thinking of bringing her to the prime minister to get it all settled. Tomorrow we would do the Old City again, but with a Jewish perspective. It's hard to be funny about Israel. Our guide said Israel is not about service. It's about emotion, something the Israelis know all too well.

DAY TWELVE

This was our last day in Israel. Today we went back into the Old City, this time doing a Jewish tour of the city. This place was very hard to get our arms around. There was so much here it would take weeks to get through it all. Even if we could, our heads might explode in the end. This was not the type of place one could ask what period something is from or how old something is. You start at 1000 BC, then you jump to 600 AD, then you are back to 70 BC, and then AD, BC, AD—it just went on. It was a mixed salad. This was a city that had been occupied consistently for three thousand years. We tried our best to soak it all in: the Western Wall, the Southern Wall, the Temple Mount, and all parts and museums in between.

I think it's interesting to note that when the Jews lost the city in 70 AD, it was 1,900 years before they were able to go back. What we saw couldn't have been done before 1967. The Israelis captured the Old City in the 1967 Six-Day War. From that day, the Israelis have been excavating and building. One of the benefits of this was the opening of the Western Wall and the Western Wall Tunnels. The tunnels were created in the sixth century when another conquering civilization built archways over the street along the Western Wall to raise the street level to wall height. In doing so, a tunnel was created that protected the Western Wall and the streets below for centuries.

It was a great tour. We entered the tunnels from the Wailing Wall and traveled under the Muslim quarter for what seemed a half a mile. When we exited, we had two armed guards who traveled with us back to the Jewish area and the Wailing Wall plaza. It seemed someone was killed in that area a few weeks earlier. I started to think that Israel was like a thrill ride: you do it because it's kind of dangerous. If you get off the ride alive, it was very exciting. If you don't, well, not so much. That was Israel: very exciting and, like a roller coaster, full of twists and turns.

Jerusalem as a whole was a great city—a little old and a little new with centuries of history. It has a beautiful charm to it. All of us were glad we came. Israel wasn't a place to come and visit as a resort experience. It was a place to visit to see the beginnings of our civilization and how it has grown. It was where one could see the best in us and the worst in us. Here we saw each level of time, one on top of the other. Should you come to Israel, you must visit Jerusalem.

Our last night here we went out for a late dinner. That was the best time to see modern Israel. People, especially youth, flooded the street. Pedestrian malls, cafés, and shops were just teeming. If there were large groups, we could see several police cars and officers with machine guns patrolling the streets. It didn't seem to stop the celebration. We felt comfortable and safe and got caught up in all the fun. As we were leaving one of the pedestrian streets, we saw a group of fifty or so Israeli army recruits sitting on some steps for a photo op. Leanne decided to take their picture and then they decided to take her picture in return. One thing led to another, and Leanne was in their group picture, then me, then Mike, and finally Diana. We were all laughing and smiling, enjoying a moment that made for international friendship. I started in the southern resort part of Israel and couldn't wait to leave. Now, after visiting the emotional part of Israel and the city of Jerusalem, I couldn't wait to come back. A good thrill ride always could beckon me back.

View of the beaches of Tel Aviv

Wailing Wall. Jerusalem, Israel

The Treasury, Petra Jordan

Flying out of Israel by private jet

New Mosque, Dubai, UAE

Indoor Skiing in Dubai, UAE

BEHIND THE IRON CURTAIN:
RUSSIA, POLAND, THE CZECH REPUBLIC, AND GERMANY
JULY 2009

DAY ONE

I always forget how long it takes to get to Europe when I make these plans. We left on the eleventh at 1:30 p.m. and didn't arrive in Berlin until 1:30 p.m. the next day. It was only two flights totaling eleven hours, but with the time change and layover, it would take same time to get on a European clock. This trip was special, as we had decided to take our daughter Chelsea with us as a present for her graduation from high school.

A driver from A&K picked us up at the airport for the short trip to the hotel. As we drove to Berlin, the city appeared very clean, and, as one would expect, orderly. I couldn't help feeling like I was coming back to the scene of a crime. Maybe it was just me. Leanne and I are both are fifties babies and remember all too well the stories of the Germans' actions in the Holocaust and the Soviets' action of splitting East and West Germany.

I don't think I would feel this way in any other German city, but this was Berlin, ground zero for some awful events. Like when passing a car wreck, I looked and asked questions. While the rest of the world tried to preserve the memory of these tragic events so we would never forget, this place tried that much harder to bury the past. Hitler's bunker where he committed suicide was buried under a children's park and any mention of Nazis was addressed uncomfortably. Berlin, too, was bombed unmercifully, so much of the city is new since the war. Many of the buildings Hitler used where bombed out and have been torn down.

We were staying at the five-star Regent hotel. It is, of all places, in what was East Berlin. East Berlin, of course, was the on Soviet side of the Iron Curtain and the physical wall that split Berlin in 1961. In 1987 President Reagan gave a speech in which he said, famously, "Mr. Gorbachev, tear down this wall." Two years later, in 1989, that wall did come down. By the time the wall came down, East Berlin was broke and broken.

The Soviets didn't build anything except monuments to their dead and left the citizens of East Berlin to starve. Today it was the most fashionable part of Berlin: the finest hotels, restaurants, and shops. It was here I came face to face with a Bugatti sports car in a fashionable showroom on a fashionable street. Only twenty years ago Germans were standing on lines for days waiting for food, any kind of food, to show up. Now they were sitting in fashionable cafés with us, paying eight dollars for a Diet Coke. By the way, the Bugatti? We could take it home for a cool $1,500,000. The last cars made in East Berlin were small and plastic and had a ten-year waiting list to get. One could now drive the Bugatti, Bentley, Ferrari, or any number of other brands out of the showroom. How things change.

DAY TWO

Today was our last day in Berlin. We met our guide in the early morning and were surprised to find out that we were going to Prague by train. I was doubly shocked to find out that it was a five-hour train ride. When I was told we were not on the high-speed express but the local, I thought I was going to die. I hate trains. I am a get-there-fast-and-now kind of guy.

The Berlin train station was spectacular. It was world-class and modern. What else would you expect? The Allies probably blew the last one to kingdom come. As we pulled out of the station I wasn't impressed with the scenery everyone talked about. I thought, *This is going to be a long ride.*

Things changed as we passed through Dresden. We were now entering the German countryside, which put a smile on my face. As we quietly rolled along, we passed the most beautiful meadows and villages. Acres and acres of yellow sunflowers fading into the green fields, stopping at the rolling hills, came into view. To remind us that we were still on earth in the twenty-first century, old windmills were replaced with wind turbines dotting the background. One town after another was a sight to behold. This was the Europe we wanted to see, and we could really only see it by train. At each charming village or town, we wanted to get off and stay.

As our train moved on, surprisingly slow, we left the meadows of Germany and followed the river into a canyon that was carved deep over the centuries. As we traveled along the riverbank we passed town after town sitting below towering cliffs. The cliffs looked to drop straight down, only to be caught by trees that seemed to come out of the mountainside horizontally and then turn quickly to the sky as they cascaded down to the riverbank. These majestic canyons were covered with more trees than I had ever seen in my life and seemed to grow right out of the rock. Every turn brought a surprise. As we followed the bend in the river, we looked up and saw a castle perched on top of the cliff overlooking the village below.

Boats meandered downriver as we rode the train in the other direction. Castles, churches, and cottages dotted the riverbank. At each stop our local train made, we wanted to get out and walk. Next time we would have to bypass the cities and travel the small villages. As we crossed into the Czech Republic I was sad to leave Germany behind. I felt like we hadn't given Germany its due only stopping in Berlin. We would have to go back. Taking this slow train, I was sure, would be one of the highlights of this trip.

As we stopped at the Prague station, our new guides were waiting to drive us to our hotel. From the moment we left the station, we knew Prague was someplace special. Everywhere we turned was a

Kodak picture spot. Our hotel, a new hotel called the Aria, was in the most fashionable part of the city, just several doors down from the US embassy. The place was themed for musicians and composers. Aria—get it? Our suite was the British music scene.

Being evening, we went on a short stroll before dinner and quickly realized we were in a real live version of Disneyland—small streets with Twelfth, Thirteenth, Fourteenth, Fifteenth, Sixteenth, Seventeenth, and Eighteenth Century buildings and castles, cafés overlooking the river ... As we looked up, medieval Europe looked down. If you are looking for a charming European city, this is it—cobblestone streets and stone mosaic sidewalks wherever you step. Old electric streetcars still commanded the roads. They reminded us that they had right of way. If you were dressed in Seventeenth Century robes, you wouldn't seem out of place here. Knights leaving the castles wouldn't get a second look. The West didn't spoil Prague. This stop was a surprise. Tomorrow I would have lot more to report as we started our tour of all that Prague has to offer.

DAY THREE

Our first day in Praha (that's how the Czechs say it) started out spectacularly. The most amazing rainstorm we had ever seen was in full bloom. We found ourselves in a torrential downpour, followed by lightning and thunder that rattled our teeth. We didn't let any of it stop us from seeing this magnificent city. With umbrellas in hand we entered our cozy van. Our first stop was the Strahov Monastery, a teaching monastery. Our stop was to visit the library.

After entering a very nondescript hallway, we waited for our guide to register at the office. What we weren't aware of was that he was arranging for us to go into the private stacks, where most tourists weren't allowed to go. The opening of an ornate door revealed the ancient and ornate theological section of the library. There we found ourselves surrounded by fifteen thousand volumes dating from the Ninth Century to the Seventeenth lining the walls. Looking up to the ceiling, we saw one of the most spectacular frescos created by Sixteenth Century artisans. It was ornate workmanship and was almost too beautiful to describe. Our guide reached for a book when no one was looking, and there in his hand was a Bible from 1549. It was around forty-five years older than Columbus's ocean voyage. After we left the theology room we entered the philosophy section. There we found stacked two thousand more volumes dating back to the twelfth century. The theme of a fresco at one end of the hall was used by Steven Spielberg to script the *Raiders of the Lost Ark*. It was special being able to come close and personal with over two hundred thousand ancient volumes in one breathtaking setting. We found it interesting that these original manuscripts were just there in the open, not protected by air control.

As we walked out of the library, the rain started to break. We were now at the top of a hill looking out at the city center. The view was magnificent and the sights were wonderful. We walked back down the hill heading to our next stop, the Chapel of Lorenzo. This was an exact copy of the chapel in Italy that was supposedly flown in from someplace by angels, for what purpose I don't remember. It was a very nice chapel. I will take this time to tell you that 50 percent of Czechs are Catholic and 50 percent consider themselves atheists. I remember that part very well.

Our third stop was Prague Castle. Prague Castle was started in the Ninth Century and only completed in 1929. The cathedral in the center was finished nine hundred years after it was started, using the same plans of the original architects. Surrounding the cathedral are Sixteenth and Seventeenth Century buildings that were still used today by the government, much like our White House. Before we walked out of the Prague Castle, we took a trip down to its dungeon. A small stairway barely wide enough for one person led us to a room once used for torture. We were surprised to still see the instruments of misery. Body chains hung in the middle of the room with a skull still locked into the headgear where a prisoner would be lowered into a pit to starve and die; we also spotted head presses with spikes used to crush skulls and collars with spikes inside and poles attached, which were used to move prisoners. Don't forget the stretching rack and leg and arm irons attached to the walls to hold waiting victims. This was a place straight from a Victor Hugo novel. This was the dark side of medieval times. Calling this a castle was a bit misleading. It was more like a small, enclosed town. The architecture here, like everywhere in Prague, was just incredible.

From the castle we traveled to the old city center across the Charles Bridge. The Charles Bridge was built in the 1300s and named for King Charles II. It linked the old city with the historic center. We were told this also was the movie location used in *Mission: Impossible*. With the sun now shining, we were dropped at the main square. From the moment we stepped on the cobblestone street we couldn't stop taking pictures. Every turn, every corner, and every alley was a perfect picture. The opulence of the buildings and the towering the church steeples made this a photographer's paradise. Each street looked like Disney Imagineers had designed it. I have to say, my mouth was open in wonder from the time I got there. We saw the building Einstein stayed in when he was teaching here for a year at the university. We also saw where Mozart stayed while putting the finishing touches on an opera. Each building told a story.

Music played a big part in the history of the city. Chopin played in the very ornate, block-long opera house. Mozart debuted his *Don Giovanni* here, and years later even the Rolling Stones played a concert in the two-hundred-thousand-person stadium right after the fall of the Communists.

As we passed through the ancient gate of the Old Town and entered the New Town, it was still a delight to the eyes. Even the modern streets of Prague's New Town had fashionable shops in buildings dating back two hundred years. Fortunately, this was a city that didn't see the devastating destruction of two World Wars.

Of course, during the Communist reign, Prague did fall into disrepair. Luckily, with the fall of Communism in 1989 and the help of governments around the world through UNESCO, the history of Prague was restored. The restoration of some of the buildings left pieces of some of the original exteriors and interiors exposed, so we could just imagine what it was like hundreds of years ago in the city. A restaurant called the Three Ostriches left exposed the original painted sign of the building as it appeared several hundred years ago, allowing us to travel back to that time.

As we strolled back to our hotel over the Charles Bridge, the natural beauty of Prague came out. The flowing river reflecting the ancient bridges in the water and the banks lined with trees gave us breathtaking views that have been recreated in famous paintings.

For those of you who are following the gastronomical part of this trip, this is for you. We went to dinner this evening at one of the best Czech restaurants known for duck. How did we like it? "Not so much," as Borat would say.

I couldn't say enough about this town. If you are coming to Europe you are missing a gem not stopping here.

DAY FOUR

For our second full day in Praha, we went a different direction, by foot, out of the hotel heading for the Jewish ghetto. Before the war, Prague was home to 110,000 Jews. Today there were less than two thousand living in the city. I expected that we would be seeing the worst side of Prague on this journey, but nothing could be further from the truth. Prague continued to surprise and never left its 1800s character. As we walked the streets, one wonderful building after the other appeared. We felt like we were strolling through a city in another time. As travelers we would get used to seeing old buildings in cities like London and Rome, which were obscured by modern structures. Not in Prague.

By 1708 Jews made up about 25 percent of Prague's population. In 1262 Premysl Otakar II issued a *Statuta Judaeorum*, which granted the Jewish community a degree of self-administration. Years later the large Jewish community in the ghetto dispersed through the city. Without the care of the Jews the ghetto became a slum by the late 1800s. At that time, due to lack of a good sewer system and running water, there were many plagues. The buildings were deteriorating. The city ordered most of the buildings to be torn down and new apartment buildings with proper sanitation installed. What were left of the original ghetto buildings were six synagogues and a very, very old cemetery.

During the occupation by the Nazis, the ghetto was once again used as a holding area for the Jews before deportation. Every man, woman, and child would eventually be transferred to the town of Terezín, where the Nazis set up a model camp to fool the Red Cross into thinking the Jews were happy and well cared for. The ruse worked for about a year. When the Red Cross figured out that the Nazis had set up a lie, all the Jews held there were transferred to Auschwitz and certain death.

A synagogue that had been unused for many years and then used for storage by the Nazis, has since been converted into a memorial for the Jews that perished. In the refurbished building, names of each person who lived in Prague and had been murdered by the Nazis have been listed on every wall of the building. In an upstairs room pictures drawn by children in art class during their stay in Terezín are displayed on the walls, grouped by subject, showing the children's dreams of a better time or the life in the camp. These drawings were smuggled out of the camp by the children's art teacher, who herself perished at Auschwitz.

Our second stop in the old Jewish area was the synagogue of the Prague Burial Society. It also has been turned into a museum dedicated to Jewish heritage. Attached to the synagogue was also the oldest remaining Jewish cemetery. The first burial took place here in 1439, and the last was in 1789, around the time of the emancipation of the Jews, which resulted in them leaving the area. There were over twelve thousand headstones here. One estimate stated that over twenty thousand people were buried in this location. Stone after stone was crowded into a very small area.

There were two famous headstones located in this cemetery. One was famous because it is the oldest burial, in 1439, of Rabbi Avigdor Kara. Rabbi Kara was one of the few survivors of the riots in the Jewish quarter and wrote a moving eulogy describing the attack on the Jews in 1389, which left three thousand dead. This eulogy is still read every year in Prague. The second was Rabbi Loew. Loew became the center of a legend in which he created the golem. According to Jewish folklore, the golem is a man made of clay that was brought to life through magic and acted as a guardian over the Jews.

Our last stop in the area was the Spanish synagogue. It was designed in the Moorish style and was one of the largest and most ornate Jewish temples I had ever seen. When we walked in, we were struck by all the gold on the ceilings and walls. The acoustics were great as well. I sneezed and it sounded like WWII all over again. I was sure this was a restoration. When the Nazis had control of it, it was used for storage. When the Communists had it, it was closed and locked. Time had to have ravaged it.

As we walked down the street out of the Jewish ghetto, it looked like it was locked in another time. I could imagine the scene fading to the turn of the century when horses used the cobblestone streets and people went about their business. I could also imagine the dark times of the 1930s, when Jews were walking the street with suitcases that held all their personal belongings, heading to the train station where the Nazis were waiting. The Jewish area here in Prague was an untouched monument to the past.

Walking back to the hotel with the sun setting over the beautiful river, we were struck by the beauty—and the tourists. The whole trip we had been by ourselves. We felt that the recession must have kept most people home, but this night, everyone came out. The streets were so crowded we could just imagine how busy and crowded the streets must be during better times.

DAY FIVE

Yesterday we left Prague and head off to Krakow, this time by plane. Getting to the airport, I was happy we bought business class until I saw the plane. We were flying Czech Air on a Russian-made turbo prop. The plane was new enough, but business class turned out to be the last two rows of the plane. The difference between business class and coach was that the drinks listed on our headrests didn't have listed prices. The rest of the world must have known it was a waste of money, because we were the only ones in the section.

After arriving at our "five-star hotel" in Krakow, we immediately noticed a stark difference between this city and Prague. Our hotel turned out to be the Sheraton, which was one of three hotels in the city. The other two were a Holiday Inn and a Radisson. It wasn't that they weren't nice—just a little different from what you expect of an international five-star hotel. On the Liz scale, they certainly were no way near five stars. I'm guessing Liz might have found it difficult to find something to her liking.

After an evening stroll to the market square, it was clear Krakow still had not recovered from its Communist occupation. Most of the buildings were in need of repair, and like most third world areas, people did anything they could to make a buck on the street. The person with the horse and carriage concession was a marketing genius. They brought in some of the most beautiful horses I had ever seen, hooked them to the newest and best carriages, and drove them with stunningly attractive uniformed male and female drivers. It was hard to pass them up.

Our first full day of touring started with a Communist steel mill. It's in this section that we saw how awful it was under the Communists. Just as one would imagine, there was nothing but gray apartments and dirty factories. Both the driver and our guide explained what it was like to live under the Soviets. The people suffered from food rationing, gas rationing, and clothes that were ill fitting—if you were lucky enough to get them. It was at this steel mill that solidarity started, which brought down the Communists. They explained that, during the Moscow Olympics, Moscow ordered all available food shipped to their city. In cities that didn't have enough food to feed the people to begin with, it was the last straw. We had the Poles to thank for the downfall of Communism. We were also surprised that the Soviets allowed the churches here to remain open. This also contributed to the downfall, because it gave the already deeply religious population a meeting place to plan the solidarity movement. The Poles are a tough people willing to fight back.

The next stop was the main castle of Krakow right outside the city square. The castle, built in the fifteenth century, was added onto over the centuries, making it very impressive. What was more impressive was the restoration. Between the Austrian army living there and using everything as firewood and the Nazis looting, the place was in horrible condition. In 1916, a restoration started to fix the Austrian damage. After WWII, they started to get back some of the property stolen by the Nazis. Unfortunately, museums around the world still had some of Poland's rich artwork.

Our next stop was the market square—and one of sixty churches and cathedrals in the city. As cathedrals go, this one was very ornate and very interesting inside. It was built using a combination of styles, which made for a great interior. After a short walk down a small back street, we found ourselves at the second-oldest university in central Europe. Guess which was older? Prague's Charles University. What Krakow's university had on Prague was its famous alumnus, Nicolaus Copernicus. Copernicus, as you may know, was the first to put the sun in the middle of our solar system and the planets moving around it. This part of the university building was from the Fifteenth Century, so it was mainly used as a museum now.

Leaving the square, we crossed the bridge to the Jewish ghetto. What I wasn't aware of was that there was no Jewish ghetto in Krakow until the Nazis created it in 1941. The Poles were always considered a tolerant people and brought many Jewish immigrants from many other European countries over the centuries. This was the ghetto that Steven Spielberg's movie *Schindler's List* was about. It was here that Schindler watched the roundup and murder of the Jewish people. Schindler had started his factory not far from the ghetto and used the Jewish labor of the ghetto and the other holding camps nearby.

The ghetto walls have long been torn down, but we could still see some of the apartments that after all this time were still being occupied. They were not nice then, and they certainly were not nice now. There was one public square that was preserved with the Nazi border gate and, of all things, a drug store. The drug store was the only business that was allowed to remain operating in the ghetto. It was run by a Pole who refused to leave. He and his employees stayed and secretly helped the Jews in the ghetto escape, hide, or get food. His store was now a museum.

Our last stop of the day was Schindler's factory. As one might expect, it's a very plain building. It was just now being restored. Until the Spielberg movie, no one believed it had any significance. It was interesting to see for those who had seen the movie. Some of the movie was filmed at the location. Schindler's heroic actions were only discovered when an author wrote a book in the 1980s after interviewing various Jews who spoke of their experience being saved by Schindler.

If Prague was Disneyland, this was not. This was an eastern European city that has been abused over the centuries and was struggling to enter the twenty-first. This was the wonder of travel. We were meeting wonderful people and seeing firsthand some of what we had only previously read about in history books, and there was so much more to learn about.

DAY SIX

Today in Krakow the weather did a one-eighty. It went from sunny skies and eighty-five on Saturday to sixty-five with rain and lightning strikes today. It seemed appropriate since the reason we came to Krakow was to go to Auschwitz. Auschwitz was an hour drive out of town through the Polish countryside. Passing farms on rolling hills and small towns, we got the feeling that Poland hadn't changed much. We didn't know what to expect when we got to our destination. Most of what we knew or thought we knew about Auschwitz we all got from movies or grainy black-and-white films.

When we arrived at the gates that morning, mist was in the air, and it was rather cold. This wasn't a place that should be viewed on a bright, sunny day.

In total there were over forty camps in the area, with Auschwitz being a compound of three main camps. When we drove up to the first camp, called Auschwitz I, we were surprised that everything looked so permanent. It was a large complex of buildings and barracks made of brick. If you removed the two-deep electrified barbed-wire fences, it could have been any complex of buildings, such as a school, hospital, or dormitory. In actuality, it was once a barracks for the Polish army, which was why the Nazis chose to begin the camp there where buildings already stood. It didn't look anything like what we imagined. Walking through the doors of the administration building, we could see why the people coming off the train didn't suspect anything. It was when we got into the buildings that we saw the horrors of the camp. It was one thing seeing Hollywood movies on the subject, but it was another seeing the conditions and the sadistic things the Nazis organized.

The first prisoners to be brought to the camp were not Jews at all. They were Polish intellectuals, teachers, politicians, Soviet soldiers, and many other non-Jewish people. Of the 1.3 million who perished in the camps at Auschwitz-Birkenau, three hundred thousand were not Jewish. It was in this camp that the Nazis experimented with poison gas on Soviet prisoners before building the chambers.

As more trains were brought in, there was a need for space. A second camp, the biggest, was added. It is this camp that is referenced in most movies and films. The camp was two miles away from the first. To see to it that there were no witnesses to what they were doing; the Germans confiscated every home and farm within two miles of the camp and tore them down. Bricks, doors, and windows were then used to build this second camp. They also leveled the forest and anything else that could be used for protection in the event of escape attempts.

Our first stop at this camp was at the observation tower of the main entrance railway station. From this viewpoint we could see the whole camp. To the left, the barracks were built from the bricks of the Polish homes torn down, and to the right the barracks were made of wood. The brick buildings to the left were for the women and children, and the right wooden ones for the men. Down the center were the rail tracks. This was where it all began.

If you have been to other Holocaust memorials, you will find that this one is different. There are photos and some of the horrific museum displays, but no video presentations or sound. This isn't a place that tells the story. This is the story. You quickly realize that this is not a museum or a monument. This is a cemetery. You want to take pictures, but you feel a bit uneasy about doing so.

At Auschwitz I a crematorium is still intact. There were two larger ones built at the Birkenau site, but the Nazis dynamited them when the Soviets arrived to free the camps. They had to know what they were doing was wrong for them to want to hide the evidence. If they thought they were doing something good, why didn't they leave it all together and stand proud? Even after sixty-five years, I still had a feeling of shock that this happened. It seems so unbelievable that the Nazis kept it a secret for so long—and that more people didn't help.

It made me wonder how the soldiers and the German people could have gone along with this. The Nazis did keep what they were doing a secret from the general public, but they didn't seem to ask questions either. So many questions and feelings went through my mind. It's good that we remember what happened here. We would like to feel it would never happen again. Sadly, it still goes on in countries around the world.

I don't know how to end this journal. There is nothing humorous here. There are no happy endings. Some Nazis paid for their crimes, and some did not.

We were told many stories by the guide, but I won't repeat them. They are horrific and sadistic and should only be told by the victims, survivors, and historians—not by tourists like us, at least not in a travelogue.

DAY SEVEN

We left Krakow and drove to Warsaw by way of Czestchowa so we could make a stop at the Jasna Góra Monastery. The monastery is to Poland what the Vatican is to Rome. It might not be its own country like the Vatican, but it has shown independence through the ages, fighting off the Swedes in the Seventeenth Century and the Nazis and Soviets in the Twentieth.

The guide for our tour of the monastery was a resident monk who had been there since 1965. He was very informative, but between the low speaking, the accent, and the fast walk, it was a job to understand what he was actually saying. Our first stop was the inside of the chapel to visit the Black Madonna. There was Mass going on, so it was packed. He explained to us why it's the Black Madonna (the face is dark brown). I think the Nazis started to call it the Black Madonna first. He explained that worshippers start their pilgrimages from Warsaw and spend ten days or more walking to get to the chapel. Once they are inside they then approach the altar on their knees. It is not unlike what happens in Mexico during pilgrimage. There was an aisleway around the chapel to allow tourists to view and take pictures. I was surprised I could take pictures during the service (no flash). The Madonna was unique in that it was also decorated. Every three years a new cloak—or should I say outfit—is draped on the painting. They use jewels from the jewelry the thankful believers donate and sew metals and jewels into various outfits that dress the Madonna painting.

Out of the chapel we received a Polish history lesson while "running" behind our guide. We stopped for pictures a few times, and he was clueless that we weren't behind him. A quick sprint and we caught up. We passed through the treasury, basement, galleries, and museums. He explained how they were able to evade the Nazis and why the Soviets allowed them to exist. (I still don't know how they pulled that one off.)

Leaving Czestchowa we were again on the road to Warsaw. We arrived in Warsaw midday. We checked into a beautiful small hotel in the New Town section of the city. They call it New Town because it's two hundred years younger than the town down the alley. This still made the hotel almost two hundred years old. Apparently the building was once the American embassy.

Exiting the hotel we went on a stroll to explore. We were pleasantly surprised. This city was every bit as charming and nice as Prague. (Honestly, Krakow needed some work). The buildings here were ornate and very central European. If you can imagine a central European style, this city has it. Granted, we are in the old tourist sections. We are not traveling to their modern cities. We can see the high-rises way in the distance.

Today was the day of touring with an actual guide. We again had a fast walker. Now, I am a fast walker, and this guy got me into a jog a few times. I think most of the pictures of Chelsea might be a blur of color. It was just as well since we had lots of territory to cover. When we first started, the guide began to explain the history of Warsaw and Polish history in general. One of our questions has always been, "If the Poles were so independent and strong, why did they fall to the Nazis?" The answer was that the Nazis attacked them on the west, and two weeks later, the Russians in the east attached them. They didn't have a chance.

Our first stop was the Warsaw Ghetto. Just like in Krakow, until the Nazis came to Poland there were no ghettos in Warsaw. The Nazis' first plan was to round up and eliminate all the Polish intellectuals and scholars and then put the Jews into the ghetto and starve them to death. When this proved too slow, they decided to build the extermination camps. Most of the Jews here in Warsaw went to Treblinka. At this camp, all who arrived were gassed upon arrival. The guide explained that one person did escape from Treblinka and made his way back to the Ghetto. When he told the Jewish elders what was happening, they thought he was crazy and admitted him to the mental hospital. The story was so unbelievable that no one listened; this was part of the problem. Lies and deceit were the main weapons of the Nazis. There were so many monuments in this area. Every place we walked there was something about the struggle and the brave who fought back.

The walls were gone, but many buildings were still standing. Then when the guide dropped a bombshell on us (excuse the metaphor): everything we were seeing was built or rebuilt in the late 1940s and '50s. Everything. Eighty-seven percent of Warsaw was destroyed during the war. He showed us before-the-war pictures and then pictures taken after the destruction. We couldn't believe it. There was so much rubble we couldn't see a blade of grass. There were no trees and no buildings, and the roads were covered with fallen brick. Our question, of course, was who did this and why. It was, of course, the

Nazis. They completely demolished the whole city—not by bombing, but with dynamite. They felt that if they destroyed the Polish culture and heritage, by the second generation everyone would only have a German heritage. Pretty sick. I am still amazed. Who in their right mind would follow perverted people like these?

Leaving the ghetto we headed back to the "street of the aristocrats" and followed that into the Old City. The Old City was within the fortress walls, and the New City was outside the walls. Again, our guide brought out pictures of Warsaw after the war, and again, it was just rubble. When I say rubble, I mean there was nothing standing. There were three- and four-story buildings before, and nothing but a pile of brick as far as the eye could see after the war ended.

So how was it that we now saw magnificent ornate Seventeenth and Eighteenth Century buildings standing? What about the ancient monuments in the square? They were all built in the 1940s and '50s. After the war, Warsaw decided to rebuild the city exactly the way it was so the Nazis wouldn't succeed in wiping out the Polish heritage. They used pictures painted by the artists in residence during the Renaissance by order of the kings. The builders used these detailed paintings and old plans to rebuild. They matched paint colors and all the exterior details. The results were remarkable. They didn't do the whole city, of course, but they did rebuild most of the New City and Old City. They also rebuilt the fortress walls and gates. We found ourselves walking through Eighteenth Century Warsaw. I would never have guessed that just sixty years ago this was a wasteland.

The last part of the tour was the Royal Palace. What a spectacular place! Although this Palace is much smaller than Versailles, the interiors were every bit as magnificent. It was made all the more amazing when we heard that it, too, was in rubble and was rebuilt in 2000. Using old plans, the king's paintings, and pieces salvaged by the staff during the war, they managed to recreate this marvelous place.

Poland was always a free and tolerant country. That was the reason so many Jews migrated to Poland. The Poles were very resilient and strong to have gone through so many devastating struggles. Before the war, one could find every nationality and group in Poland. After the war, there were only Poles. I think that bothered our guide. I don't think he would be inviting the Germans to come back soon. For the rest of the world, WWII ended in 1945. In Poland it ended in 1989, when they finally got their freedom from the Communists.

DAY EIGHT

Today we are leaving Warsaw and concluding the central Europe part of our trip. We were very excited to be heading to Russia. Maybe it was because Leanne and I were born in the fifties during the time of the Cold War. Going to Russia during our youth was unthinkable. We didn't know what to expect, but we knew it was going to be an adventure.

We left the old town of Warsaw in the morning and had the opportunity for the first time to see the more modern sections of the city. As I said before, the whole city was razed during the war, so what we were going to see while leaving was built after the war. Heading to the airport, we found a mix of crumbling gray buildings interspersed with modern high-rises and new shopping malls. Warsaw still had a long way to go to become a world-class business destination. It was a very historic and charming town in the Old City, and I would recommend it to travelers.

It was a short flight to our first Russian destination, Saint Petersburg. When we landed we were greeted at the gate for our VIP arrival. Our airport host saw to it that we didn't have to wait in lines. When we reached baggage he surprised us by going behind the baggage carousel, finding our bags, and making sure they were the first ones off, just like VIP dignitaries.

Outside, only minutes after we landed, we were in our car with our driver and guide, headed for the hotel. After a quick change we were ready to get started. Our tour this day was starting at four and ending at eight. No worries—sunset wasn't until after eleven.

Leanne and I were almost giddy to get started. Being seasoned travelers and having seen so much, we still felt it was like our first time visiting Paris. I think we drove the guide crazy with questions.

What about the food lines? What about the czar? What about Lenin? What about Stalin? What about …? We just couldn't get enough. Poor Chelsea—I think she thought we were crazy. In a few short moments we were getting a history lesson of Saint Petersburg going back to 1703.

Our first stop before it closed was the Peter and Paul Fortress and Cathedral. The fortress was the first built in Saint Petersburg by Peter the Great to defend the area and drive out the Swedes. The fortress now encircles the cathedral. This was where the czars were all buried, starting from Peter the Great, as were their wives and most of their children. Also buried here is Catharine the Great. It looked to us that being czar was a very dangerous occupation. Most of them were murdered, either by rivals or, in the case of one czar, by his wife. I mentioned that some of the children were buried here. The czars must have also had bad genes, because most of the czars' children died at very young ages, or the czars were not able to have children at all.

The cathedral was very bright inside and very ornate, like most churches of Eighteenth Century Europe. Peter the Great was well traveled and loved Western architecture. With large windows letting in light and a brightly painted ceiling, the cathedral seemed much bigger than it was. The cathedral also housed the bodies of the last czar, Nicholas II, his family, and all of his servants, all of whom were slaughtered. He was, as you may recall, murdered with his family and servants during the 1917 Russian revolution. It is a very sad story. It was only after the fall of communism that the KGB told the world where the bodies were buried. All but two of the children were buried here. Alexei and one of his sisters, Anastasia, I believe, were only recently found.

The rest of what was remaining of the day was spent driving through the city to get an overview of what we would be seeing in the coming days. This city was a jewel and just stunning in beauty and architecture. Everywhere we looked was a treat. Leanne calls this city "eye candy." We stopped briefly for pictures at the river, just to gaze at the palaces lining the banks. If the Communists were here, we couldn't tell, now. It seems they did do the right thing and kept many of these buildings restored and in good shape.

In the car again, we traveled down the main street, which housed the best shops of Europe. Our guide pointed out a very interesting and rather large Eighteenth Century building that was the main department store. There, in 2009, you could get most anything you wanted. It was open during Communist times, but our guide pointed that although the store still existed, during those times it had very little to sell. We noticed one more thing. It was extremely crowded. Both the sidewalks and the roads were full with either traffic or shoppers. Traffic was a nightmare here. If it rolled it was on the road; everything from 1950s Communist-era cars to large SUV limos.

We feared that this once again would be a gastronomical disaster. Chelsea would only have French fries for dinner. I had beef stroganoff; what could they do wrong to that? It had very little meat and lots of my favorites: mushrooms—yuck! Leanne had a rack of lamb that had a funny taste and was tough as nails. We still wouldn't stoop so low as to go to McDonald's or Pizza Hut. Oh, well, the bread was great!

It was picture perfect today and we just couldn't wait to get started and see the treasures of Russia.

DAY NINE

On our second full day in Saint Petersburg, we set out for an eight-hour walking tour of the city. Ouch! Our first stop was the house of the hermit. You may know it by its Russian name, Hermitage. It is one of the most famous museums in the world. The treasures housed in the Hermitage were collected by Catherine the Great and kept hidden behind these walls for her alone to enjoy—thus, the house of the hermit. She was very selfish and felt, at the time, that all the artwork was only for her enjoyment and was to be shared only with the mice!

Entering the Hermitage, we were actually entering the Winter Palace of Catherine. Our guide had everything planned out perfectly. We arrived at an appointed time and were in the great palace within minutes, enjoying the grand staircase. As one would expect, the rooms were very ornate and covered in gold, marble, and precious stones.

Famous paintings graced the walls, and precious objects lined the floors. We were surprised that so much still existed after the Soviets came to power. It seems they sold more paintings than artifacts and furnishings. If it was made of gold they kept it. We were also surprised that they took care to restore the palace and museums. We in America thought they only made arms and munitions.

After a half hour of touring, we headed to the basement, which our guide had set up a permission to enter—and visitors definitely need an advance reservation. No large groups need apply. The treasures in this room rivaled those found in the tombs in Egypt. The gold objects in the first section were from the first millennium BC and had been found in burial sites in Siberia. It seems the Russian nomads buried their dead with gold treasures as well. The intricacies of the designs were spectacular. It would be difficult doing these designs today. As we walked through this large gallery there were more and more gold treasures, some dug up at burial sites, some given as gifts to the Czars, and some just found buried. We were the only ones in this gallery, and we had a special Russian guide for this section. Our regular guide translated the stories of each piece. The collection of gold dates from 1000 BC to gifts presented to nineteenth-century czars. All of this was hidden from view in the basement of the Hermitage.

We resumed our tour back upstairs in the galleries. It would be hard to describe it all. Catherine, as well as most of the royalty of Russia, loved European art and were an avid collector. Their palaces were also designed in the style of the western European arts and architecture. At the Hermitage there were old masters as well as modern impressionists. The impressionists were added by the Soviets when they "nationalized" the palaces of the aristocrats (another way of saying *confiscated*).

After two and a half hours we left the Hermitage and were ready for lunch. We dropped into a Russian café close to our next stop, the Church of the Savior on Spilled Blood. This little café was famous for their pies: meat pies, fruit pies, and vegetable pies. Of course, that's what we ordered—salmon pie and strawberry pie. To us it tasted like Jewish challah bread stuffed with salmon, and the other with strawberries. It was at this moment that I realized that the many Jews were eastern Europeans and Russians—where else would this stuff come from? We are all one big, interrelated family.

Now, on we went to the Church of the Savior on Spilled Blood. This was probably the only building in Saint Petersburg that was of Russian architecture. This was really a memorial for Czar Alexander II, who was mortally wounded on this very spot. The place he fell on in the street was enclosed and preserved in this church—cobblestone street and all. They even narrowed the canal next to the church to fit the building over it. The outside and the inside were remarkable. The outside was what I had imagined Russian architecture to look like: many large, brightly colored enameled cupolas jutting from a granite and marble structure. The interior was decorated with precious stones, marble, and acres of mosaics. They were everywhere—on the floors, ceilings, and walls. There was not an empty space that was not decorated. The mosaics took one year for every nine square feet completed.

We left the church and started our stroll down the fashion street of Saint Petersburg. Again, this fashionable street got its design from western Europe. Large boulevards and fashionable Nineteenth Century shops lined the sides. This was where the excitement of the day happened. A gang of pickpockets tried to steal my wallet. I was walking with Chelsea when five or six guys started to push us around. Chelsea got pushed to the side and I was bumped several times. As I reached behind I hit the hand that was on my wallet. I jumped off the curb and turned to the group, who were now just acting innocent. I grabbed Chelsea and had a story to tell. I won; they lost. Be careful here in crowds. They had waited for me to stop at a crosswalk light.

Continuing our walk, our guide pointed out a few interesting buildings, such as the poet Alexander Pushkin's home and a sign left over from WWII advising the citizens to walk on the opposite side of the street. The southern side of the street was a safer place since the Nazis were bombing the northern part of the city. We also passed a Russian battleship from the beginning of the twentieth century. The gun on this ship was fired in 1917, and that sound was the signal that started the Russian revolution.

Our last church was the Saint Isaac's Cathedral. This was your typical European church. It had lots of paintings and lots of gold. It was massive. The front and back were lined with forty granite columns that must've been fifty feet tall. Inside the church they had a mock-up of how they were able to stand such large pieces of granite on end to build the church. They also had a model of framing showing how the very large dome was made. All of this was very interesting.

At the end of the day we decided we should take in a little Russian theater and culture. We booked seats for "Feel Yourself Russian," a folk dance and folk music show. To Leanne and me the most interesting part was in the audience. Here we were, three Americans watching a Russian show in the ex–Soviet Union, and in walked a group from Iran. For two hours, Americans, Russians, Iranians, and many other groups from other countries enjoyed a show together. We were all smiling, clapping, and laughing together. None of us seemed much different. Too bad governments couldn't be run by the people.

We left the theater at nine thirty with the sun still shining and walked back to the hotel, my wallet still in my back pocket.

DAY TEN

I couldn't think of anywhere in the world where there were more ornate and spectacular palaces and cathedrals than Saint Petersburg. I had to hand it to the Communists. They couldn't feed their people, but they had managed to meticulously restore these special places. It was all the more amazing since they didn't believe or support religion or the aristocracy. Between fires and the Nazis many of the treasures and buildings we have gone through had been either destroyed or stripped of their valuables. The Communists in the early days of the Soviet Union also abused these monuments. Later in the century the Communists saw these as Russian treasures and converted many palaces and cathedrals into museums. The Church of the Savior on Spilled Blood, which I wrote about earlier, was almost demolished three times in its recent history. It almost happened twice by the Communists, who believed it didn't fit the European architecture of Saint Petersburg.

Today we headed out of Saint Petersburg into the countryside. The countryside was very beautiful and full of green fields and plenty of forests. We left through the civic center, or town, and traveled through the industrial area. This was not like the States. It had wide-open spaces, and fields separated factories and warehouses. Our destination was Catherine Palace. This was the summer palace of Catherine I, the second wife of Peter the Great, who founded Saint Petersburg. She was not the famous Catherine the Great. This was just one of nine palaces the czars had in that countryside.

I thought the Hermitage was over the top. The summer palace even outdid the famous Hermitage in grandeur. This was the palace that housed the famous Amber Room. Walking into this room we were engulfed in a golden amber glow. This room was very different from the European style of the rest of the palace. The Amber Room was made up of thousands of carved amber pieces put together in a mosaic. The walls were covered completely in amber. Even the frames on the walls were made of carved amber and jewels. What wasn't covered in amber was covered in gold—not an inch of paint or stucco anywhere. This room existed in the time of Catharine the Great. The Nazis actually stripped the walls of the Amber Room and hauled it away. Unfortunately, the Nazis hid the sheets of amber, and they have never been found. Craftsmen worked from 1979 to 2003, rebuilding this room from photographs that had been saved. They did a remarkable job recreating the room—truly spectacular.

The rest of the rooms in the palace were very impressive as well. There was a hall of golden rooms that just took my breath away. Over 220 pounds of gold was used on the exterior walls and statues. They had to have used at least that much inside. Although the Nazis never marched into Saint Petersburg, they did have control of the countryside and this palace. Unfortunately, the Nazis totally stripped this place down to the bricks and then set it ablaze when they left. What a shame! The Soviets again did a fantastic job restoring it to its original glory. We saw pictures of the gleaming Hall of Gold, which was stripped down to a bunch of brick doorways after the war. Much credit must also be given to the servants, staff, and army that protected the castle. Before it was captured by the Nazis they did manage to get many art objects and furnishings out of the palace into safe hiding places throughout Russia. Imagine our capitol sacked and burned to the ground and our White House stripped and set ablaze. Well, I guess it was, back in 1812. Oh, well. We have never seen the destruction that these countries have. Our country is very lucky not to have had such destruction and pillage on our soil.

As we left the palace we walked out to Catherine's garden. At home we wouldn't call this a garden. This was a park—acres and acres of grounds meticulously manicured. In the center was a very large lake for boating, surrounded by pavilions, bathhouses, and boathouses. Marble bridges crossed streams as we strolled the perimeter of the lake. There was even a gallery building, which had to be forty thousand square feet, overlooking the lake. It was complete with a veranda where Catherine I and Catherine the Great could stroll if it should rain. These women were extravagant, tough, and stingy with their possessions.

Our second stop for the day was the Russian Museum back in the city. The Russian Museum was a duke's palace that was converted to a museum in late 1792. These days it was used exclusively to showcase the art of Russian artists and foreign artists who worked in and lived in Russia. Each room was opulent and full of Russian art and sculpture. These works of art were like the great masters of Europe. We went from the paintings of the religious period of the icons that adorned the churches starting in the ninth century, to the nineteenth-century landscape painters painting in the classic style. Some of these paintings were huge, taking up entire walls of a very large palace. Our guide was very knowledgeable in Russian art and was able to explain key pieces to us, which made the visit that much more enjoyable. We could see the rich history here. As I mentioned, most of the art was done in the European style. It seemed less unusual when we found out that the Russian czars had very little Russian blood. Like in most of Europe, marriages were mostly arranged with nobles from other countries. Many were more German than Russian. I found that kind of ironic. They were more German than Hitler, who was born in Austria.

At the end of our day we took another shot at Russian cuisine. Our guide brought us to a great Ukrainian restaurant. It was decorated with family possessions from the Ukraine, and the interior was like a country cottage. Not only was this place darling, but the food was good as well. Some of it we actually recognized. I had the chicken Kiev. It really is Ukrainian.

It was a Friday night and the weather was wonderful. We decided to walk to the riverbank and have a drink at the *Flying Dutchman*, an eighteenth-century boat docked on the river. As we passed plazas we could see young Russians dancing in the streets and having fun. As we were sitting on the deck of the *Flying Dutchman*, boats passed with still more people dancing on their decks. Readying to leave, a large Russian red yacht approached and docked on the deck where we were sitting. A very rich Russian stepped off, surrounded by security. This was the new Russia.

We had one more stop tomorrow at yet another palace before we flew to Moscow. Saint Petersburg was all we had hoped for. There was so much here it would be hard to describe it all. This place was a combination of Paris, Venice, London, and Amsterdam, with a little bit of Egypt thrown in for good measure. Say what you will about the Communists, but their care and restoration of these Russian treasures should be applauded.

DAY ELEVEN

Our day today was a trip to Peterhof to visit yet another palace. We were up to four, now, and we hadn't scratched the surface. There were one hundred palaces open as museums here. If we did four each trip, we would be done in twenty years. Peterhof Palace was famous for its fountains. I don't know what these czars could have possibly done to create something more impressive then the summer palace.

The drive to Peterhof is a boring one-hour trip though industrial areas, so our tour operator sent us there the same way Peter the Great arrived. We went by boat. We actually took a hydrofoil. We guessed it was a little faster than Peter's boat in 1710. Leaving the dock by the

Winter Palace, we traveled down the Neva River until it opened to the Baltic Sea. We took a right turn toward the Gulf of Finland and soon found ourselves at Peterhof in a picturesque thirty minutes.

After debarking from the hydrofoil we walked alongside the canal that flowed from the palace gardens. In Peter's day he would have sailed up the canal and stepped off into the garden. Our walk ended at the cascading fountain. I wouldn't call this a mere fountain. It cascades with water from three stories up into a pool that shoots water high in the air. Everywhere we looked there was water shooting up, sideways, down, and any other way you can imagine. The fountain was made up of gleaming gold statuary that spouts water from every conceivable orifice: gold lions, gold turtles—everywhere was gold, gold, gold. The structure of the fountain was granite and marble, again dressed in more gold. This was pure Las Vegas. This was the main fountain, but it was only one of 165 on the property that were still working today.

Our tour company always had a special treat for us, and this stop was no exception. While scores of people toured the outside of the garden, we had a special tour of the grotto behind the fountains and the inner workings of the fountains. All of the fountains on these hundreds of manicured acres were fed by gravity through a labyrinth of pipes. In Peter's time they were made of wood. Today they were steel. There was a small display case above the grotto that showed the uniforms the fountain staff wore to maintain the system. Over fifty men in uniform were in charge of seeing that the fountains on the grounds operated properly through the day. We walked the grounds for over an hour and could not have possibly seen it all. Maybe we saw twenty of the 165. The grounds and garden themselves were immaculately groomed; not a bush was overgrown. It even looked like the trees making up the forest were placed and maintained in a perfect manner.

It was now time to enter the palace. Surely all the energy was spent outside. Nothing could be further from the truth. This palace was a bit smaller than Catharine's palace, but it made up for that discrepancy in incredible detail. Here there were rooms in different periods. Each czar left his special touch. There was Peter's oak study, one of the first rooms of the house and still original. Hand-carved, intricate oak panels lined every wall. Catharine Palace had the Amber Room; Peter's had the Oriental Room. Hand-painted silk and Chinese period furnishings and floors dazzled us. There were many gifts that had been given to Peter from the Chinese emperor. I am not a Chinese décor fan, but this won me over.

Catherine I and Peter added the Baroque Room, with its shining gold, massive chandeliers and mirrors. It was similar to the summer palace, but on a slightly smaller scale. Catherine the Great added the Classical Room. Each palace we visited was our favorite. Now this was our favorite and shouldn't be missed.

Our time was up in Saint Petersburg, and we must now go. Our trip this afternoon was taking us to Moscow. We would be flying on our first Russian-made plane. It was an A Tupolrv TU154 (ever heard of it?). This plane was first built in 1960 and was now out of production. This was one old plane. Inside it still looked like something from the 1960 dawn of the jet age. Everything about it was 1960s, even the flight crew and service—lots of beautiful, young, long-legged Russian blondes. These women weren't close to being born when this plane was made. More likely their grandmothers were flight attendants on this plane. When it was time to listen to the flight safety talk I didn't take my eyes off of them for a minute. I hung on every word. They looked like the old Pan Am stewardesses, white gloves and all.

The terminal was a hoot. They dropped us about three hundred yards away and we walked up with our bags. The terminal was small and only flew domestic to Moscow. We couldn't check our bags until a designated time, so passengers who arrived early had to sit and wait with their bags. When it was time to go to the gate—yes, there was only one—they came with a bus to pick up the twenty economy-class people flying. They told us to wait. Sure enough, another bus arrived to take the four business class passengers to the very same plane. The same thing happened when we arrived. It didn't seem very efficient!

Once we were in the air it was time for our meal service. With starched white gloves and form-fitting uniforms, the flight attendants served us a full meal and drinks with linens and china. Mind you, this was a one-hour flight. Flying in a 1960s metal cigar tube with two beautiful Russian blondes was totally worth the risk. I was not the only one who said so. Leanne was constantly talking about how many tall, skinny, long-legged, blue-eyed blondes there were here. Chelsea just rolled her eyes at me.

The flight was very smooth, and we arrived early in Moscow. We landed at the domestic airport, and I must say, it was even older than the plane we were on. The skycaps were not blond, and they were not beautiful.

Our car and driver whisked us away to downtown Moscow. The drive coming in was like driving down Queens Boulevard in Forest Hills, New York—lots of apartment buildings, some old buildings, some new. The new had some great designs. We arrived in the downtown area, where we are staying at the Ritz Carlton. You can't beat the Ritz—especially a Ritz that was built less than a year ago. (Liz would definitely love this one!) This hotel was just a block from Red Square. This was the same hotel where President Obama stayed when he met with Putin just a month ago. Moscow is a big city of eleven million people, and we would be ready to attack it in the morning.

DAY TWELVE

Today was the day we had been waiting for. Two kids brought up during the cold war were going to enter the Kremlin. What we expected was a large, Soviet-style building veiled in secrecy. What we found was much, much different. It turned out that the Kremlin isn't a building at all. *Kremlin* means *fort*. The Kremlin was the original Moscow fort from the fourteenth century. It covered seventy-two acres surrounded by a large wall and two rivers and was the residence of the founding czar. It also included churches, an armory, and many other buildings to support the ancient military and service the czar. During Soviet times they did build a new assembly hall for the Communist party. During the time of the czars, the Kremlin also housed a museum.

Now that the Communist party is gone the Kremlin has been transformed back to the presidential residence and armory museum.

The name "armory museum" is even misleading. The museum housed not only medieval armor, but also the coaches of the czars, clothes, costumes, and wonderful artifacts. The armory rivaled anything one could possibly see at the Smithsonian or the royal museums in London. One could even say it was a combination of the two.

The section with the royal coaches was just mind-blowing. I have seen movie set coaches and English coaches. I had never seen anything as wonderful as these. The hall of costumes was another area that was magnificent to see. But the place to be is the Diamond Room. This separate area behind tight security housed the Russian jewel collection and several display cases that held buckets of diamonds. I mean *buckets*. We are not talking small stones here. If you have seen the Crown Jewels in London you have seen the Macy's collection. Here we have the Tiffany's collection. The Communists even sold some to raise hard cash. It's hard to imagine the collection could have been larger. This was a rich country. Siberia seemed to hold most of its riches. Diamond, gold, and silver mines, tons of oil, and many gorgeous semiprecious stones were there.

The museum housed so many treasures that it would be hard to describe or even mention them all. Here there were porcelain, clocks, furs, furniture, and artifacts going back centuries. All of it was in exquisite condition. The Kremlin Armory houses the greatest collection of British royal silver in the world as well. It seemed Cromwell melted down Britain's royal silver to make coins. The Russians saved theirs. It seemed they saved everything. They had displays of magnificent treasures that had been given to the czars from foreign countries over the years. Each country's gifts were displayed separately. The czars and even the Communists were big on culture and museums. We could have stayed the day here, but like this travelogue, we must move on.

Our next stop is Red Square. I always thought it referred to the Communists—or maybe it meant spilled blood. It doesn't. The Russians say *red* for *beautiful*. And that it was. The square had a large department store on one side, the wall of the Kremlin on another, the Natural History Museum building on a third side, and, of course, the famous Saint Basil's Cathedral at the end.

Saint Basil's is one of the most famous and recognizable cathedrals in the world with its nine colorful cupolas. When the average person thinks of Russia, this is the image he or she conjures up. I must have taken one hundred pictures. I couldn't get enough of it. It was so Russian and so unique. Ivan the Terrible was so taken by the beauty of Saint Basil's that he asked the engineers and architects if they could build another as beautiful as it. When they answered yes, the czar promptly had them blinded to protect this treasured cathedral. Czars will be Czars.

The other buildings in the square were also breathtakingly beautiful. The Natural History Museum next to the gates, with its red brick façade and silver steeple roofs, looked to have perpetual snow on it. I must have taken at least fifty shots of this one. The department store on the right was also a sight to behold—amazing architecture. During Soviet days there wasn't much to buy there. Today one would find the finest displays and designer fashion from around the world.

This wasn't the vision I had of Russia when I came here. Where were the Soviet-style gray utilitarian buildings? The gray days? Where were the people who were depressed and in despair in the street? Russia had problems, but most of that was American propaganda. Moscow, even during the Communist rule, had a tremendous amount of resources, vast forests, great architecture, and a preserved ancient heritage. It's a shame that the Communists deprived their citizens and the world of this treasure.

We ended our city walk going through Saint Basil's, which was very different from most of the cathedrals we have seen. We also made a stop at the medieval birth home of the first Romanoff czar, Michael. Michael's parents were nobles. Czar Michael's grandson wanted to promote the family name back in the eighteenth century, so he bought all the Romanoffs' ancestral homes and turned them into museums. The one we visited today had just been restored and opened.

These were not the palaces of Catherine. They were well appointed, and for medieval times, were very well decorated and impressive. We found them small, hot, and claustrophobic. I think winter would be a good time to be in these homes—summer, not so much. The history of the time is fascinating. The rules they lived by are bizarre by our standards. Although they were Russian Orthodox, we found the customs to have Muslim traditions and roots.

We ended the day with a little culture, Troy style. No, we didn't go to the Bolshoi or the opera. We went to the Moscow Circus. What fun! We found it to be much different from ours. The Moscow Circus was a little Las Vegas showgirl, a little Cirque du Soleil, and a little bit Barnum and Bailey. Put them all together in a very intimate setting with laser beams and a big tank of water with fountains, and you have the Moscow Circus. This is worth seeing if it comes to the States.

We tried to get the political feelings here. What we found was that the Russians were not very political. The Russians we asked said that was always up to the government. Since news was blacked out, they had nothing to talk about. Even during the Cold War, they told us, the citizens were fond of the people of the United States. I believe them. Before the Communists the Russian people loved everything Western. After the fall of communism, they didn't take long to embrace it again.

One item we found curious was that there were stories that were believed here that Osama bin Laden is made up, created by the CIA. People have written about it so some believe it to be true. It is interesting to see how propaganda works. Another item we found interesting was the way different people look at history. The Polish people told us many times to be very afraid to go to Russia. They believed it was very unsafe there. They kept reminding us that the Russians invaded Poland just two weeks after the Germans left during WWII. The Russians we saw seemed to be delightful and we felt very safe. Their story was they went to Poland to fight the German invasion of Poland, not to attack Poland. Someplace between these different perspectives was the truth.

DAY THIRTEEN

This was the second-to-last day of our trip. Today we were seeing the surrounding city to get a true feel of living in Moscow—sort of. Our first stop was the sculpture park, or, as it's been called since 1991, the

Park of Fallen Idols. Here were many of the old Soviet-era statues and monuments that were torn down from around the city after the fall of the Soviet regime. Many were broken and had to be restored. (I told you they saved everything here.) There were a number of statues of Stalin, Brezhnev, Lenin, and others. If you want a picture of the hammer and sickle, this is where you have to go as well.

This definitely was a catchall day. After the Park of Fallen Idols, we headed to a cemetery. This cemetery was similar to LA's Forest Lawn. Many famous people were buried here: actors, poets, composers, soldiers, and Russian leaders. Brezhnev, Yeltsin, and Khrushchev were all buried here. This cemetery was very entertaining. Most of the headstones included either carved likenesses or statues of the residents, all in poses that reflected their lives. For instance, a businessman may be seen talking on a telephone, a composer writing music, or a ballet dancer doing a pirouette. There was even a clown who eventually became the director of the Moscow Circus. It was surprisingly fun to look at. Brezhnev, Boris Yeltsin, and Khrushchev didn't have such statues. Hmm, I wonder what that may mean.

Our next stop was the last remaining working monastery in Moscow. It was built in the fourteenth century and was famous for being the place where Peter the Great sent his first wife. Apparently since he did not like his wife and the Russian Orthodox Church forbade divorce, the only solution was to ban her to this monastery. Sending her to a monastery was thought of the same as sending her to another world. Having done that, he was approved by the church to then marry his true love, Catherine. Look, he could have beheaded her like good old Henry VIII. Peter also sent his sister there for plotting to overthrow him. So much for monastery history.

The next stop was, yet again, a cathedral. While walking up to get a picture, guess what happened? We ran into the Iranian group from the folk show in Saint Petersburg. They recognized us, and we them, so we got a few pictures together. I don't think they knew America and Iran didn't like each other. We need to figure out how to get rid of governments.

Our last stop for the day was by far the most fun and interesting.

We had seen the pictures on the Internet and never believed them, but they were true. We spent the afternoon riding the subway of Moscow, getting off and photographing all the stops. I think we got off at some ten different stations. Each was spectacular, and each had its own theme. One station had bronze sculptures, barreled ceilings, and bronze and crystal chandeliers; the next had stained glass panels lit from behind. All of this was 1,200 feet underground.

It didn't stop there. Some stations had mosaic ceilings, some mosaic walls, and some hand-carved plaster. All were decorated with marble, granite, and elaborate chandeliers. We are not talking in one area; we are talking the full length of the platforms and entryways. Every thirty feet or so we would see chandeliers, wall sconces, bronze statues, stained glass, or mosaics—all created by famous artists. It was a sight to see.

You could also eat off the floor. It was amazing—there was not a paper wrapper anywhere, nor a mark on the walls. The tracks looked like they had just been installed. Even the trains, no matter how old, were spic and span. What was even more amazing was there wasn't a trash can to be found. Leanne had two water bottles to throw out, and we couldn't find a trash can. Apparently what you brought in with you had to be brought out by you. I looked up at the chandeliers and sconces and didn't see a speck of dust anywhere. The walls, if they were not decorated with granite, marble, or wall carvings, were painted in fresh bright colors. Whether we were at a station opened in 1938 or one opened in 2008, they were magnificent.

As an American I was embarrassed with how our citizens act and treat our public projects. Even the new stations just opened last year were decorated in a modern motif of granite and marble with grand chandelier lighting. The subway was built by Stalin. He had two reasons for the massive maze of deep tunnels, and he also had a reason to make it so grand. First, he felt the ordinary people should have "grand palaces" of their own. The true reason might have been a bit different. Stalin knew that war with Hitler was inevitable. He built many more tunnels than he would have needed just for the trains. These tunnels were to be used as bomb shelters during the war and to provide ways of moving troops and tanks underground. Only 20 percent or so of these tunnels were actually used for public transit.

The grandness of the stations was a little smoke and mirrors, you may say, to prepare for war without letting the public know. The effect worked. If I showed you pictures of the stations you would think they were of one of the noble palaces.

I lied. We had two more stops, both off the metro. One was lunch in a Russian restaurant, which was actually one of the oldest dining rooms in Russia. This restaurant was built in a monastery in the 1600s and was recently discovered buried behind offices. It had since been restored to its original look and purpose: a restaurant. It was like eating in a cathedral. It had lower ceilings but the same fresco painting.

The last stop was a very fashionable pedestrian street that was still being restored to its Nineteenth Century grandeur. Here we found street artists like in Montmartre in Paris. It had a similar feel to the pedestrian mall in Santa Monica. We would have to come back when it was finished. The next day we would visit Lenin's tomb, and then we were heading home. I shall only bother you with my ramblings one more time. All of Russia had been an amazing adventure. We so enjoyed seeing its rich history and people.

DAY FOURTEEN

This is the last of my travel logs.
We went to see Lenin's tomb today.
He is still there, preserved in argon gas.
He looks good, still dead—just like communism in Russia.
Dasvidaniya!
Good-bye from Russia with love!

St Basils, Moscow Russia

St. Basils at night, Moscow Russia

Red Square, Moscow Russia

Peterhof Palace, St. Petersburg, Russia

Hermitage Museum, St Petersburg, Russia

Old Soviet monument and sign grave yard, Moscow, Russia

Subway station, Moscow Russia

Subway station, Moscow Russia

Subway station, Moscow Russia

Church on the Savior on Blood, St Petersburg, Russia

Auschwitz Concentration Camp, Krakow Poland

Floating in our balloon high over Prague, Czech Republic

Shindlers Factory, Warsaw Poland

Colorful Row Houses, Warsaw, Poland

PARIS; THE ONE AND ONLY

DAY ONE

It was the best of times, it was the worst of times, no this is not a dickens novel. It's how I describe an American coming to the most fabulous city in the world with the American greenback. We arrived in Paris the afternoon of May 5. The weather couldn't have been more perfect. Spring is the start of the high season for Paris and if you skip April and come in May, you are almost certain for the best weather.

We were in Paris to meet up with our close friends the Eshkar's who have been traveling through Italy while we made our trek around Morocco. The four of us hit the ground running. Checking into our two bedroom suite at the hotel we hardly had enough time to unpack and change for our dinner reservations at Jules Verne which is on the second level in the Eiffel Tower.

Jules Verne is one of the most famous and sought after reservations in Paris. Taking a private elevator mid way up the tower we were lead to our table right on the window with a spectacular daylight view of the city and the river Seine. Three and a half hours later the sun was down and so were our wallets. The bill in Euros was not too bad, but converting it into devalued dollars our bill was 40% higher coming in at a staggering $1,150.00 for four people. That's with having only one bottle of the cheapest wine on the menu. (This is the worst of times.)

The best of times was walking down the private stairs of Jules Verne to the mid deck of the tower with the lit city of Paris at our feet. The tower began twinkling in the night sky as the clock struck the hour. We thought about taking the final elevator to the top only to be pushed back by the line of people waiting in the queue which circled the total circumference of the deck only to end in a Disneyesque maze. We decided it was best that we escape to the comfort of Jules Verne for our ride down, leaving the trip to the top for another day.

The next morning was reserved for our city tour. Our guide for the next couple of days was a wonderfully knowledgeable Parisian woman named Eliana. Right on time with our driver, we set out to revisit the city. Our hotel, the Raphael, is located just off the Champs Élysées next to the arc d' Triumph. Pulling out of the driveway we found ourselves right in the middle of the Triumph circle roundabout during Friday morning rush hour. Here, if you are not aggressive, you could find yourself circling the monument mindlessly until lunch time. Our driver luckily was very adept at playing chicken. It's the only square in Paris where if you have an accident responsibility is shared 50/50. For that reason most Parisians opt for the slower outer circle with its multiple stop lights.

Our first stop was a plaza some distance from the tower. If you don't already know the city of Paris, it is designed much like the city of Washington DC. Or, should I say, Washington DC is designed after Paris. It has long wide boulevards spiking out in all directions from central roundabouts. Imagine standing on the steps of the Lincoln memorial with Dr Martin Luther King Jr as he gave his "I Have A Dream" speech and looking out at the Washington monument with the capitol dome in the background. This is the view we had only with the Eiffel Tower in the center and the dome of the Parisian military academy on the opposite end. Take out the Washington mall reflecting pools, add park like grass and you are now in Paris. We were standing at one of the many pavilions created along with the tower for the 1889 Paris world exhibition.

Let me give you a few interesting facts about the Eifel Tower. First, did you know when it was built it was painted orange? Yep, it started out orange, and then yellow before someone had the idea for the more pleasing bronze we see today. Second, did you know it was only supposed to stay up for ten years after the Paris world's fair? The towers demise was prevented by the army who argued that it was a perfect place to put another new tower of the day, the Marconi wireless tower. Thirdly and my favorite, did you know it was the catalyst for the creation of the Ferris Wheel? After the Paris exposition the long winded politicians of Chicago (get it, Windy City) wanted to top Paris. Not wanting to just create a "me too" tower, they had a competition where they chose George Ferris' wheel as the winning entry. Rising to 264ft with each car holding 60 people for a maximum capacity of 2,100 riders it created the uniqueness of this marvelous feat of engineering before us.

Paris is undoubtedly the most beautiful city in the world. Designed by Napoleon III, the famous general's nephew, it was inspired by the streets of London. What's so spellbinding about Paris, is it is pretty much unchanged from the 19th century. Height and design restrictions keep Paris looking much like when Napoleon walked the streets, with its distinctive French style architecture (maximum five or six story height limit) and wide boulevards. If Napoleon returned today I think he would easily recognize his beloved Paris. Should George Washington return to New York he would be hopelessly lost.

Every street we traveled was a picture postcard. Beautiful French facades accented with Paris' famous icon, the Eiffel Tower ~majestic in the background. Our tour took us to 6pm and we didn't scratch the surface, yet tomorrow is another day. Still today we need to rush back to make our dinner and show reservations for the evening.

Like all of the Troy trips this one too is timed in military precision. Our dinner reservations were at the fashionable restaurant L'Avenue just two blocks from Avenue George V. With only 15 minutes to run up and change our clothes for dinner we made arrangements that our car and driver wait to save time. It was important not to be late so we could make our first of two famous Parisian shows. Tonight we were going to the Crazy Horse, a landmark since 1951. It is known for its beautiful matching dancers, each dressed only in colored light. Each woman is the same height with the same body type. They performed in unison sensual routines bathed in the creativity of light. If you have never been to the show I recommend it, it's very tastefully done. In a way it represents Paris. All the buildings the same height like the girls, the same classical style and form all bathed in the colorful lights of Paris. Maybe this is why they call Paris "the city of lights." The night ended shortly before midnight with a stroll down the famous Champs Élysées.

The next morning we were up and out early again. Today we were going to brave it to the top of the tower. Our tour operator had wisely made a reservation for the four of us at 9:30 am but that wasn't a guarantee that we could make it to the top without a wait. Our guide Eilena warned us that fighting the crowds to the top of the tower could take possibly 3 hours. Our reservation would only get us as far as the 2nd floor, the same observation deck of Jules Verne. After that we fought the crowd like everyone else. To our surprise when we reached the second deck the queue to the top was empty. Due to great planning by our guides we made it to the top of the tower in just under 30 minutes. I have to say, there's nothing like seeing Paris from 980 feet. So if you are visiting Paris and want to go to the top, get a reservation before 9:30am and keep moving until you reach the summit. You can't walk down from the top of the tower anymore, but you can from the 2nd or 1st decks. I will leave it to you to guess which we walked down?

Our next stop was the Louvre, undeniably the most famous museum in the world. We have been to the Louvre 3 times over the last 40 years so there is always a need for a brush up visit. For our friends the Eshkar's this will be a first. Eilena, our guide, as usual is incredible. There isn't a piece of art that she didn't know the history or providence. Even so, we just had to do the most important classics such as the Mona Lisa, the Winged Atlas, and the Venus d' Milo, and many others.

We all agreed one of the most interesting parts of the tour was a section they opened in 1993 which shed the history of the actual building the Louvre is housed in. Judging by the crowds most visitors miss it. The Louvre wasn't always a museum. Like the Hermitage in St. Petersburg in Russia it was converted from a royal palace. But, before it was a palace is where it becomes interesting. The museum started out as a small windowless walled fort and arsenal on the Seine surrounded by a moat. The fort slowly, over the centuries, expanded adding wings, windows and different roof structures slowly morphing into the large structure it is today. Sometime shortly before 1993, curators discovered the original basement and moat from the fort. They have since been able to preserve it and open this section for tours. With years of excavation you can walk on the floor of the moat (sans water) and walk around the massive walls and ramparts of the Fort including the embankment wall of the moat. If you have gone to the Louvre and made a direct be-line to the Mona Lisa you missed a true treasure.

Returning home we chose to take the long walk along the Seine walking up the Champs Elysées to our hotel before dinner. Strolling Paris is magical, but it does burn up the time. We arrived back just in time to shower change and grab a taxis to one of Paris' oldest and most famous showrooms, the Moulin Rouge night club. Dating back to 1889 it is where the famous Toulouse-Lautrec got inspiration for his painting and where the French Can-Can was born. Going to the Moulin Rouge brings you back to another era in entertainment which Las Vegas has long abandoned. Just standing on the sidewalk facing the historic red windmill brings you back to how Paris was at another time.

The next morning was to be our free casual unstructured day. Leave it to me to add just a little structure. It turns out it's very easy to navigate and walk the streets of Paris. Walking the Champs Elysées turning on avenue George V we crossed the Seine for the tower. Our destination was a two hour lunch cruise up and down the river. The boat sails to the end of the city limits and turns back past the tower before it turns again right in front of a smaller version if France's gift to America, the Statue of Liberty. This statue was given to France in 1889 by the Americans living in France in celebration of France's revolution. It sits high in the middle of the Seine. It was such a pleasant day to begin a spring day in Paris. Disembarking from the boat we crossed the Czar Alexander Bridge with its gold winged lions guarding the passage. Just then, we all caught a glimpse of a large poster advertising the current issue of the French newspaper Le Point. There, bigger than life, was a front page picture of President Barack Obama with the headline, "America's Back". These are the best of times.

Did you notice the Eifel Tower?

CALIFORNIA YANKEE IN CUBA
APRIL 2013

DAY ONE

Before we even arrived at the airport, our travel agent warned us of the difficulty and time it would take to check in and get our boarding passes for our charter flight to Havana. Our flight leaves at 9:00 a.m. out of Miami, and we were told we needed to get to the airport by 5:00 a.m. Ugh!

Despite all the dire warnings we received about the process, it actually wasn't too bad. Unlike most check-ins, we had to go to four different desks to get our travel documents and boarding passes, check our luggage, and, of course, pay for overweight bags (over forty-three pounds), even though they were underweight. My bag was thirty-eight pounds and Leanne's was forty-two. I'm not sure where the attendant found the extra forty-four pounds I was billed for. Everyone paid overweight. Once we got into the rhythm, it went pretty smoothly. That four hours required to check in took us thirty minutes.

Oh God! I flew coach. Not only that, but I had a middle seat across from the galley and right in front of the bathrooms. I didn't know what Cuba would be like, but it had to be better than this.

Hallelujah! Someone in the exit row said they could not speak English so were not eligible to handle the emergency door. We quickly volunteered for the task. The flight to Cuba was a quick forty-five minutes.

April is one of the best times to visit Cuba. As we flew over the island, we could see that it was still lush and green. I could swear I noticed a few mansions on a lake. I was told there are no rich Cubans, but they also tell me no one knows where Fidel and Raúl live. I think it's that large Mediterranean palace I passed over.

Again we were warned that immigration could be intrusive. Nothing could be further from the truth. The process was very quick, pleasant, and smooth. Going to Cabo, Mexico, was more difficult.

Stepping out of the airport, we were met by our guide, Laura. We would spend the next eight days with her and our driver. Yes, the island was flooded with old 1950s pre-revolution automobiles. Pretty cool. Most were kept together with spare parts from everything from washing machines to old farm equipment, I was told.

We were staying at the Melici Cohibia hotel—a nice, modern hotel, but like much of the equipment and buildings here, in need of maintenance and sprucing up. What our room on the Royal Floor lacked in decor was more than made up by the incredible ocean view. Looking out our window, we felt like we were sitting in the ocean. To the right out the window, Havana lay before us.

CALIFORNIA YANKEE IN CUBA: DAY TWO

For our first day in Cuba, we had nothing organized or planned and were on our own to explore the town around the hotel. The first order of business was to have lunch. Strange as it might seem, the Ritz in Miami didn't have twenty-four-hour room service, so since we left at five in the morning, breakfast was impossible. The guide recommended Atelier, a place within walking distance from the hotel. Heading out of the lobby, we were told the restaurant was two blocks on the right. After three blocks we still couldn't find it. We asked at another restaurant, where the waiter was sure it was several more blocks up the road and decided to guide us himself, leaving his own diners behind. After four more blocks, we realized he didn't have any more idea where the restaurant was than we did. Abandoning our new guide, we set out asking everyone we passed if they knew where the restaurant was. Not one person we asked had a clue. We realized since most of the Cubans couldn't afford to eat in a restaurant, they wouldn't have any reason to know.

The walk wasn't all in vain, though. We were heading down a wide boulevard where stately mansions once occupied by rich Cubans still stood majestically. They were in surprisingly good shape for not being cared for in over fifty years. Some could've used a good coat of paint before welcoming their past owners. Several of the larger and more ornate of the homes had been restored and turned into government buildings and museums.

After walking back to the hotel to ask for directions again, we headed out, once again, to find lunch. Again, we were told to walk two blocks up and now down the side street to the right. Yet again, we were hopelessly lost. This time we decided to just circle the streets and hope for the best. Voilà! Forty-five minutes after we set out, we found it. Up two blocks and to the right—go figure.

Evidently the Cubans were not the only ones who didn't know about this place. Although we had a reservation, there wasn't another soul in sight.

The café was really very nice and occupied the second floor in one of the older mansions on a side street. Stark white walls, the dark, carved wood ceiling, and the checkered tile floor gave us the true feeling of being on a Caribbean island. The art on the walls was very interesting as well. There were paintings of Jesus and what looked to be Mary naked, lying across his lap in a provocative pose. One strange painting had Christ crucified upside down with his tunic falling back against his chest, exposing his genitals—my kind of religious art!

No matter what the US government thought, Cuba wasn't that isolated. I ordered a Diet Coke from Mexico and wine from Chile, Spain, and France. Cuba had these wonderful old '50s cars as well as a few newer cars that were imported from France, Germany, Japan, and South Korea. I counted eight Mercedes, BMWs, and Audis just in front of our hotel—and not the cheap ones.

Let's not forget the entertainment. Music and movies were pirated off the Internet or the hotel satellite TVs (I'd wondered how they knew

Beyoncé). Other US goods like skintight blue jeans covering little round young butts came here via Venezuela or the country of manufacture. The ones wearing or using these goods were in the tourism industry, I suspected. Cubans survived on tourist tips for the CUC money. The CUC is different from the Cuban peso. CUCs bought the extra goods the Cubans need to survive. The CUC was set up on par with the US dollar and was supposed to be used to soak tourists and get the hard currency needed to trade. The Cubans now depended on it to survive. Interested in a George Forman grill? It would cost you 118 CUCs, about $130. Want a new Samsung side-by-side refrigerator? It would set you back a whopping $2,000. The average official pay for a Cuban citizen was between twelve and fifty dollars a *month*. So tips were necessary to make it through the month. Who knows what else one might deal in to earn hard tourist currency? The Cubans call this new Cuban currency kooks.

For dinner the guide recommended La Maraleja. The taxi drivers were very friendly and informative. Tips, remember? During our drive up the coast, we passed the US mission. Yes, we had a mission for our "special interests." We also passed a beautiful old colonial hotel. It looked like a place Liz would stay—very nice indeed. I came to find that she had indeed stayed there. I'm never sure why the tour operators pick the hotels they do. I am very fussy, and I make that perfectly clear. Don't get me wrong, our hotel was nice. I just hate it when I see a hotel and think I should have been there. I was assured ours was the nicer hotel.

Our destination that night was a charming restaurant in what was obviously a very ritzy area prerevolution. The mansions on both sides of us were huge and very ornate. They don't take credit cards in Cuba, so I had to take lots of cash. I can already tell I should have taken more. It's not cheap here for tourists. The wine list has many bottles north of one hundred dollars. At lunch when our waiter brought our bread he said it was a gift. I didn't think much of it until we arrived at dinner. We were asked if we wanted bread. Jokingly I asked if it was a gift. The response wasn't so funny. "No." What were we thinking? We ordered lobster, French chardonnay, and bread. I thought that I might have to walk the streets for tips to get out of there.

The young ladies waiting on us were just delightful, not to mention beautiful. One young woman just lit up the room with her smile. After dinner we were presented with complimentary Cuban cigars and a nice bottle of Cuban rum. Let's just say, leaving the restaurant, it was hugs for everybody. We'd just gotten a flavor of this wonderful country, and we were already in love. I couldn't wait to see more and learn about life here and all the history.

CALIFORNIA YANKEE IN CUBA: DAY THREE

Today was our first tour day here in Cuba. Just from our walk around yesterday we could tell that this trip would be special. Cuba has everything a writer or tourist could want. I could tell I would have a wealth of information to write about—and Cuba didn't disappoint. Again we passed that old hotel that I found very intriguing yesterday. It turns out it was not where Beyoncé stayed. That was the Saratoga Hotel in Old Havana. This grand-looking hotel was the National Hotel. As I thought, it has a great history. The National Hotel was the holdout of the mafia when they were running gambling here in Havana. Mayer Lansky, Lucky Luciano—they all stayed here. I knew I really needed to stop there while we were in Cuba.

Our first stop was at the Plaza de San Francisco, which is anchored by the Basilica San Francisco de Asis. It is a magnificent limestone baroque-style cathedral built in 1730. The plaza was originally built back in the 1590s. It was the main market for the city. Today it houses the basilica, a hotel, a few homes, and the port office for unloading cargo. The basilica is no longer a church. Today it's set up for concerts. As luck would have it, there were musicians practicing a symphony piece, and we were able to enjoy the acoustics of the towering stone walls and baroque ceiling. Passing through the church and out into the courtyard, we could see where monks once walked.

Next we headed straight up into the bell tower. Climbing the old, narrow wooden stairway and ducking under low arches past the bronze bells, I pictured Quasimodo climbing these stairs. Finally reaching the top, we had an unbelievable view of the city. One of the more interesting buildings in the distance was the Bacardi building with its bat logo sitting on the tower. Bacardi is long gone, and the building is well maintained now as a real estate company office. I will speak more about real estate in Cuba a little later.

Our next stop in our walking tour was the old market square. This was the main market after it was moved from Plaza San Francisco. It appears the monks didn't find all the sounds and smells of the market conducive to great thought and meditation! This new square has been totally restored. It is surrounded by large, old, baroque-style homes, which have been converted to stores and museums on the first floors and apartments on the upper floors. Out of all of the plazas, Old Market Square makes you feel like you are someplace very special. It's exciting that this plaza has been restored to its eighteenth-century grandeur.

And to think—during the Batista era, the dictator turned this place into a parking lot. There are before-and-after pictures of the square. It has undergone a remarkable transformation, all thanks to tourism dollars. You will also find several chain stores here: Paul and Shark men's store, Colors of Benetton for women, and a Perfumeria. Most Cubans don't shop here; it's just another way to shake CUCs out of the tourist.

Another observation I made is that all of the power lines in the historic old city have been put underground. We have cities in the United States were we are still trying to do this. There is a tremendous amount of construction and restoration happening here in the old city. All those tourist dollars are going into restoring the past heritage of the city—not weapons, like some other unnamed countries.

Much of what is happening is thanks to the opening up to tourism in 1993. What's the significance of that date? It's right after the collapse of the Soviet Union. All of a sudden, the financial support from Russia was cut off. This was the direst of days for the Cubans. To get hard currency, it was decided that tourism should be allowed, and this new CUC currency was created. Most of the goods Russia supplied now have to be purchased from other countries, and they are expensive. Cubans have to pay for all manner of goods with CUCs. If your

1950s-era refrigerator goes out, replacing it will set you back 1,000 CUCs ($1,150) or more. So most just patch them up—just like the '50s-era cars. Air conditioning is out of the question for most Cuban homes. Believe me, you need it here. Today was ninety-one degrees with 95 percent humidity.

Next we went to Cathedral Square. Another beautiful 1700s baroque church dominates the plaza. Walking into this church, we saw beggars for the first time. They were sitting right by the entrance. In a strange irony you can blame the United States for them being there. Our guide explained that begging is illegal in Cuba and that there are many places they could go for help. Strangely the government is worried about arresting them for fear some tourist will record it and circulate it as yet another human rights violation. Who would have thought?

Moving on, we headed to the hotel where Hemingway lived in 1932. Before we got there we passed a small outdoor cart that was selling the best piña coladas in the city. Offered were regular piña coladas and, for 1.50 CUCs extra, Hemingway piña coladas. What's a Hemingway piña colada? It comes in a pineapple. For some reason I doubt Papa, who wrote about wars and revolutions, drank his piña colada out of a pineapple. Anything goes to get another CUC out of the pockets of the tourist.

Continuing on from the Hemingway Hotel to the Governors Palace, we passed the Santa Isabel Hotel, where Jack Nicolson, Jimmy Carter, and numerous other famous people stayed when they came to Cuba. It seems everyone has traveled here but us.

One of the last plazas we visited was occupied by the Governors Palace. It was another wonderful and imposing building and has been lovingly restored and now houses a museum with furniture, art, carriages, and accessories from the old colonial era. It is quite remarkable, actually, that there are still so many historic items. It reminds me of what we saw in Russia. Like in Russia, none of this stuff was made here. All the items shown were imported here by the rich colonialists.

How can any walking tour through Old Havana end without a

stop in Hemingway's favorite bar, the Floridita? We just had to have his favorite drink, the daiquiri. They say it was invented here at this bar. Again, I can't imagine Papa sipping a frozen strawberry daiquiri out of a straw—a mojito, maybe. That also was invented here in Cuba. I don't know about Hemingway, but the Floridita makes a great daiquiri. Leaving the bar, we passed the Hotel Saratoga. You might all know it. It was made famous by Beyoncé and Jay-Z just a week ago. It's a very nice hotel—small, colonial, and five-star. The Saratoga has the history; our hotel has the ocean view. Boy, it's a toss-up. But I think I would go with the historic, as long as the air conditioning is working. It should be—the hotel was a Hilton before the revolution.

This is a special place, and this is the best time to come—no Starbucks, T-shirt shops, or Louis Vuitton. I think the Cubans are more afraid of the invasion of Starbucks than they are of the US military. And I don't blame them. If we ever do have normalized relations, I have to hope that this preserved colonial city is not McDonaldized.

Let's talk embargo for a second. Did you know that a 2012 Gallup Poll published in TIME Magazine, showed that 83 percent of Americans think we should end the embargo. Polls for the last seven years have shown that the majority of Americans favor ending the embargo. Even influential Cuban dissidents think we should end the embargo. So why is it still in place? What a surprise—the answer is money, six billion dollars' worth. That's the amount of the judgments held in the United States against Cuba for nationalizing American factories and the property and homes of former Cubans. Pissed off Cubans vote, and politicians want those votes. Oh yes, what about the human rights violations? We don't see citizens being mistreated. We understand there are "political prisoners," and we want them released. TIME magazine published a very good article in 2013 pointing out the weakness in America's position. It stated that our argument has been weakened ever since we began storing our political prisoners, just a few miles away from Havana, at Guantanamo.

Then there is the Cuban economy. Did you know we are their fifth-largest trading partner and supply almost 7 percent of their imports? Under Clinton, congress voted to supply Cuba with humanitarian aid in the form of food and medicine—humanitarian aid that the Cuban government has to pay for in cash. The US government kept in place the restriction on American tourists coming here. This then prevents Cuba from collecting the hard dollars necessary to buy the so-called aid. Is this all starting to sound a little stupid to you?

Now let's get back to touring. We ended our day driving under Havana Harbor to the sixteenth- and eighteenth-century fort that the Spanish built to protect the harbor. It is a large, imposing fort with cannons pointed at the lane leading to the harbor. It is easy to see why it was built here. It has a great view looking back into the city. The strategic position of the fort worked wonderfully for over two centuries until the British cleverly attacked it from behind and captured Havana.

The English occupation was short-lived, though. The British decided to trade Cuba back to Spain in exchange for Florida. It was the American colonists who then had the last laugh during their revolution when they took Florida from the British. Cuba, it seems, has been dependent on, or occupied by other countries since the landing of Columbus in 1492—first the Spanish, then the English, the Spanish again, then the Americans (yes, Cuba from 1902 up until the revolution was a US territory), and finally Russia. After five hundred years of occupation, Cubans are having a hard time finding their way on their own. We ended the day with dinner high on a rooftop with yet another panoramic view of this amazing city.

CALIFORNIA YANKEE IN CUBA: DAY FOUR

If you know anything about Cuba, your knowledge certainly centers on their world-renowned cigars. So, naturally, we had to make a stop at the place where it all happens: a Cuban cigar factory. This is not just any Cigar factory; it's the one that makes the most famous cigars in the world. Indeed, the factory makes a number of the most famous brands. Here you will find Cohibais, Fidel's favorite; Romeo and Juliet, Churchill's favorite; and the H. Upmann Petit, Kennedy's favorite. Pierre Salinger, Kennedy's press secretary, claims Kennedy ordered him to go to Cuba to get 1,200 of his favorite cigars before he ordered the embargo. It would have been nice if he'd tipped the rest of us off.

This factory, one of four in Havana, produces twenty-five thousand cigars a day made by four hundred workers. Entering the factory, we joined a factory guide and translator, whom we followed upstairs to the crafting room. There we found row upon row of workbenches divided into small workstations where men and women handcrafted a particular brand. Personally, we had no idea how a cigar was made. Moving to a single workbench, we watched as a worker chose different types of tobacco, bundling them together and layering them by flavor of a particular brand. Then he twisted the outer leaf around the filler tobacco until a perfectly shaped cigar was produced. At this point the cigars looked a little rough around the edges. Never fear, cigar aficionados—the craftsmen clipped the ends. Next, a worker placed an umbrella piece of tobacco over the mouth end and then placed the cigar in a shaping press that smoothed it out for that perfect look. When he was done, the cigars went to the quality control area to check for density. Too much or too little tobacco would get a cigar rejected. The craftsman we were watching had a daily quota of 150 cigars for this brand. For that he made about twelve dollars a month in Cuban pesos. He also got a few CUCs and four of the rejected cigars a day. Trying to sell your allotment of cigars can get you fired. Cigars are a major export for Cuba. Here in Havana, 92 percent of the production is exported overseas. The ones coming into the United States are sniffed out and sent to Arnold Schwarzenegger. Just kidding. Apparently it is also very common here to see women smoke them.

Leaving the factory, we headed back to Old Havana. As we drove away from the factory, we passed through a seedier part of town: Centro Havana. Here is where the lower-class workers, prostitutes, and people who may have been let out of prison live. You will find some grand architecture here; though, unfortunately, like the area might imply, it is very far from restoration. These are the areas that should welcome Starbucks for revitalization. Maybe one day.

We continued driving past the remains of the old fort walls of the city. We passed the Art Nuevo train station where trains from the

1950s and earlier still operate. Unlike in Mussolini's Italy, these trains, we heard, don't run on time.

Finally, we arrived at our second location of the day: an old-convent-turned-college-turned-senior-activity-center. The old convent takes up a full city block with several interior courtyards. Unfortunately, only one of the courtyards has been restored, and it is occupied by seniors. Entering the massive doors was like stepping into a beautiful riad, much like you might see in Morocco. wide, colorful loggia circled the courtyard, which was planted with cooling shade trees. Seniors were engaged in crafts, dominos, conversation, exercise, and card games.

It would be wonderful if all the other courtyards could be restored to welcome additional seniors as well. It comes down to money. The Cuban aid workers managing this project are desperately short of supplies. This one courtyard was not the work of the Cuban government. It was the work of many foreign sponsors who sent money, the United States notably absent from that list. It would seem that this would be a great place for humanitarian aid. Upstairs in this quadrant is a daycare. Rounding the corner, the kids got a glimpse of us and started running and screaming with excitement toward us. Ages one through five—they were just adorable. Apparently most of these children were the children of institute workers or children from dysfunctional families. It was a wonderful setting with its high ceilings and large, airy windows overlooking the lush courtyard below.

It was now time to continue with a drive far out of the city to see Hemingway's home, which he bought in 1940 and lived in until he left the island sometime in the very late 1950s. We seemed to drive and drive and were surprised how far out of town the house was. The small towns looked like those in Mexico. It didn't seem like a drive Hemingway would have enjoyed. Back in Hemingway's day this road would have been through the forest. The buildings we were passing weren't here when he bought his eight acres with a house. These shabby buildings were built in 1948 or later.

Turning off the main road, we traveled up a dense, tree-lined driveway, which lead to Hemingway's home. The trees we were passing were from different parts of the world, including Wyoming, Africa,

Europe, and Cuba. These were all favorite trees of Hemingway, and he apparently planted them after he bought the house. It makes for a very lush, cool, and serene setting. The original house on the property was built in the 1880s and is preserved just as Hemingway left it. He was obviously expecting to return. His books are on the shelves, and his typewriters are still on his desks. You can't walk through the house, but you can walk around it, peering in the windows to take pictures. The furniture is well maintained as if the owner would return any moment. One interesting area was Hemingway's bathroom. Behind the door, Hemingway had a medical scale. He weighed himself every day. He then wrote his weight and the date right on the walls. Line after line shows his weight gain and loss over the years. Hemingway was a diabetic and obviously was concerned with his weight and controlling the disease. Where sweet frozen daiquiris fit in I am not sure.

After Hemingway bought the house, he did add a guesthouse and a large pool. Legend says Ava Gardner swam naked when she visited. I have to believe she wasn't the only goddess to grace the pool naked while visiting Papa. Being a museum, the property also houses Hemingway's fishing boat, the famous *Pilar*, flagged out of Key West, Florida. On this boat he fashioned *The Old Man and the Sea*, using his friend and sea captain as a model. Walking back to our car, we passed a sugarcane press and stand making a local beverage out of sugarcane and rum—not good if you are a diabetic, not so bad if you are visiting Cuba. The drink was surprisingly good and very refreshing.

After a very full morning, it was now time for lunch. Today we were going back to Old Havana to what was supposed to be the best "government-owned" restaurant. I hate when I hear I am going to a government restaurant. That typically means bland comrade food. Entering the building, I became even more concerned when I saw the name, Castropol. The sign says it was founded in 1929. Walking around the first floor and mezzanine, we found a construction zone. Oy vey.

Entering the dining room on the second floor, we were pleasantly greeted by a nice decor and a very welcome blast of air conditioning. I was feeling better. Getting the menu, I was really happy to see a nice variety of dishes. The ones that caught my eye were the pineapple ceviche and the local lobster. This was going to be a meal of lobster, lobster, and more lobster. I ordered mine sautéed in garlic, and Leanne ordered hers in a mixed grill. The food was very, very good. The best part of the meal was our conversation with our waiter. When we said we were from San Francisco, he started talking about Napa cabernet. He said that everyone who worked in the restaurant wanted to go to America. He also told us that of all of the visitors to Cuba, they liked the Americans best. It would be a theme we would hear several more times again today.

After lunch we made two more stops, the first at a neighborhood where we met an artist named Salvador. In 1990 he started painting African murals on all the walls of the local buildings. Two things stuck out as strange: first, that they allowed it, and second, that he wasn't African. When he started painting, most Cubans thought he was crazy. Not so. Now he has a small studio where he sells paintings to visiting tourists. They are very nice, but I felt the same way here as I did when I was ushered into the Arab rug stores.

Our last stop was our most memorable, arriving at the largest cemetery in Havana. More than 2.5 million people were buried here. It was the first place you could actually buy real estate in Cuba. It was expensive. The place is just huge. Marble slabs are so close together you have to walk single file between them. There are four past Cuban presidents here and over seventy thousand marble works of art decorating the plots. There is a spectacular one built for thirty-four fallen firemen who died in an explosion back in the 1800s. As they responding to a fire, the store's proprietor failed to tell the responding firemen he was storing explosives in the basement. The monument has much symbolism built into the statues. There was also an ornate mausoleum for a bartender. It just so happens he was Hemingway's bartender and the inventor of the daiquiri.

There was also a very emotional crypt. It appears to be the resting place of Amelia. Superstition says that when two brides marry on the same day, one will have lasting bliss, and the other tragedy. Amelia was the latter. She and her baby died in childbirth. She was buried in her grave with her baby at her feet.

As I mentioned, this cemetery has 2.5 million occupants. Like Mexico, the dead here can only be buried for two years. Then their bones are put in a center communal grave on the plot, and the next person is laid to rest. When they opened Amelia's grave to inter her father-in-law, they found that Amelia's baby was lovingly resting in Amelia's arms, not at her feet. Shocked at the miracle, they left Amelia and her baby to eternally rest where they lay. To this day, her grave is visited by people from around the world and rubbed for luck in a very sweet ceremony we took part in.

By far our most memorable time at the cemetery and possibly here in Cuba was our visit with our cemetery guide. He was very candid and forthcoming with his assessment of Cuba today. I had asked him for his opinion of Cuba's health care system. He was quick to point out that the doctors were some of the best of the world. They have become very skillful due to the fact they have very old equipment and instruments to work with. He also said that Cuba is suffering a brain drain. There are thirty thousand Cuban doctors practicing in Venezuela alone. Engineers also are going overseas to work. It is tough for these professions here in Cuba. You study for years to get your degree, and the most you can make here in Cuba as a doctor is thirty-five dollars a month—not nearly enough, even in this socialist country, to support a family.

He explained that 70 percent of university graduates want to leave Cuba when they graduate. I would suspect that 70 percent of the remaining population would like to leave as well. He told us that the government, as of January, had made it easier for Cubans to leave, but with the high cost of exit visas and limitations on immigration around the world, it was still out of the reach of most Cubans.

The government also has allowed for the sale of real estate. Many Cubans own their own homes. If you owned a home before the revolution and either hadn't abandoned it or been involved in illegal activities, you still owned your home. So if you chose to sell it to move or possibly leave Cuba altogether, you were able to do so. When you combine all of this with the new CUC currency and private ownership of businesses, you can see capitalism creeping in.

Since I have been here I have been wondering what it would be like to ride in one of the many 1950s-era American cars here. As luck would have it, our tour operator scheduled for us to travel to dinner tonight in a purple 1955 Buick convertible. Like most of these '50s-era cars, it was pretty rough with a decent paint job, which, of course, hid the fact that it didn't have the hand cranks for the windows. Not to worry—it didn't have windows, either. But who cares? We were back in time with the wind blowing through our hair, cruising through Revolution Square and headed to dinner.

Our last stop of the evening was one of the hotels that had most fascinated me: the Hotel Nacional. This hotel was the mafia's headquarters for gambling on the island and the site of one of the biggest gambling halls in Havana. We were there to explore the 1930s grounds and the hall of fame. It was here that the rich and famous stayed from 1930, the opening of the hotel, to its closing in 1959. Should a hotel guest return today, they would see the hotel exactly as it was when guests visited in the 1930s, '40s, and '50s—sans the gambling, of course.

The hotel also has a Parisian showroom, which has a Cuban-style floorshow. This is where the likes of Frank Sinatra, Jimmy Durante, and Nat King Cole used to perform. Today it's a combination Las Vegas–Carnival–style show. We weren't expecting much and planned to leave early since it was getting late, but we found ourselves mesmerized by the dancing, costumes, colors, and, my favorite, the tight little butts of the show girls. What can I tell you? I'm still a guy. All Leanne could say was how much it reminded her of Ricky Ricardo (Desi Arnaz). Oh yeah, he was Cuban!

Traveling back, we had a stark reminder that all of this—the restaurants, shows, five-star hotels, and shops—are all for us, the tourist. These places are all out of reach for Cubans because of the cost. Driving back, there were hundreds, if not thousands, of young people sitting along the long sea walls with nothing to do. It reminded me of a line from one of my favorite movies. To paraphrase, it goes, "Communism is dead. Don't blame me; I didn't do it. It was dead when I got here."

Stephen Troy and Leanne Troy

CALIFORNIA YANKEE IN CUBA: DAY FIVE

We are halfway through our visit to this the largest of the islands in the West Indies. Traveling from the hotel we headed to one of Cuba's most modern buildings, the National Museum of Fine Arts. The museum houses Cuba's finest colonial and pre- and post-revolution art. In the interest of time Leanne and I decided that we would be most interested in seeing the more modern Cuban art ranging from the 1950s to the 1990s.

Passing through the entrance we were greeted by a stunningly beautiful, slender, tall, black Cuban young lady. She would be our guide for the next hour, leading us through the decades of Cuban art. Like the cemetery, the best part of our tour was listening to our guide's views, problems, dreams, and aspirations. Like many Cubans she was a trained to be a teacher and had to leave her chosen profession because she couldn't live on a teacher's pay, which didn't provide for the ability to earn CUCs.

Before we even started, our guide apologized for the lack of air conditioning. It seems this very modern building has a modern, complicated air-conditioning system, and no one knows how to fix it. She was concerned for us and for the art due to the hot, humid days here in Havana this time of year.

The first room we entered showcased the work of several artists of the '50s and the progression of work pre- and post-revolution. One large canvas painted by a young Cuban artist before the revolution was of men showing confidence, strength, and hope. His painting just across the room, which he painted after the revolution, showed the same faces in a more shadowy, contorted feeling of despair. Many had high hopes for the revolution and its mission of making everyone equal. For this artist, however, who happened to be gay, equality wouldn't extend to him. Gay artists played a role in several of the more interesting art pieces in the hall. Before the revolution, there were many gay artists, and they suffered from discrimination. After the revolution, human nature being what it is, the discrimination didn't stop. It was interesting to see that, like in Pompeii, the art during this period had a heavy

278

emphasis on a particular male private part. Most gay artists would eventually leave Cuba in the '90s with thousands of others.

As we progressed through the decades, we could see through the art what was happening in Cuba and how the people felt. After the revolution, military leaders, not art curators, were put in charge of the Ministry of Culture. These military men were charged with deciding who could create art. As a result, the art of the '60s became less symbolic and interesting and focused more on the revolution. Many of the great Cuban artists were prohibited from practicing their craft and switched to other occupations. By the '70s, art started a renaissance, and by the '80s and into the '90s, it started to again represent the feelings of the people. It was wonderful to have this lovely woman pointing out the symbolism in each piece. I have to say, I don't think I have ever enjoyed a tour of modern art as much as I have in this museum. Where else in the world can you see the feelings of the people represented in art in a place that has changed radically over fifty years?

Our next stop was the Museum of the Revolution, which houses the boat that Castro and nine of his men traveled on from Mexico in 1957 to launch the revolution. For some reason, this was not on our schedule, but after passing it several times in the car, I thought, *How can we leave Cuba without seeing the boat and understanding the revolution through the eyes of the people who lived it?*

The museum is housed in the old Presidential Palace. The palace—or I should say museum—is a gorgeous limestone building in colonial style taking up close to a city block. Fidel's rebels stormed this building trying to capture the dictator Batista. After a firefight that left bullet holes in the walls, the rebels broke through, but they missed Batista, who slipped out via a hidden stairway. The interior of the building of the building is what you would imagine of a palace: tiffany fixtures, high domed ceilings, and grand halls. Two of the highlights were Batista's private office with its gold phone given to him by the mafia (a prop which played a prominent role in *The Godfather: Part II*) and the balcony off the hall of mirrors where Fidel gave his long revolution victory speeches.

Here in the museum you can read the other side of story of the revolutionaries. You can view pictures of the Batista era here in Cuba and how brutal his rule was. You can contrast that with the blood-soaked shirts of the freedom fighters who fought to end Batista's rule. It was a time filled with corruption, gambling, drug dealing, and the oppression of the farmers. You get the feeling that things had to change. Sometimes change isn't pretty and the outcome is not what everyone was hoping for.

Leaving the palace building, we were greeted by Cuban soldiers, all at attention. Two of the officers stood at the exit, and a band was ready to play. Could it be they heard it was our anniversary today? Nope. It turns out that April 19, 1989, is when Fidel dedicated the Cuban equivalent of the Tomb of the Unknown Soldier.

We stopped to listen to the national anthem and to watch the laying of the wreath before we crossed the courtyard to see Fidel's boat, the tanks he used to fire upon the presidential palace, various jeeps with the occasional bullet hole, and vestiges of the Cold War. The tail section of a US bomber, the turbine of a U2 spy plane the military shot down in 1962, and a skiff used to transport Cuban counterrevolutionaries at the failed Bay of Pigs Invasion were included in the display.

Lunch was located at another Hemingway hangout, La Bodeguita del Medio. The Floridita was Hemingway's favorite spot to have a daiquiri. La Bodeguita was his favorite spot for a mojito. The bar and restaurant are now owned by the government since the original owner who opened the bar in the 1920s fled the city. In Hemingway's time it was a bar with a small restaurant. Today the restaurant has been expanded in the rear for the visiting tourist. La Bodeguita is one of the most popular sites to visit in Havana. Famous people have been drinking and eating here for decades. Nat King Cole ate here, and his table has been hung high up the wall. What we noticed when we entered the building was that the walls were covered with handwritten signatures and messages of just about everyone who has ever visited. Our guide Laura tipped off the band that it was our anniversary, so our lunch was accompanied by fun Cuban music. One song went on so long I thought it was the Cuban equivalent of the twenty-minute rendition of "MacArthur Park."

One of the reasons American are allowed to come here is to be able to visit with the Cuban religious community. Our stop after lunch was to a synagogue, which has one of the few Holocaust memorials in Latin America. Cuba has played a large role for Jews for over the last five hundred years. The first white European to step foot in Cuba was Luis de Torres, a Jew, who came to Cuba with Columbus in 1492. It is believed it was Torres who recognized the value and importance of the local tobacco crop. The Holocaust display here at the synagogue was the work of a Los Angeles resident, Stanley Falkenstein, who donated the funds for the project in 2011. The display depicts through pictures and video the suffering and persecution of the Jews in Europe. Jews have settled here in Cuba for centuries. They established shops, factories, and restaurants. Refugees from Antwerp even established a diamond-cutting industry in 1944. By 1952, there were twelve thousand Jews in Cuba. Today there are only about 1,500. Most of the others left right before the revolution.

Our last stop of the day was at the Habana Club Museum of Rum. You can thank Columbus for the rum industry here in Cuba. It was Columbus who introduced sugarcane to the island. If you have sugarcane, you have molasses, and that's the ingredient for making rum. It is not possible to go to the actual factory, so Cubans built a model of the factory right here in the city. The tour ended, as you would expect, in the gift shop and tasting room. I was very happy we are not allowed to bring rum back to the States. That way I didn't feel bad when I didn't buy the top-of-the-line rum for a staggering $1,900 a bottle. No way! Yes way.

Dinner tonight was on our own. We were hoping to get a reservation at La Guarida, the restaurant where Beyoncé and Jay-Z had dinner. Unfortunately they were booked. We had to settle for a new restaurant in Havana called Ratatouille. We were without our car and driver and hadn't a clue where this place was, so we had to cab it. Getting into a cab, we gave the taxi driver the name and the address of where we wanted to go. We were headed inland into a main residential area. The homes all seemed to be in great condition and well maintained. The architecture seemed to be more of a Caribbean/ Spanish influence as opposed to the eighteenth-century colonial you see in the city. It was like any middle-class area you might find in Miami.

Soon we realized that not only did we not know where we were going, our driver was totally clueless. When he stopped to ask directions, I knew, based on my experience trying to find lunch the other day, it was going to be pointless. I was right. Driving a cab must be a new profession here. A couple of more inquiries, and—what do you know—we found it, deep in a residential area of Cuba. Ratatouille is in one of the old mansions out here in the suburbs. The home has been totally restored, and every room downstairs has been turned into a private dining room. Again we found dining rooms that were totally empty. Interestingly, that didn't stop our waiter from seating us next to the kitchen. Why do they do that? I felt like I was in one of those old black-and-white movies where the couple is dining at home with musicians playing in the background and the butler and maid serving dinner. There we were, the only ones in the house, with a duet and several servants waiting on us hand and foot.

Both of us had the seafood grill of lobster shrimp and fish. I only mention this because the Cuban people don't eat any of those things. You would think that, the island being surrounded by water, fish would be a staple. The Cubans don't eat fish here, because they have no boats. Even if they had a boat, the government has restricted fisherman from going into the main fishing areas. Those areas are reserved for me. Fish, lobster, shrimp, and beef here are reserved for the restaurants and hotels—in other words, for me. While we were chowing down on lobster, the average Cuban was dining on chicken, rice, and beans. It reminded me of the other day when our cemetery guide quoted George Orwell's *Animal Farm*. For the record, the restaurant was very, very good.

Our last stop of the evening was the Buena Vista Social Club. It is a bar right off the Plaza de San Francisco. We were told we would see a show with Cuban music. Walking into the club, we could see it was loud and rockin'. There, right past the front tables where we were sat, was a ten-piece jazz band that was wailing away. Up front there were five old men between the ages of sixty-five and eighty-five singing Cuban jazz. We were told the show came with two drinks. You could have anything you wanted as long as it was a mojito. I'll take the mojito, please.

After every song the group changed lead singers and styles of music. You haven't lived until you have seen a seventy-year-old Cuban who looks like Bill Cosby rock out to "Old Time Rock and Roll" in Spanish. The audience went crazy. For an hour and a half, these men and women rotated in and out, singing, dancing, shaking their booties, and bringing the house down. When was the last time you were in a conga line and not at a bar mitzvah? I smiled and laughed until it hurt. It was just the right mixture of great jazz, Cuban style, rock and roll, dancing, and schmaltz. It was just adorable. It was like a Cuban Club Med. If you come to Cuba and miss the Buena Vista Social Club, you will miss the heart and soul of the country.

Thank God we found a taxi driver who knew how to get us back to our hotel.

CALIFORNIA YANKEE IN CUBA: DAY SIX

There is more to Cuba than the city of Havana, so for the rest of the trip we are going exploring. Today we were headed west to Pinar del Río, the westernmost province of Cuba to view the Guaniguanico mountain range with its pine forest, rich farmland, and hump-shaped limestone hills that have been carved by centuries of rain and flowing rivers, which have also created caves and caverns inside the mountains. Our drive west out of Havana took us down what Cuba calls its Fifth Avenue. This was Fifth Avenue before the revolution—maybe more Park Avenue. It's the area where the rich and famous lived in their mansions and partied at their country clubs and golf courses. These are by far the largest and most beautiful of the homes we have seen to date. Some of the homes are still owned by residents who didn't abandon them during the revolution, and others have become hotels, restaurants, and embassies. Most of the embassies occupy one of these majestic homes and have been meticulously restored. The Russian embassy, on the other hand, is a '50s-era cement fortress that looks like it hasn't been pressure washed in decades.

The most impressive and largest of the buildings on the block was the old "country club" clubhouse. You could just imagine the 1940s and '50s Cadillacs, Lincolns, Mercedes, and even a few Rolls-Royces pulling through the tall, massive iron gates and circling to the front door, where they would have been greeted by a doorman. For some reason, today it sits abandoned and deteriorating. What a shame. From the look of the façade, I think there is still hope for it. Where's Starbucks when you need it?

We so enjoyed driving through the city, which was filled with the lush green and tropical foliage of the countryside. We headed down a modern-looking four-lane divided highway out of town. As nice as it looked, it was one of the bumpiest rides I have had outside of India. Sometimes impressions don't fit with reality. The drive to the Guaniguanico Mountains would be three bumpy hours each way. The mountain range surrounds the most fertile and gorgeous valley we have ever seen. Our first stop was on a high ridge where we could get a view of the limestone mountains with their unique shape. Their beauty is not duplicated in any other place in the world. The Viñales Valley below our feet was stunning. The land seemed to stretch on forever, dotted with small, irregular farms, many of which grew tobacco, fruits, vegetables, and sugarcane.

The thing that stands out the most about these farms is their small size and the lack of farming equipment. Here you will find men swinging sickles, driving oxen, and transporting goods on small two-wheel horse-drawn wagons. The farmers here all own their land. The difficult part of the farming here is that they just don't own any of the production. Just about 90 percent of all of they produce must be delivered to the state. From the remaining 10 percent the farmer has to pay his workers and the cost of planting and then hope to have money left over to feed his family. If the government is going to take 90 percent of your production, why expand and give yourself more work and additional expenses? What's the incentive? It is interesting that with all of this fertile land, Cuba still can't produce enough to feed its citizens, let alone export for hard currency.

We saw firsthand what happens to the 10 percent production. Person after person lined the highway, offering food for sale. We saw one woman sitting with a single basket of tomatoes, a family offering whole dead goats on the hoof, and another waving a block of cheese. When we thought it couldn't get stranger, we saw men holding long, horizontal sticks from which a row of eight to ten whole fried chickens where hanging. Oh, there was also a whole dead pig for sale. It became less appetizing when we saw the 1950s Plymouth in front of us belching black smoke onto the chickens. I guess now they can charge extra and advertise them as smoked—zing!

For our next stop, we headed to one of the many tobacco plantations located here. This valley grows the best tobacco in Cuba. Tobacco, we were told, starts out as seeds planted at the riverbanks. When the seeds sprout, they are then moved to the valley and replanted close to a drying barn. Every tobacco farm has a large barn made of a combination of wood and thatch with row upon row of rods to hang tobacco leaves to dry. Thousands of leaves are hung over the rods from floor to ceiling and from wall to wall. It was very interesting, and I am sure if I smoked cigars it would be titillating. Last time I smoked a cigar I tasted like an ashtray for four days. Not my thing.

As we got out of the car at a small rest stop, we saw an old man who had put a saddle on a big tan ox. For a donation of whatever we liked, we were more than welcome to go for a ride. If you put a saddle on it, we are ready. Being cowboys at heart and owning horses ourselves, we climbed up for one of the slowest and wobbliest rides ever around the parking lot. The pictures are great.

Next stop: the caves. As we got closer to the limestone mountains we could see the caves peeking from the long green vines that cascade down the sides. Thousands of years of rain have carved a view you would only expect to see in an Indiana Jones movie.

Finally arriving, we turned into a small park at the base of the mountain. We walked up a staircase past a guitar player at the entrance hoping for tips. Turning a corner we came to a small crack in the side of the mountain with a small, slippery set of steps heading back down. As we climbed lower, the cave started to get larger, then smaller, and then larger again. The ceiling, in places, rose to thirty or forty feet and then dropped to six or seven feet. The river that ran through here carved a series of caverns, peaks, and stalactites. As we walked, we soon hit a line of people. At first I thought they were just holding us up by taking pictures. What they actually were doing was waiting for one of three boats that would take them on a tour of the cave by river, eventually floating back out to the valley. I felt like I was in Disneyland, winding through the Matterhorn, waiting to get to the roller coaster. Inch by inch we wound around, never knowing where the end was. Finally, like in Disneyland, we were above the river watching people loading on to the boats, knowing it would be our turn soon.

Stepping onto the small skiff with a small outboard engine, we left the dock and started up the river. It stopped feeling like the Matterhorn and started feeling just like the Pirates of the Caribbean. They even pointed out the bows of Columbus's Niña, Pinta, and Santa Maria, all lined up and jutting from the wall and all made from limestone naturally carved from years of erosion. You had to have a good imagination. Finally we saw land! Through a small crack in the wall we were finally led outside to an exit dock. Turning back after we exited, we were up close and personal with a scene from *Raiders of the Lost Ark*. Disney couldn't do it better.

Dinner tonight was at Café Laurent Paladar, one of the many private restaurants that have sprung up over the past several years. Our tour company assures me that it's one of the best on the island.

Our car once again was waiting at seven thirty to whisk us through the city to our dinner destination. I never tired of traveling through Havana. The architecture is so interesting and wonderful to look at while thinking about Cuba. Arriving at the block of the restaurant, we still couldn't figure out where we were going. Cuba is not like most places in the world. Here you won't find any advertising or signs pointing you to your destination. Eating in a restaurant here in Cuba requires that you know where you are going. Luckily our guide Laura was here to assist us. We crossed the street to a very nondescript five-story apartment building. We entered for the short elevator ride to the rooftop. Walking into the small lobby brought back memories of my grandmother's apartment building in Queens. I could swear this was the same model Otis elevator she had in her building that was built in the 1930s. In general, it is hard for me to enjoy the best restaurant in a third-world county. I am always a bit concerned about the meats, so I inevitably order the lobster. Tough life, huh? And so be it—lobster for everybody, or at least for the tourists.

CALIFORNIA YANKEE IN CUBA: DAY SEVEN

Where's the beach? We have been in Cuba for six days, and we have yet to see a beach. I have to say, my expectations of Cuba were of a Caribbean island where European and Canadian tourists come to lie on the beach sipping daiquiris outside their hotel. That's Jamaica, not Cuba.

We checked out of our Havana hotel today, heading southeast to the town of Trinidad, where I still have hopes of finding white sandy beaches. Our drive to Trinidad would be a staggering nine hours with a few stops along the way. After about two hours of driving, we turned off the highway down a small two-lane road through a swamp leading to a bay. Not just any bay—this bay was the Bay of Pigs! This was where the United States got its ass kicked in April of 1961. Driving down the road, our guide pointed out large stone memorials dotting the roadside. These locations apparently are markers where Cuban fighters fell in the fighting. At one point we stopped at a railroad crossing—really more on it then at it! At the blow of a whistle I got a close-up look at the trains here in Cuba. I was expecting Butch Cassidy and the Sundance Kid to ride up any second.

As we drove we passed a tourist attraction of an Indian village as it might have looked at the time of Columbus's landing back in 1492. You won't find any descendants of native Indians here. Apparently Columbus and the conquistadors killed them all off after the Indians taught them how to cultivate tobacco. Why? We still haven't gotten an answer to that one. Continuing on, we started to notice that the road was littered with hundreds of red and white splattered circles stretching hundreds of feet. It was then we saw a few red crabs scurrying across the road. We could tell that they were in a hurry. Unfortunately many didn't make it across. I would think someone would stop and load these little things in a bucket for tonight's dinner. But what's the incentive?

We continued driving through the Zapata Swamp. This is the area that represents the people who were most helped by revolution. Here, swamp people lived in horrid conditions, with no electricity, schools, hospitals, or decent housing. These people had to subsist on making coal out of burnt wood for their livelihood of a few pesos a month while Batista and the mafia made millions partying with the wealthy who gambled in Havana. When Batista was overthrown, he escaped, taking with him a $300 million fortune.

As we continued down the road, driving through little villages, we saw where kids and adults were engaged in Cuba's favorite pastime: baseball. Cubans loves their baseball. In the States it's America's game. Here it is Cuba's game. No soccer, no football, no cricket—just baseball. Finally we reached the site of the first landing of Cuban exiles at the Bay of Pigs. I was totally unaware of how large the invasion was. The invasion started April 15 with an air attack, followed by a land assault from the sea. The invasion couldn't have been botched any worse. It reminded us of planning by Jimmy Carter, not Dwight D. Eisenhower. I know John F. Kennedy was president at the time. In truth, we know now that an incompetent CIA planned the invasion. The only thing the CIA accomplished with the invasion was to strengthen the Castro revolution. At a gathering of the Americas, Che Guevara sent Kennedy a note thanking him for strengthening the revolutionary cause in Cuba. In front of the museum there was an American plane that was captured and various tanks and antiaircraft guns that were used to shoot down the invading planes. Inside, of course, was the Cubans' side of the story, talking about their great victory. Isn't that how it is? The victors write the history. Over two hundred Cuban exiles were killed and 1,197 taken prisoner. After public interrogations by the Castro government, Cuba traded all 1,197 for $53 million in food and medicine.

Anyway, there was still no beach at the Bay of Pigs. I guess I was expecting a beach like Normandy that has been transformed to a resort with umbrellas and people sitting in the shade sipping daiquiris. The bay is a gorgeous blue, and I'm told there are a lot of scuba adventures done here, just no beach. There is a small hotel, I am told, located at the site of the first landing of exiles.

Next stop on our nine-hour trek was the town of Cienfuegos. Cienfuegos was the last town established in Cuba, founded in 1819 and thus new by Cuban standards. The town has the longest boulevard in Cuba, which goes from the start of town to the beautiful harbor. We stopped for lunch here at a very cute little private restaurant called El Tranvia, "The Streetcar." The waiters wear conductor uniforms and hats, and the inside is decorated with all types of stuff reminiscent of the days the streetcars ran through the town, from 1913 to 1954. The streetcars stopped running when General Motors came into town and bought the line and promptly shut it down, ripping out the tracks. From a three-cent fare to five-dollar-a-gallon gas—I guess that's our fault too. Get over it; they did it in LA also. I'll bet you can't guess what we had. After lunch we went to the main square, which is surrounded by Art Nuevo buildings, most of which have been restored. There we found the old city hall, a college, a cathedral, and the Terry Theater given to the town by Tomás Terry, a slave trader who was trying to cleanse his reputation.

Our next adventure was to travel down the boulevard toward the harbor. We passed several delightful bright mansions as we drove. One was a very ornate old building that was once the Cienfuegos Harbor Club—no doubt reserved for the rich plantation owners and cattle ranchers. A stately white color, it seemed to have been completely restored and stood facing the harbor. Passing the harbor club, we pulled into the parking lot of a magnificent, intricately carved, Moorish-style palace built sometime in the 1700s. Even in Morocco we didn't see such detail on such a well-preserved building. It stands out of place across the parking lot from a '50s-style hotel built by the brother of Batista. The palace is now a restaurant. We had just eaten lunch, so this stop was just for drinks to enjoy the sweeping harbor views from the rooftop, which is accessed by a series of spiral staircases up three floors. I was almost dizzy by the time they handed me my cocktail.

By now we'd been traveling for seven hours now, and we were still eighty kilometers away from Trinidad. We were not traveling super highways here, so it's a bumpy ride. As we got within forty kilometers, what did we find? A beach. It's not the white sandy beach I was expecting, but it's a small beach with people swimming and a few thatched umbrellas on the heavy granular sand. Finally after nine hours we rolled in front of the Iberostar Grand Hotel in the city of Trinidad. It's a lovely hotel that would be perfect if we could get CNN on the TV. Leanne is just going to have to read about the Boston bombing on the Internet. Damn, that isn't working, either.

This hotel, like the Cohiba in Havana, is in partnership with a hotel company out of Spain. You would expect there to be more of these partnerships and investments by other international companies. America is the only with an embargo; none of the other countries of the world restrict travel to or investment in Cuba. The reason you don't see investment is the terms of any deal. Cuba demands 55 percent of the revenue from any venture, and in addition, after so many years, the properties, along with all improvements, revert back to the government without compensation. It's not a great investment when you put millions—if not billions—into a venture here.

CALIFORNIA YANKEE IN CUBA: DAY EIGHT

Trinidad is a town frozen in time. Founded in 1514, it was Cuba's third city. Walking the cobblestone streets here is like walking through a living museum. Before we took a walking tour of the town, we first took a drive out to the valley that supported it. Traveling about ten minutes outside the city, the scenery changes to a large, green, unspoiled valley framed by the mountains in the background. Our destination was one of the original sugar plantations on the island. The hacienda and the slave houses sit pretty much as the planters left them back in the 1870s after the plantations and mills were destroyed by rebellion. The original hacienda has been restored and showcases the life of the wealthy plantation owners with its original doors, unique ceilings, and traditional carved wooden bars on the windows. The original eighteenth-century wooden bars are a focal point of many of the buildings in Trinidad.

The street leading up to the master's hacienda is lined on both sides with the old slave homes that were on the plantation. Some have been modified somewhat, but others look like they are the originals from the 1800s. The hacienda was interesting, but the focal point of the town is the tall tower. The tower rises 147 feet on a narrow base of maybe a thirty-foot square. It raises section upon section, each layer getting narrower as the tower gets higher. The tower was apparently used to keep watch on the slaves working the plantation. It housed a large bell that would be used to start and end the day, as well as to warn if a slave was escaping. It is still possible to climb the tower, and Leanne and I, like other tourists, decided to venture up. The path leading up was made up of steep, wooden, ladder like steps. These steps rose up to an even narrower landing, where you find the base of another, even steeper ladder. Round and round we climbed into tighter and tighter spaces. At one point I began to wobble. Looking down, I realized it wasn't the stairs, just me. I can only describe descending from the tower as walking down the steep steps of the galley of a small boat; these just went on and on and on.

It was now time to head back to town to resume our walking tour of the city. We arrived at the perfect time: high noon, when the streets were the hottest. Ha! Man, it was hot today. As I have mentioned, Trinidad is much like what you would have seen in the late 1800s. Colorful buildings line the cobblestone streets. You see very few cars here. What you do see are two- and four-wheel carts pulled by the skinniest horses I think we have ever seen. It's also not unusual to see a couple of caballeros riding horses through town. It's not for tourism; it's their means of transportation. This is what is so special about Cuba at this moment. It's undeveloped and free of the clutter of capitalism—no advertising, very little begging, and streets incredibly clean of litter, even though there wasn't a trash can in sight.

There are no national restoration projects going on here in

Trinidad like the ones in Havana. The brightly painted buildings are the responsibility of the residents who own them. I think if we'd come to the town ten years ago we would have had a different impression. Since 2001 the Castro government has allowed private ownership with special licenses so the citizens can start businesses. Here in Trinidad they have taken full advantage of it. The town is teeming with festive bars, restaurants, galleries, and rooms for rent. The additional tourist income comes from renting out rooms and selling locally created crafts, textiles, and paintings. The extra money has allowed the citizens to put a fresh face on a town that must have been pretty shabby twenty years ago. Limited capitalism has been allowed to flourish here in Cuba. You just can't get too big. To make sure that doesn't happen, the government taxes you progressively higher if you add employees. It also forbids multiple locations. This assures that expansion won't be profitable. It's a strange idea, given Cuba's current unemployment problem after laying off 1.3 million government workers. That's 10 percent of the population of the country.

As we strolled down the streets we stopped to visit some of the seventeenth- and eighteenth-century churches that still stand in town, as well as a hotel that has a revolution museum. The hotel in the center of town sports a bell tower you can climb to get a view from above. The hotel's museum features vehicles in its courtyard, along with a makeshift boat with two machine guns mounted on the bow and stern. This was one of the boats used by the Cuban rebels resisting the Castro regime. Every last one of the rebels was either killed in battle in the mountains or caught and executed by firing squad during the six years between 1959 and 1965.

I'd had enough of the glory of the revolution, so I took the trip up the stairway to the bell tower to get a few aerial pictures of the town. Due to some stairs that were separating from the floor beams, I decided to cut my ascent short and climb onto the ledge of a window just under the bell. Ducking carefully under the outer edge of the bell, I came up a little too soon and conked myself on the head with the clapper. Boy, did I ring my bell. I can't tell if the headache I have is from the heat or the run-in with the bell.

Walking through town isn't easy. I am sure some of you have walked on cobblestone streets before, but you have not walked on anything like this. These are rocks, and they haven't been reset in some three hundred years. As I said, this city is frozen in time. I tried to understand why this town was built here in the first place. There is no river, and it's not near the ocean. Why settle here? As best I can tell, it was a place away from the plantations where the wealthy could have second homes and enjoy some city culture. The main square of the town has a very Spanish colonial feel. The plaza is circled with bright blue, yellow, white, green, and orange mansions, which were once the homes of the rich of the region. Today they are museums or restaurants. The plaza's painted railings are done primarily in bright yellows and whites. There are dozens of green and cream-colored urns on pedestals lining the palm tree-lined walkways. Standing here makes you almost feel ten degrees cooler.

Starting our walk back to our hotel for lunch, we ducked into a little bar on a corner. Sitting at a little table by the window, we sipped our cool piña coladas and watched the horse cart vendors pass by selling mangos. There is no place left on earth that can bring you back to an authentic, unspoiled time like you can find in Cuba.

A CALIFORNIA YANKEE IN CUBA: DAY NINE

The downside of traveling nine hours out to Trinidad is that you have to spend nine hours driving back. Going back we traveled by way of the town of Santa Clara. Driving on a Cuban highway is a little like riding the ten-cent stage coach you used to find outside the grocery store, rocking back and forth and bouncing up and down. The rough roads here are a result of the poor-quality asphalt used and the searing heat baking the streets, a combination that makes for waves, cracks, and potholes. Another element you will notice on Cuban highways is that they seem to narrow and widen every several kilometers. It's a strange occurrence, because you also see bridges that go nowhere. One minute you are on a divided highway, and then you have to move and share the road with oncoming traffic. Lack of money prevents vast sections from being finished. The other odd occurrence is the plethora of people on the road waving money in the air. These are all Cuban hitchhikers. There are hundreds along the road and sometimes even in the roadway, all hoping someone in need of a few pesos will stop and pick them up. Public transportation here looks to be lacking and infrequent.

Two hours after leaving Trinidad, we pulled into the city of Santa Clara. As we turned off the highway, we continued driving through the outskirts of the town. Here we saw the very drab Soviet-era cement apartment buildings while we worked our way to the city center.

Santa Clara might be the most important town in Cuba, not for what residents make, but for what happened there back in December 30, 1958. It was here in the small town of Santa Clara that a young Ernesto "Che" Guevara halted the Batista army, giving the Castro guerillas a clear pass to victory.

Our first stop was the historic area where Che and a band of little more than eighteen guerillas fighters, along with help from local residents, trapped and captured the reinforcements and supplies sent by Batista to support army troops fighting in Santiago, a town on the southeastern part of the island. The train was stocked with $4 million in US supplies, guns, and ammunition to support the army for two months in its battle against Castro's guerillas. The park and monument at the site of the derailment contain some of the original cars from the convoy as well as pictures and artifacts from the original contents of the train.

Batista had assembled seventeen freight cars in Havana, modifying them with double-walled armor and filling them with wet sand, making the cars impenetrable by bullets. The train left Havana loaded with 350 troops, a cache of ammunition, guns, mortar, and bazookas. What Batista didn't know was that there were workers in the rail yard who sympathized with the guerillas and didn't want to miss the opportunity to notify Castro. Before the trains moved from the rail station, sympathizers sent a note to Che informing him of the train's departure, its cargo, and its weakness: the wooden floor.

When the train reached the town of Santa Clara the engineer

noticed the bridge was blocked. Backing up to retreat, the engineer found the tracks behind him were now split. Che, arriving in time from the mountains, had used a local farm tractor to rip out thirty meters of track, trapping the train, the troops, and the vital army supplies. Falsely believing his three engines could crash though the blockade, the engineer sped the train right into a second tractor blocking the track, ultimately derailing the train. With only small windows at the very top of the train, the army had no way to see what was happening around them. Now the Batista army was at the mercy of Che's small group. With the help of local sympathizers, they lobbed Molotov cocktails all around and under the train. To the soldiers who couldn't see, it would have seemed as if they were surrounded by hundreds of guerillas, when in actuality there were only eighteen. The commander of the army, after only twelve hours, had no choice but to surrender. The Che- and Castro-led revolution now had the arms and munitions they needed for an all-out assault. Batista's days as a dictator were numbered, and he escaped shortly after.

The next stop on the road to Havana was Santa Clara Leoncio Vidal Park, the central plaza of the city. The centerpiece of this park is the large gazebo erected in 1911 that is still in use today for public concerts. Looking around the park, we found beautiful classical European architecture dating back to the seventeenth and eighteenth centuries—that is, until we came upon the ugliest and very out-of-place twentieth-century building in the plaza. This was once the Santa Clara Hilton. The outrage over the ugliness of this building alone could have launched the Cuban revolution.

Moving on, we had our last stop before returning to Havana: a visit to the memorial and resting place of Che Guevara. The memorial houses a museum dedicated to Che, along with many of his personal belongings and pictures of him as a boy, teenager, and young doctor. His resting place is really very beautiful. It's a place that you might want to take decorating tips from. The ceiling is lined with irregular blocks of exotic wood, and the walls are done in a dry stack stone. Recessed in the wall are round bronze platters with the pictures and names of the thirty-five guerillas Che fought with in Bolivia, where he was killed. In the center is a pillar where the remains of Ernesto "Che" Guevara rest.

Our tour was now coming to an end, and the three-hour drive back to Havana gave me time to put all of the information I had collected together. Was I for the embargo, or was I against it? What were my thoughts on the revolution and the subsequent Castro government?

Sometimes revolutions are necessary. Americans should understand that—we had our own in 1776. Our revolution was over taxes and representation. The Cuban revolution was against a brutal dictator in partnership with the mafia to rape the country, leaving the Cuban people in horrid poverty. I have to say, I now understand the Cuban revolution much better. It is what happened after that I found baffling. Except for a period in the 1980s, the Cuban people have not prospered, and life has not been easy.

The Russians wanted a location close to the United States during the Cold War, so they completely supported the country and its people financially. When Russia's own economy failed, it was forced to stop the handouts and support it was giving to Cuba. When the handouts stopped in 1992, the plight of the people became downright dire. The loss of the support of the Soviet Union sent the Castro government scrambling to find revenue. After 521 years, Cuba had to finally try to support itself. The government decided to allow foreign tourists in 1992, which was a start, but it wasn't until 2010 that private enterprise and private ownership were allowed. Only when they allowed the sale of property did things start to get better here. Cuba has a long way to go before it can realize the dream of a good life for all.

To date, the Cuban government has tried everything to hold back full-blown capitalism. The citizens are patiently waiting for things to change. When I ask why the government has taken so long to recognize that the system is not working, Cubans just shrug and say, "It's complicated." From where I sit, it's not so complicated.

The Chinese have discovered that capitalism is necessary, and I am sure Cuba will come to that realization as well. I would hate to see this wonderful, unspoiled country invaded by Pizza Hut, Kentucky Fried Chicken, McDonald's, and Starbucks, though. Sadly, to be part of a world economy, foreign investment is required. Coffee, chicken, hamburgers, and pizza may one day be what brings success to the Cuban revolution.

And by the way, there are resorts and beaches here in Cuba. They are apparently found to the east of Havana. Many European tourists come to experience the traditional Caribbean vacation at these resorts. We chose to emphasize the history, people, and culture.

Cuba is a very interesting and beautiful Caribbean island with a rich, preserved history, lush landscaping, and very open and warm people. I was surprised how open and willing the people were to discuss past, present, and future desires for Cuba. One day all these hopes and dreams will be realized. Everything in life has a birth, life, and death—people, businesses, plants, the sun—and yes, even governments.

Hasta la vista, baby!

CREDITS

Cuba Travel Arrangements	Ronen Paldi, Ya'lla Tours
US Travel Arrangements	Jan Morris, Peak Travel
Guide in Cuba	Laura Gonzalez
Driver while in Cuba	Miguel Garcia
Car Used	Peugeot
Charter	World Atlantic Airways
Host Hotel in Havana	Melia Cohiba
National Museum Guide	Marilyn Rueda Sanchez
Host Hotel in Trinidad	Iberostar Grand Hotel

Centro, Havana

Tail section of US jet shot down during the Bay of Pigs invasion, Cuba

Tobacco drying shed

Guaniguanico Mountains, Cuba

Horse drawn delivery cart, Trinidad, Cuba

ACKNOWLEDGMENTS

I would like to acknowledge and thank Jan Morris of Peak Travel in San Jose for her tireless work in making all of our trips, even the small ones, special and trouble free. The same goes for Abercrombie and Kent and their incredible network of international guides, drivers and local greeting staff. Without someone like A&K we could never have covered as much ground, learned as much about local culture or survived what could have been overwhelming schedules.

I would especially like to thank Frank Mosier, my High School English teacher who I have reconnected with after 40 years. He was very instrumental as my editor, to make sure I didn't make a grammatical fool of myself. If I don't get an "A" on this book this time around, its part his fault.

INDEX

C

Café Laurent Paladar, 285–86
camel rides, 96, 99, 186
camping excursions
  Dubai, 186
  India, 39–42
  Morocco, 97–100
  Peru, 154–55, 159
canopy walk, 154
capitalism
  Cuba, 276, 292, 296–97
  India, 5–6
carpets, 18–19, 93, 120, 186
cars, in Cuba, 265, 277. *See also*
  driving/driving experiences
Casablanca, Morocco, 82–84
casbahs, 98, 106, 118
cash economies
  Argentina, 146, 149
  Cuba, 266
castles and forts. *See also* palaces and
  grand houses
  Cuba, 271
  Czech Republic, 217–18
  India, 20–21, 45, 56–57, 58
  Jordan, 192, 193
  Poland, 223
  Russia, 231
Castropol restaurant, 274–75
catacombs, 177
Catharine the Great, 231, 232–33
cathedrals. *See* churches and
  cathedrals
Cathedral Square, Havana, 269
Catherine I, 236, 245
Catherine Palace, 236–37
cave sites
  Cuba, 285–86
  India, 10–13
  Jordan, 196
  Peru, 177

cemeteries. *See* burial sites and
  cemeteries
Centro Havana, 272
Chandr Mahal palace, 35–36
Chapel of Lorenzo, 217
chariots, 191
Charles Bridge, 218
Charles University, 223
China, international relations,
  61–62, 65–67
Chopin, Frédéric, 218
Christ the Redeemer statue, 130
chukkas areas, 122
churches and cathedrals. *See also*
  temples and monasteries
  Bethlehem, 205
  Brazil, 133–34
  Cuba, 267–68, 269
  Czech Republic, 217
  Jordan, 192, 196
  Peru, 172–73, 174–75, 177
  Poland, 222, 223
  Russia, 231, 234, 235, 243, 245
Church of Saint Francis of Assisi,
  177
Church of the Nativity, 205
Church of the Savior on Spilled
  Blood, 234, 235
Cienfuegos, Cuba, 289–90
Cienfuegos Harbor Club, 289
cigar factory tour, 271–72
Circus, Moscow, 244
Classical Room, Peterhof Palace,
  240
Clean Agra, 47
clothing, 117, 201
coaches, 242
cobblestone streets, walking
  challenges, 293
Cold War, relics of, 280
communism/communist influences,
  218, 222, 231, 244, 247, 277

E

earthquakes
Morocco, 101
Peru, 169, 176
eating out. *See* dining and food-related experiences
economic observations. *See also* slums
Brazil, 127, 131
Cuba, 266, 272, 273, 290, 292, 296
Eiffel Tower, 257, 258–59, 260
Eilat, Israel, 198–200
Einstein, Albert, 218
Eklingji temple, 24–25
elephants, 33–34, 35
El Tranvia restaurant, 289
embargo, of Cuba, 265–66, 270
Emirates Palace Hotel, 187
environmental practices, Bhutan, 60, 63
Eshkar family, 257
Essaouira, Morocco, 121–23
Estancia los Patos, 143–45
Estrada, Ángel de, 143–45
Everest, Mount, 59
exchange rates. *See* cost, of travel

F

Faena Hotel, 142
Falkenstein, Stanley, 281
farms/farming museums
Bhutan, 63
Cuba, 284–85
Jordan, 190
Peru, 160–61, 162–63
Fatehpur Sikri, India, 43–44
Ferris Wheels, 259
Fez, Morocco, 85–86, 90–94
FIFA World Cup event, 132
fishing boats, Morocco, 121
flags, of prayer, 64

Floridita bar, 270
food. *See* dining and food-related experiences
foreign workers, Dubai, 184, 187, 188–89
forts. *See* castles and forts
fountains, at Peterhof Palace, 239
France
as colonial power, 86–87
Paris, 141, 257–61
frescoes, 48, 194, 216–17
Frost, Peter, 161
fusion architecture, 4

G

Galilee, Sea of, 202
Gandhi Museum, 5
Ganges river, 51–53
garbage and pollution
Bhutan, 72
Brazil, 129
Dubai, 183
India, 11, 47, 53
Peru, 176
Garcia, Miguel, 297
gardens
Argentina, 147
India, 56–57
Morocco, 114
Russia, 237
Gardner, Ava, 274
Gate of India, 3
Gate of the Sun, 168
gauchos, 144
gay artists, in Cuba, 278–79
gazelles, black, 19
gender segregation, 187
Gerash/Gerasa, Jordan, 191
Germany
Berlin, 213–14
countryside of, 215

Humayun's tomb, 57
hydrofoil ride, 238–39

I

Iberostar Grand Hotel, 290
Ifren, Morocco, 95
Iguaçu River/Falls, 134–36, 137–40
Imperial Hotel, Delhi, 55
Inca civilization, 162–63, 166, 170,
    171–72, 174–75. *See also* Machu
    Picchu
Inca Trail, 167, 170
India
    Agra, 44
    Aurangabad, 14
    Bharatpur, 43
    Bhutan and, 65–67
    culture/scientific contributions
        of, 28
    Delhi, 55–58
    described, 1, 11
    Fatehpur Sikri, 43–44
    Jaipur, 31, 33–36, 37–38
    Jodhpur, 16–17, 20
    Khajuraho, 48 50
    Mumbai, 2, 3–6
    Orchha, 47–48
    population of, 70
    Shahjahanabad, 56
    travel to, 1–2
    Udaipur, 22–24
    Varanasi, 50–54
Indian village, Cuba, 287–88
injuries, 140
Inkaterra
    Amazon River Resort, 151–57
    Machu Picchu, 166–67
Ipanema Beach, 129, 132
iPhone
    loss of, 150
    uses of, 68, 97

Iranian tourist group, 235, 245
iron chains, bridge of, 65
irrigation tunnels, 100–101. *See also*
    water systems
Islamic culture, 88, 93, 107–8, 187,
    201. *See also* mosques
Ismail, Sultan, 87, 117
Israel
    complexities of, 205–7
    Eilat, 198–200
    Jerusalem, 202–7
    Masada, 192–93
    security, 198–99
    service in, 199–200
Israel Museum, 203
Ivan the Terrible, 243

J

Jahan, Shah, 47, 56
Jahangir Palace, 48
Jainism/Jain sites, 8–9, 22
Jaipur, India, 31, 33–36, 37–38
Jai Singh, 33
Jasna Góra Monastery, 226–27
Jaugards, 38
Jemaa el Fna Square, 115
Jerash, Jordan, 191
Jerusalem, Israel, 202–7
Jesus
    historic sites associated with, 204,
        205
    representations of, 130, 172, 265
Jews/Jewish history
    Cuba, 281
    Czech Republic, 219–21
    Israel, 202
    Morocco, 86 87, 88, 93, 117
    Poland, 223, 228–30
    Russia, 233–34
Jigme Dorji Wangchuck, King, 61
Jodhpur, India, 16–17, 20